DAME KATHLEEN KENYON

PUBLICATIONS OF THE INSTITUTE OF ARCHAEOLOGY, UNIVERSITY COLLEGE LONDON

SERIES EDITOR: Ruth Whitehouse
DIRECTOR OF THE INSTITUTE: Stephen Shennan
FOUNDING SERIES EDITOR: Peter J. Ucko

The Institute of Archaeology of University College London is one of the oldest, largest and most prestigious archaeology research facilities in the world. Its extensive publications programme includes the best theory, research, pedagogy and reference materials in archaeology and cognate disciplines, through publishing exemplary work of scholars worldwide. Through its publications, the Institute brings together key areas of theoretical and substantive knowledge, improves archaeological practice and brings archaeological findings to the general public, researchers and practitioners. It also publishes staff research projects, site and survey reports, and conference proceedings. The publications programme, formerly developed in-house or in conjunction with UCL Press, is now produced in partnership with Left Coast Press, Inc. The Institute can be accessed online at *http://www.ucl.ac.uk /archaeology.*

ENCOUNTERS WITH ANCIENT EGYPT SUBSERIES,

Peter J. Ucko, (ed.)
Jean-Marcel Humbert and Clifford Price (eds.), *Imhotep Today*
David Jeffreys (ed.), *Views of Ancient Egypt since Napoleon Bonaparte*
Sally MacDonald and Michael Rice (eds.), *Consuming Ancient Egypt*
Roger Matthews and Cornelia Roemer (eds.), *Ancient Perspectives on Egypt*
David O'Connor and Andrew Reid (eds.), *Ancient Egypt in Africa*
John Tait (ed.), *'Never had the like occurred'*
David O'Connor and Stephen Quirke (eds.), *Mysterious Lands*
Peter Ucko and Timothy Champion (eds.), *The Wisdom of Egypt*

CRITICAL PERSPECTIVES ON CULTURAL HERITAGE SUBSERIES, Beverley Butler (ed.)

Beverley Butler, *Return to Alexandria*
Ferdinand de Jong and Michael Rowlands (eds.), *Reclaiming Heritage*
Dean Sully (ed.), *Decolonizing Conservation*

OTHER TITLES

Andrew Gardner (ed.), *Agency Uncovered*
Okasha El-Daly, Egyptology, *The Missing Millennium*
Ruth Mace, Clare J. Holden, and Stephen Shennan (eds.), *Evolution of Cultural Diversity*
Arkadiusz Marciniak, *Placing Animals in the Neolithic*
Robert Layton, Stephen Shennan, and Peter Stone (eds.), *A Future for Archaeology*
Joost Fontein, *The Silence of Great Zimbabwe*
Gabriele Puschnigg, *Ceramics of the Merv Oasis*
James Graham-Campbell and Gareth Williams (eds.), *Silver Economy in the Viking Age*
Barbara Bender, Sue Hamilton, and Chris Tilley, *Stone World*
Andrew Gardner, *An Archaeology of Identity*
Sue Hamilton, Ruth Whitehouse, and Katherine I. Wright (eds.) *Archaeology and Women*
Gustavo Politis, *Nukak*
Sue Colledge and James Conolly (eds), *The Origins and Spread of Domestic Plants in Southwest Asia and Europe*
Timothy Clack and Marcus Brittain (eds), *Archaeology and the Media*
Janet Picton, Stephen Quirke, and Paul C. Roberts (eds.), *Living Images*
Tony Waldron, *Paleoepidemiology*
Eleni Asouti and Dorian Q. Fuller, *Trees and Woodlands of South India*
Russell McDougall and Iain Davidson (eds.), *The Roth Family, Anthropology, and Colonial Administration*
Elizabeth Pye (ed.), *The Power of Touch*
Miriam C. Davis, *Dame Kathleen Kenyon—Digging Up the Holy Land*
Marcos Martinón-Torres and Thilo Rehren (eds.), *Archaeology, History, and Science*
John Tait, *Why the Egyptians Wrote Books*

DAME KATHLEEN KENYON

Digging Up the Holy Land

Miriam C. Davis

Left Coast
Press inc.

WALNUT CREEK, CALIFORNIA

Left Coast Press Inc.

LEFT COAST PRESS, INC.
1630 North Main Street, #400
Walnut Creek, CA 94596
http://www.LCoastPress.com

ISBN 978-1-59874-325-8 hardcover
ISBN 978-1-59874-326-5 paperback

Library of Congress Cataloguing-in-Publication Data:
Dame Kathleen Kenyon : digging up the Holy Land / Miriam C. Davis.
    p. cm. — Includes bibliographical references and index.
        ISBN 978-1-59874-325-8 (hardback : alk. paper) —
        ISBN 978-1-59874-326-5 (pbk. : alk. paper)
        1. Kenyon, Kathleen Mary, Dame. 2. Women archaeologists-Israel-Biography.
3. Israel—Antiquities. I. Title.
DS115.9.K395D38 2008—[B]
2007050633

Printed in the United States of America

The paper used in this publication meets the minimum requirements of American ∞ National Standard for Information Sciences-Permanence of Paper for Printed Library Materials, ANSI/NISO Z39.48-1992.

08 09 10   5 4 3 2

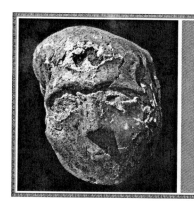

CONTENTS

For my grandmothers
Velma Massey Thompson and Lucille Williams Reynolds

ILLUSTRATIONS

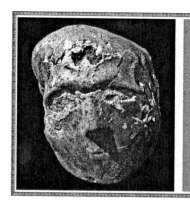

PREFACE

I NEVER MET KATHLEEN KENYON. I discovered her when, as a teenager, I read her obituary. At about the same time my grandmother took me on a trip to the Holy Land and an interest in perhaps the most famous female excavator of biblical lands was born. For many years I waited for a biography to Kenyon to appear. When one never did, I took matters into my own hands.

This is not an academic or intellectual biography of Kathleen Kenyon. That remains to be written. It is rather the book I wanted to read as a young person interested in archaeology, Biblical Studies, and extraordinary women.

ACKNOWLEDGMENTS

I am grateful to the many people who helped make this biography possible. I want to thank all of the people mentioned in the notes who willingly (and in some cases eagerly) shared with me their memories of "the Great Sitt." Only lack of space precludes listing all their names again here.

Special thanks are due to Doug and Maggie Tushingham for furnishing me with an initial list of contacts, as well as members of Kathleen's family: Colonel John Kenyon, Janet Heath, Jeremy Ritchie, and Elspeth Ritchie Panichi. Janet and Alan Heath provided me with the most pleasant archive I've ever worked in.

The book could not have been written without the cooperation of a number of professional societies and organizations: the Bodleian Library; the BBC Written Archives Centre; the British Library; the British Red Cross Museum and Archives; Baylor University Libraries; Council for British Archaeology; Council for British Research in the Levant; the British Academy; the Jewry

Wall Museum; the Palestine Exploration Fund; the St. Albans Museums; St. Hugh's College; St. Paul's Girls' School; Somerville College; the Institute of Archaeology, University College London; the Society of Antiquaries of London; Oxford University Archives; University of London Library, Historic Collection; the Surrey Archeological Society; and the Surrey History Centre. I am deeply grateful to the highly professional, and very kind, staffs of these institutions.

I am particularly indebted to the archaeologists who were willing to read part or all of the manuscript, save me from embarrassing mistakes, and answer what must have seemed like endless questions: Sarnia Butcher, Martin Biddle, Rupert Chapman, Felicity Cobb, Thomas Holland, Peter Parr, Sebastian Payne, Margreet Steiner, and Ron Tappy

Others, non-archaeologists, were willing to read early drafts and provide helpful criticism: Michael Burger, Maxine Davis, Tim Davis, Sharan Newman, Maggie Tushingham, and Janet Heath. Corey-Jan Albert was such a good editor that she deserves her own sentence. Many others read parts of the manuscript for accuracy, for which I am grateful. Also, several anonymous reviews made helpful suggestions.

I owe several librarians much gratitude: Lloyd Busch, Diane Coleman, Gail Gunter, and Ielleen Miller.

The following deserve special thanks for a variety of reasons: Cindy Buob, Sara Callaway, John Crowfoot, Hal Drake, Joel Drinkard, Margaret Drower, Aileen Fox, Shane Gong, Stuart Laidlaw, Nancy Lapp, Louis Mutch, Kay Prag, Diana Rowley, Charles Scott-Fox, Hershel Shanks, David Spurgeon, Helen-Margaret Stevenson, Peter Titchmarsh, Rosemary Tripp, and everyone at the Bean Counter.

If I have neglected to mention anyone who has earned my thanks, please believe that it is a failure of memory, not one of gratitude.

And finally, thanks to Michael who, although he neither typed the manuscript nor compiled the index, read (so he claims) a million drafts, and fed me ice chips and barbecue as needed.

The earliest known example of realistic human portraiture had just been discovered, and Vivienne Catleugh was annoyed. Everyone was packed and ready to go. After three months of roughing it in the Judean wilderness, people were ready to leave the expedition camp in Jordan and return to more conventional lives in England, Canada, America, or wherever. In charge of running the camp for her long-time friend, Catleugh was as ready to go as anyone, anxious to do a little sightseeing in Syria before going back to her Red Cross job in London. Then the skulls were found.

The Jericho Expedition Camp was ruled by Vivienne Catleugh's close friend, the Great Sitt—Arabic for "Lady" or "Madame." And one of the Great Sitt's strict rules was that one did not gouge holes in the straight, clean walls of the trenches. But at the urging of an enthusiastic and able assistant, Peter Parr, she had relented and made an exception. Now he showed up at what remained of the camp with something the likes of which no archaeologist had ever seen before—an 8,000 year-old[1] human skull, molded with plaster to have surprisingly life-like human features. Moreover, Parr reported that two more skulls were now visible in the hole where this one had been dug out.

The Great Sitt cancelled plans to leave. Catleugh complained, but she stayed. Others complained, but they stayed as well. Even at the site of biblical Jericho, where they had come to find Joshua's walls but found instead Neolithic walls—and thus 2,000 more years of town life (so far)—human portrait skulls were extraordinary.

Over the next five days, as the Jordanian summer grew hotter and hotter, the Great Sitt and a select crew painstakingly removed six more skulls from the gaping hole in the trench. Complete with shells used to simulate eyes, they were individual re-creations of men dead for millennia. Everyone was relieved when the last one was removed and no others were visible. They could finally go home.

The Great Sitt and the Neolithic portrait skulls were covered in newspapers all over the world. They made the front page of *The New York Times*. At the age of forty-seven, having been an archaeologist for half of her life, the solid figure of the Great Sitt suddenly became one of the most recognizable in the archaeological world.

Although she had been born into the heart of the English scholarly community, and had all the help that influence and connections could provide, she had become one of the foremost excavators in Great Britain through hard work, commitment, and a flair for dirt archaeology. Despite coming from a world of horses and country houses, she was never happier than when living in a tent and trenching through the past in some distant and uncomfortable part of the world.

In many ways an uncomplicated and conventional person, she led an unconventional life, devoting herself to her career and rising to the top of her field when it was unusual for a woman to have a career at all, leaving the dull, domestic details of life to be attended to by Vivienne Catleugh. She was a modest woman who had confidence in her own judgment, a kind woman who did not suffer fools easily, and a pioneer in her discipline who many found insufficiently "academic." She was known for her love of dogs, pink gin, and digging.

The Jericho excavations would make her famous, but they would not be her most important contribution to archaeology. Although her name would be forever associated with Jericho—and later Jerusalem—her most important contribution to archaeology would be the methodology that would bear her name. Her love of digging, which would contribute so much to her success, would also account for her greatest failures.

The Great Sitt was Kathleen Kenyon. She was, in the eyes of many, the greatest field archaeologist of her generation and the greatest woman archaeologist of her century.

KATHLEEN MARY KENYON'S birth had been awaited with great anxiety. Her mother had lost two previous children at birth due, according to family tradition, to the incompetence of the doctor where they lived in Harrow-on-the-Hill, a suburb of London. Indeed, Kathleen's birth was rather difficult, as she came out arm first. Nevertheless, the baby was delivered safely on January 5, 1906, and congratulations poured in from delighted friends and relatives.

She had been born in a nursing home just north of Regent's Park in London, but Kathleen had also been born into the English landed gentry. Her father's family came from Shropshire. Frederic Kenyon himself had been born in London in 1863 where his father practiced law, but on the death of his grandfather in 1869 moved to Pradoe, the family estate in Shropshire where he grew up. The Kenyons were a distinguished family. Pradoe had been bought in 1803 by the Honorable Thomas Kenyon, son of the first Baron Kenyon, who had served as Lord Chief Justice from 1788 to 1801. Frederic's father, John Robert, a younger son of the Honorable Thomas, married Eliza Hawkins, daughter of Edward Hawkins, a noted scholar and a Keeper of Antiquities in the British Museum. John Robert Kenyon was himself a prominent lawyer, the Vinerian Professor of Law at Oxford and a judge of the Vice-Chancellor's court.

Frederic was the eleventh of fifteen children, ten of whom survived childhood. He had an upbringing typical of his day and class, starting Greek and Latin at home before being sent off to a preparatory school, then to Winchester College, and finally to New College, Oxford. Fred, as he was called by his family, showed distinct academic promise at an early age, winning prizes in biblical history and in literature at school. As a scholar at New College he took a First

Class degree in "Mods and Greats"—that is, classical languages, literature, and philosophy. He continued to win prizes at Oxford, being awarded a Greek Testament Prize in 1885 and the Chancellor's English essay in 1889. After receiving a fellowship at Magdalen College in 1888, Frederic became an Assistant in the Department of Manuscripts at the British Museum in 1889.

In 1891 Frederic married Amy Hunt, who also had roots in Shropshire. Her father was Rowland Hunt of Boreatton Park, Shropshire, an estate only a few miles from Pradoe. Amy's artistic and musical inclinations were an agreeable complement to her husband's scholarly detachment. She sang, sketched, painted, and, in later life, took up cross-stitching and woodcarving. Her husband was not immune to her influence. Although not musically inclined himself, after his marriage Frederic applied himself to learning all he could about music, becoming very fond of Wagner as well as Gilbert and Sullivan.

By the time Kathleen was born in 1906, Frederic had established himself as a scholar of some reputation. Soon after his arrival at the British Museum, the museum acquired a number of Greek papyri that he was given to examine. Thus, Frederic came to identify, among other things, the lost treatise of Aristotle on the Athenian constitution, and eventually to produce both an edition and translation. This and other works, such as the catalogue *Classical Texts from Papyri in the British Museum* (1891) and *Handbook to the Textual Criticism of the New Testament* (1901), led to numerous academic honors. He received honorary doctorates from Durham University and Halle University in Germany, and was elected a corresponding Member of the Berlin Academy in 1900. Frederic was involved in the establishment of the British Academy and was himself elected to membership in 1903, becoming a member of its Council in 1906. In addition to his scholarly works, Frederic also wrote for the general public, publishing such popular works as *Our Bible and Ancient Manuscripts*, *The Story of the Bible*, *The Bible and Archaeology*, and *Literary Criticism, Common Sense, and the Bible*.

In 1909 Frederic Kenyon, who had been promoted to Assistant Keeper in 1898, was appointed Director of the British Museum. While his scholarly reputation and the high opinion in which he was held by his colleagues would seem to make this unsurprising, his appointment was unusual in that he had served neither as a First Class Assistant, nor as the head of a department. With characteristic modesty he later claimed that he would not have been promoted if the other senior keepers had not been considered too old.[1] He was awarded a knighthood in 1912, apparently at the insistence of King George V himself.[2]

Frederic and Amy lived at Harrow-on-the-Hill, Middlesex, in the early years of their marriage. But the house they lived in after their daughter's birth was apparently unsuitable for the adventurous Kathleen, who as a toddler insisted on repeatedly falling into every rosebush in their small garden. In 1907 the Kenyons moved into a house they had built in Godstone, Surrey, which they called Kirkstead. The neighborhood was appealing not only because Frederic had family there, but also because it was both within commuting distance of London and in the countryside that they both preferred.

The Kenyons moved into Kirkstead in November of 1907, and Kathleen's sister Nora was born the following February. When Frederic was appointed Director of the British Museum, the family moved—at least during the week—from Kirkstead into the residence of the Director, which was attached to the museum, in the Bloomsbury area of London.

Frederic went from the house into the museum every morning at 9 am, attired in morning coat and tails. He was, perhaps, one of the great directors of the British Museum, committed to making the national treasures of the museum accessible to the general public. He set up, for example, a system of guided tours intended to introduce visitors to the museum rather than leaving them to be overwhelmed by its contents. He was known to join one of these tours, unobtrusively, on occasion. He was also known for his commitment to keeping the museum free to the public.

Frederic Kenyon—a small, dapper man—was also painfully shy. Although sometimes giving the impression of coldness and aloofness (he was not noted for his small talk), he was, in fact, a very kind man dedicated not only to the education of the public, but also to the well-being of the staff who worked under him. If his essential reserve made him appear aloof, it did not mean he was concerned with his own dignity. One of his subordinates, writing after Kenyon's death, recounted that Frederic had gently rebuked him for formally addressing him in a letter as "Dr. Kenyon." Unlike his predecessor, he did not insist that the staff remove their hats when they passed by him.

He was temperamentally suited to administration. Once, a colleague recalled, when as Director Frederic had to deal with a miscreant, the tact and prudence with which he disposed of the matter won the admiration of the offender himself. He would have been, this colleague added, an excellent judge because of "the clarity and impartiality with which he [could] have summed up a perplexingly complicated issue."[3] Years later, a student of Kathleen's would remark that Frederic Kenyon's qualities were very similar to Kathleen's own.[4]

Although she preferred the country to life in London, Amy—more outgoing and effusive than her reserved husband—took her responsibilities as the wife of the Director very seriously. She threw frequent dinner parties and was "at home" to visitors every Monday afternoon. The two little girls were dressed up, told to be on their best behavior, and brought down to the drawing room after tea to shake hands with visitors.

Kathleen, or K as she would come to be called, and Nora had a pleasant childhood. Attended by their nanny, their first playground was Russell Square, whose twisting paths the girls found fascinating. They played with the neighborhood children there and went to tea parties. Amy and Frederic, having waited fifteen years to have children, were attentive, loving parents. Shortly after Kathleen's birth Amy wrote: "It is frightful how precious that wee mite is. Of course I know one ought to do one's best and then not worry but it is very difficult."[5] From an early age the girls added "kisses to Daddy" to Amy's letters to Frederic and soon began writing him letters of their own. On one occasion Amy included a letter from the seven-year-old Kathleen to her father, noting that she was a bit embarrassed about her handwriting,[6] something that might seem ironic to those who would later have to try to read Kathleen's impenetrable handwriting.

Kathleen took after Frederic, having fair hair and bright blue eyes (Figure 1.1). It must also be said that at an early age she showed the determination—some might say hard-headedness—that would later characterize her. In a letter to her husband when Kathleen was only a few months old, Amy reported that "Baby has taken a crank into her funny little head and refuses to feed from the left side. . . . She is quite determined on the subject."[7] A few years later she wrote, "I did not put the net over Kathleen last night [,] making her promise not to get up and she was very good. It was really making a virtue of necessity as the little monkey now undoes it at the corner herself and was discovered sitting on the rail [,] which is really dangerous."[8]

She did not always play well with other children. At her first tea party, while her mother was pleased that K was the prettiest baby there, she complained that she tried to poke out the eyes of her other young guests.[9] When K was about two, Amy noted that she very much wanted her own way when playing with her cousin Nina.[10] Later Nora would say that K always insisted on organizing all of their childhood games, and if she was not allowed to do so, would go off by herself.

The Kenyons were rather unusual for the time in that they were content to let their girls grow up as tomboys. With their blouses tucked into their bloomers, the girls played Indian, climbed trees, fished, floated toy boats in a stream near Kirkstead, and generally led a rather unfettered existence. They also engaged in

FIGURE 1.1: Kathleen Kenyon as a child. *Courtesy of Studio D Photography.*

more traditional pursuits such as ponies, bicycles, and lawn tennis. Both Amy and Frederic played tennis and, in fact, had a hard court built at Kirkstead when such courts were still unusual.

Although the Kenyons were far from rich, Frederic Kenyon did experience one unexpected stroke of good fortune. In May 1914 he inherited the estate of Rose Hill in Erbistock, in north Wales, from a distant cousin, Gertrude Girandot. Mrs. Girandot's only son had died, she was unhappy with her other near relatives, and she was looking around for someone to whom to leave her estate. Meeting the young Kathleen at one of Amy's "at home days," she was apparently quite taken with the charming child. According to K's own version of the story, when she and several cousins visited Rose Hill, she was the only one to write Mrs. Girandot a thank-you letter. When the estate was left to Frederic, Kathleen liked to take the credit. Although money was needed at first to pay death duties and servants' legacies, eventually Rose Hill could be rented out.

When the First World War broke out at the end of the summer of 1914, Sir Frederic, a company commander in the Inns of Court Rifle Volunteers, was at his annual military camp. Upon learning of a request for officers to be sent to France as censors, he immediately volunteered. Amy was appalled by the whole idea, complaining that his only weapon would be the pencil of a censor. Frederic tried to reassure her that a pencil would be less dangerous than a pistol, but Amy remained unenthusiastic. She did not feel, she wrote, "inspired with patriotism enough to risk your life for a beastly little state like Serbia."[11]

Amy need not have worried. Her husband had left for France without obtaining the permission of the Trustees of the British Museum and, although everyone understood his motives, the Trustees, the King, and the Archbishop of Canterbury were soon united in an effort to get him back. On September 9 he received orders to return to England, presumably to the relief of his wife and certainly to the delight of his eight-year-old daughter, who wrote "I am so very glad you have come back."[12] While Amy and the girls remained at Kirkstead for the duration of the war, Frederic was stationed at Berkhamsted, just outside of London, where he could manage the British Museum from a distance.

The girls reacted to the war by playing war games. They used the pony cart as an "aeroplane" and played at the dropping of bombs. They also dug an air-raid trench in their garden. This trench was quite realistic, being based on the description of young men they knew who were in Flanders, complete with a bend in the middle and a roofed dugout. They must have retained their high spirits, for Amy wrote Frederic that their "joie de vivre" kept her cheerful.[13]

After the war, life returned to normal. Amy began spending a part of each summer in France at spas, dieting and taking the baths. During these times Kathleen and Nora, and often Frederic, would go to Shropshire to visit relatives. K wrote lively, affectionate letters to her mother, giving the details of picnics, hill walking expeditions, and tennis parties. It is in such letters that K's great love for dogs first becomes apparent. From time to time K mentions her own dogs in her letters, and in a letter to her mother from Boreatton Hall she reports on a "delightful puppy," a spaniel with an unhappy tendency to bite. This habit does not appear to have disturbed K: "She has been crawling over me and biting me most of the time I have been writing this letter, so you must excuse [my] writing."[14]

THE WAR DID AFFECT Kathleen's and Nora's education. Like most children of the time, Kathleen and Nora had begun their education at home. They started with Miss Sankey, a friend of Amy's who taught the girls the alphabet, then moved through a series of governesses. Nora, although two years younger, insisted on doing whatever K did, and so was taught along with her sister. Nora later acknowledged that they did not demonstrate any particular interest in learning for its own sake, and the governesses found it easier to keep the girls quiet than to teach them anything. One governess, a German, was hired with the expectation that she would teach the girls French and German. When she left at the outbreak of the war, the girls informed Amy that she must have been a German spy because she had tried to teach them more German than French.

Because of concern with air raids over London, Amy and the girls spent the war at Kirkstead, and in 1917 Kathleen and Nora began at Eothen School in Caterham, about three miles from Godstone. A school that prided itself on its social exclusivity, Eothen also boasted that it was a place where schoolwork was more important than games.[15] The girls stayed at Eothen for about a year, until December 1918. The teaching must have been fairly good because, as Nora later remembered, they were well prepared to enter St. Paul's Girls' School in January 1919.

St. Paul's Girls' School (SPGS) was the most distinguished girls' school in London. Although the High Mistress, Frances Gray, insisted that the goal of St. Paul's Girls' School was the preparation of future wives and mothers, the education provided did not seem to reflect this. The curriculum was geared to getting scholarships to Oxford and Cambridge, at which SPGS was quite successful. One near contemporary of Kathleen Kenyon's would later observe that in fact there was little effort to educate the girls as future homemakers; their curriculum was virtually identical to that of the boys' school.[16] Presumably the education they received at SPGS did encourage girls to think outside the realm of marriage and motherhood, for a list compiled in the 1920s of the professions of former Paulinas includes architects, bank employees, civil servants, solicitors, secretaries, nurses, doctors, journalists, teachers, and poultry farmers.

SPGS did not practice the kind of social snobbery of Eothen. Indeed, according to Gray, one of the advantages of the school was its mixture of social classes. And it was religiously open, accepting not only Jews but also agnostics. Because it was known as the best girls' school in London, its students tended to be the children of the intellectual elite.

Although the school emphasized academics, both Kathleen and Nora were very active in sports. K played hockey, lacrosse, and cricket; comments in the school's magazine, *The Paulina*, reveal the repeated criticism that while K was a solid cricket player, she tended to be a bit slow in the field. A younger contemporary has a vivid memory of the rather stocky Kathleen, pigtail flying, charging down the hockey field at her.[17]

Frederic Kenyon was clearly concerned with his daughters' education and with their intellectual development. He regularly gave his daughters books—school atlases, story books, Bibles, volumes of Shakespeare—and inquired about the books they were reading. On one occasion he warned of the dangers of limiting one's reading: "One can go on liking stories all one's life, but people who read *only* story books are apt to get stupid."[18] He understood the importance of self-education, for he noted that he himself learned while at Oxford mainly by reading on his own. He wrote to Amy at the end of the war: "I don't think their education has really suffered, since they are of an age to educate themselves to a considerable extent, and as they have the taste for reading and a certain amount of intelligence. I think they are doing so, and their minds are really developing satisfactorily."[19]

Sir Frederic took a particular interest in his daughters' religious education. The Kenyons were a devout family. A critical scholar of the Scriptures who also believed they were divinely inspired, Sir Frederic encouraged his daughters to understand them.[20] This early training must have had some effect, because K remained a regular churchgoer to the end of her life and, according to her family, a deeply, if quietly, religious person.

Both Kathleen and Nora did well in school. Inspired by a gifted history teacher, K showed a particular fascination with the study of the past, becoming active in the History Club, and an avid consumer of teenage literature. She always denied that growing up in the British Museum instilled into her any particular interest in antiquity. But having the director of the museum as a father was, she recalled, an advantage as "it was most useful to have the national collection at one's disposal, added to which were the joys of accompanying my father by the light of an electric torch to select books from the great catalogue in his Reading Room."[21]

Although a good student, Kathleen did not like exams any more than most students. Writing to her mother after completing the Oxford entrance examination, she was highly critical of her own performance. On the English General Essay topic of "Wars in self defense are not the only righteous ones," K wrote, by her own account, "eight pages of awful bosh with great difficulty." Of the experience she concluded, "on the whole I think I haven't utterly disgraced myself in the exam, but I know I haven't done strikingly well."[22]

Kathleen must have been confident that she would do well enough because she sat only the Oxford entrance exam, not the Cambridge Higher Local Examination that would have given her entrance to lesser universities. The teachers at SPGS must have thought well of her academic abilities because she left the school with the Mary Willson History Prize in 1925. But she also received what was, in some ways, an even greater accolade in her final year, recognizing as it did her capacity for leadership. To no one's surprise in retrospect, and to her sister Nora's amazement at the time, at a school assembly in December 1924 Kathleen Kenyon was declared Head Girl.

Upon leaving St. Paul's K would enter Somerville College, Oxford. Her father's friendship with Margery Fry, soon to be its next principal, may have played a role in this decision. Certainly the fact that her father was the product of two Oxford colleges did. K received a scholarship from St. Paul's, a Leaving Exhibition, for three years at Oxford. Of the three Exhibitions awarded by the Governors of the school, K won the third by such a slim margin that the school provided extra funds in order to provide a fourth Exhibition for her competitor.[23] But win it she did, and at the beginning of the Michaelmas term of 1925 Kathleen Kenyon entered Somerville College.

KATHLEEN ENTERED OXFORD UNIVERSITY with no intention of becoming an archaeologist. Later rumors that as a child she had dug a trench in her back garden because she anticipated her future were only that: rumors to explain the origins of the "Mistress of Stratigraphy," one of the greatest field archaeologists of her generation. Despite being the daughter of the Director of the British Museum, despite being born into the heart of the British academic and archaeological establishment, despite her first-rate education at St. Paul's Girls' School, Kathleen arrived at Oxford in the fall of 1925 with no idea what she would do with her life.

K had chosen Somerville, the most popular of the women's colleges, which lacked the religious affiliation of the others, and enjoyed a reputation for liberalism and serious scholarship. Although there were weekly tutorials and essays, she could attend lectures as she liked. What K chose to do—or not do—was her own responsibility.

She enjoyed her freedom, throwing herself into an active social life, giving tea parties in her room, attending debates, the cinema, and the theater. She dabbled in politics, joining the Conservative Club. Her later penchant for committees showed up early; she served on the Junior Common Room Committee for three years, holding the office of treasurer her final year. Her talent for leadership was evident even in small ways: she organized a team of freshers for a snowball fight against the older students, in which they soundly defeated their seniors.[24] Her only real problem that first year, as she said to Nora, was running through her funds: "The trouble about the accounts is that I always seem to have spent just a little more than I have got."[25]

Despite the freedoms of undergraduate life, Oxford was governed by a formality foreign to later generations, including a multitude of rules. The rules of Somerville College required that an undergraduate have the permission of her tutor and the principal to leave Oxford during term time or to be out of the college after 9 pm, and obligated them to return to the college before 11:00 pm. Kathleen thoroughly disliked such restrictions, complaining when she and her friends had to miss the last scene of a play in order to get in by the appointed hour.[26] She wasn't above ignoring the rules when it suited her. Once, having taken a train out of Oxford to have Sunday lunch with friends of her family, she accepted a ride back with a young man. She fully realized that this violated all the chaperonage regulations, but, as she wrote unrepentantly to her mother, she "wasn't found out."[27]

In those days Kathleen only dabbled in archaeology. Even the co-presidency of the Somerville College Archaeological Society was evidence of her social life rather than career ambitions. Known as "Ark," it was, in fact, not much of an archaeological society. It had degenerated into what K described as a social society "of which you are made officers chiefly if you are considered funny and capable of making amusing speeches."[28] Existing primarily to bring freshers and seniors together socially, its activities revolved mainly around scavenger hunts.

Even so, she was sufficiently interested in archaeology to become a member of the Oxford University Archaeological Society, which had begun to admit women only five years earlier. The Society met on Friday nights for lectures and sponsored excursions to local places of interest. Some members took part in nearby excavations, such as those at the Romano-British site at Alchester, about ten miles north of Oxford. Kathleen, however, did not participate in any of these excavations and demonstrated no particular interest in archaeological sites.

In those early days archaeology was a minor interest at best. Kathleen's major interests were of a much more social and less intellectual variety. She joined the Dramatic Society, and in her first year helped produce the freshers' play, to much acclaim.[29] In her final year, K took to the stage herself, costumed in uniform, wig, and bushy mustache in a Pirandello play.[30]

The ever-social Kathleen liked dancing, was quite good at it, and usually found a partner for the college's Saturday night dances. At the same time the hearty, athletic K wasn't the most sought-after of young women. As a result she occasionally had real difficulties finding a partner, in one instance asking seven young men, who all refused her invitation. But she persevered until she found a "very unattractive man who . . . was longing to come" to the Somerville dance. The "unattractive man" did not stop her from having a very nice time; once there, she did not lack for other partners.[31] One of her favorite dancing partners in these days was the young Christopher Hawkes[32]—who was also to become a well-known archaeologist—then an undergraduate at New College.

K seems to have spent more time on sports than just about anything else (Figure 1.2). In the 1920s Somerville had a particularly high reputation as a sporting college, and Kathleen made the most of it. She spent most afternoons playing sports of one kind or another—lacrosse and hockey for the Somerville College teams, and hockey for the University team, for which she was eventually awarded a Blue. In addition, she belonged to the Tennis Club, went ice skating and riding when she had the chance, organized ad-hoc games of cricket, and at least considered signing up for ju-jitsu lessons.[33] More than once she wrote home that she had played games "every day this week."[34] Even as she played to win, Kathleen's good nature was evident. In her letters home, whether

FIGURE 1.2: K at play, probably mid to late 1920s. *Courtesy of Janet Heath.*

a game was good or not did not depend on whether her team won. She was tough, as well, playing hockey even while recovering from a badly sprained ankle she got while jumping down a flight of stairs.[35]

Her remaining time was devoted to the degree course. Her subject, Modern History, was, along with English, one of the most popular subjects among women undergraduates. "Modern history" at Oxford meant "not ancient history" and covered Europe from the early Middle Ages to the modern period, with an emphasis on English constitutional history. In later years K would be accused of not being a real intellectual; nothing in her Oxford career contradicts this. For the future principal of an Oxford College and the daughter of a classical scholar, she was remarkably unpreoccupied with intellectual endeavors. When the Dramatic Club read Pirandello's *Henry IV*—an admittedly overtly philosophical and metaphysical play—she disliked it on the grounds that it was "rather deep and complicated, and . . . took us a long time to discover what it was driving at."[36] When her tutor gave her a long list of books on the nineteenth century to read in preparation for an exam, K was not very enthusiastic, admitting to her mother that she would probably end up relying on what she remembered of her father's reading of the historian Trevelyan.[37]

If K was not "intellectual," she was bright and, above all, dutiful. If she went weeks without going to lectures,[38] and could write to her sister that she was "feeling very end-of-termish and above work,"[39] she was also capable of working seven, eight, or even twelve hours in a day to catch up.[40] Because she opted for the medieval options of the modern history course, Kathleen's tutor at Somerville was Maude Clarke, a distinguished medieval historian who was also an excellent tutor. Miss Clarke seems to have been reasonably satisfied with K's academic work, although it was not her intellectual powers she admired most. "Miss Kenyon can be relied upon to carry out with intelligence and energy any duties that she may undertake," she said in her evaluation of K. "She is incapable of doing anything—games or work—in a slovenly or half-hearted way. The all-round ability, loyalty and unselfishness which have made her a most valuable member of the College should ensure her popularity as well as her success wherever she goes."[41]

K's attitude toward her academic studies is evident in her handling of one of the hurdles of her first year—Divinity Moderations, known as "Divers," an examination on the New Testament required of all undergraduates. Originally a study of the New Testament in Greek, by K's time one could choose to be examined on either the Acts of the Apostles and two Gospels in Greek, or the Acts and all four of the Gospels in English. K chose the option of the Acts of the Apostles and the Gospels of Matthew and John in Greek. She did not put much effort into preparing for the examination, warning Nora in advance that she might fail because of her lack of effort.[42] In fact, she found the exam something of a joke. The actual translations seemed easy enough, but she had difficulty putting the verses in context, because they were "the sort of vague phrases which . . . might come in anywhere." She responded with equally vague answers. "I didn't definitely get them wrong," she wrote to her mother and sister. "That was only because I didn't put anything definite at all."[43]

After the written exam she then faced a *viva voce* that would allow her to make up any deficiencies of the first exam. In the end she passed the entire exam with little effort but thought the *viva* ludicrous because all she was asked was the names of the tentmakers who hosted the Apostle Paul in Corinth. Her answer, "Priscilla and Aquilla," ended the exam. Of the two girls who failed the *viva*, K could only remark, "I can't think how they can do it."[44]

Despite the fact that the Oxford University Archaeological Society had only recently begun to admit women, and then only after heated debate, by K's final year it had decided it needed to attract more female members. Somebody seems to have suggested that a woman president might help. As daughter of the Director of the British Museum and co-president of the Somerville College Archaeological Society, K was an obvious choice. Thus, in her third year, at the instigation of undergraduates who had known her when Sir Frederic was a Warden of Winchester (including future archaeologist Christopher Hawkes), Kathleen became the Oxford University Archaeological Society's first female president.

Her inaugural lecture took place on November 4, 1927. To prepare for it, K had greater resources than the average undergraduate, borrowing slides belonging to the British Museum[45] to speak on "Everyday Life in Medieval England."[46] According to Nora (who by this time was also at Somerville), the lecture went quite well and seems to have succeeded in its main goal: not only was the lecture hall full, but most of the audience were women.[47]

Kathleen's undergraduate career would, of course, culminate in "Schools," the series of final exams that would determine the class of degree she received. In the end, her preoccupation with other matters caught up with her; K did not do spectacularly well on her finals. She took a Third Class degree, which put an end to any hope of an academic career in history, if that had appealed to her. Certainly Frederic Kenyon had hoped for at least a Second and was keenly disappointed.[48]

It is worth remembering that Thirds were perhaps more common in the 1920s than they became later. Of the twenty-eight Somerville students who took degrees in 1928, only one took a First Class degree. Thirteen got Seconds, twelve got Thirds, and there were two Fourth Class degrees. Of the eight who took degrees in modern history, one received a First, three took Seconds, and four (including K) obtained Thirds. So, Kathleen's performance was not as catastrophic as one might think. It was, nevertheless, clearly a disappointment and was remembered throughout her career. At one of her memorial services fifty years later the speaker brought up the Third.[49] She could never quite get away from it.

At this point Margery Fry, the Principal of Somerville College, stepped in, with significant consequences for K's future. Margery Fry had become head of the college in 1926. As in so many instances throughout her life, K had a previous connection. Miss Fry already knew Frederic Kenyon, having served with

For much of the nineteenth century, archaeology was simply treasure-hunting. In the early nineteenth century, for example, Bernardino Drovetti and Giovanni Belzoni collected antiquities by essentially ransacking Egyptian tombs. In the 1870s Heinrich Schliemann hacked recklessly through a number of occupation levels at Hissarlik in his search for the legendary Troy. This cavalier approach was changing, however, as the century came to an end.

A major figure in this revolution was Flinders Petrie. Beginning in 1883, his excavations in Egypt introduced a more systematic and methodical approach to digging that emphasized the recording of all objects, even the humblest fragments of pottery, and careful attention to both stratigraphy—that is, the different layers of a site—and the objects in them. In the course of his work he also established typological sequence dating for the ancient Near East. Using groups of artifacts that appeared together consistently in Egyptian graves, he was able to establish a timeline of the relative chronology of the different styles of pottery for pre-dynastic Egypt. At the same time Petrie pioneered a dating method known as cross-dating, whereby objects of a known date in a particular archaeological layer are used to date objects of an otherwise unknown date in the same level. He was, for example, able to date Mycenaean pottery to ca. 1500–1000 B.C. because at a site called Ghurab he found it in association with Egyptian artifacts that he knew dated to the Eighteenth Dynasty (1570–1293 B.C.). Petrie's accomplishments were such that, despite little formal education, in 1892 he became the first Professor of Egyptology at the University of London.

In 1905 the British Association for the Advancement of Science sent David Randall-MacIver, an archaeologist trained by Flinders Petrie in Egypt, to investigate the ruins of the Great Zimbabwe. In his excavations Randall-MacIver noted that artifacts found in the lowest levels were very similar to those of the surrounding African population. Moreover, he was able to use cross-dating to date the site. Many of the foreign artifacts—Chinese, Arab, and Persian—came from near the bottom of the archaeological layers and could be dated to the later medieval period. But his conclusion, reported in *Mediaeval Rhodesia* (1906), that the Great Zimbabwe had been built in the fourteenth and fifteenth centuries by black Africans, was difficult for many to accept. Richard Hall responded by publishing *Prehistoric Rhodesia* in 1909, arguing that the Great Zimbabwe was beyond the capabilities of native Africans and suggesting again that it was the work of outsiders, perhaps as long ago as 2000 B.C. Many agreed with him that such impressive buildings could not have been constructed by indigenous Africans.

Some twenty years later the controversy continued. In 1928, wanting to settle the matter, the British Association invited Gertrude Caton-Thompson to examine the site again and report to the Association at its meeting, to be held in Cape Town in July and August 1929. Caton-Thompson, too, had learned archaeological method from Petrie. Blessed with a private income and largely educated at home, she began her study of archaeology in 1921 at the age of thirty-one by attending his lectures at University College, London. She then joined Petrie's excavation at Abydos in Egypt later that same year. After spending a year studying at Newnham College, Cambridge, she excavated with Petrie again at Qua in 1924, and was sufficiently skilled to begin her own excavations at Fayum, in northwest Egypt in 1925.

Caton-Thompson accepted the commission to investigate the Great Zimbabwe, and Margery Fry urged her to take Kathleen Kenyon as her companion. Kathleen, anxious for a little adventure, was eager to go. Unfortunately, she was also completely untrained in archaeological excavation. K's lack of experience meant that Caton-Thompson required some persuading.

Now it was Sir Frederic Kenyon who intervened. Kathleen Kenyon would always deny that she became an archaeologist because of her father, but he certainly facilitated her early career. She first met Gertrude Caton-Thompson at lunch at the British Museum, where Sir Frederic had invited her to discuss the possibility of his daughter accompanying her. He offered to pay Kathleen's traveling expenses if the expedition would pay her living expenses.[1] Caton-Thompson was willing to take K, finding her intelligent and eager. She suggested that Sir Frederic put his proposal to Professor (later Sir) John Myres, General Secretary of the British Association, Wykeham Professor of Ancient History at Oxford and himself an archaeologist, with whom Frederic Kenyon was already well acquainted. Caton-Thompson hoped that the Kenyons might be persuaded to foot all of Kathleen's expenses, although Sir Frederic maintained he couldn't afford this. Caton-Thompson was unsure how far the expedition's funds would go in southern Africa, a region with which she was unfamiliar, and insisted that a trained assistant was necessary. She wanted to take Dorothy Norie, a professional architect, who would do the surveying and drawing of plans but who could not pay any of her own expenses.[2] In the end a deal was struck: the British Association agreed to pay Kathleen's maintenance, but not her travel expenses.[3] In late February or early March 1929, Kathleen joined Dorothy Norie on a boat bound for South Africa.

The St. Albans dig did not begin until July, but the ever industrious K made sure she had plenty to do in the intervening months. She spent much of January and February doing research in the British Museum,[6] for she had agreed to contribute a chapter to Caton-Thompson's book on the excavations, which was eventually published as "Sketch of the Exploration and Settlement of the East Coast of Africa" in *Zimbabwe Culture: Ruins and Reactions* in 1931. She also published several articles, illustrated with her own photographs, in *The Kodak Magazine*, a popular magazine for amateur photographers. Helping with an exhibit on Zimbabwe at the British Museum in April and May of 1930 and giving lectures on the excavations took up yet more of her time. Her more serious pursuits didn't keep K from recreational activities: tennis, hockey, dances, and tea parties.

The period between K's return from Africa and her departure for St. Albans also presented a social difficulty. Although she had an active social life, Kathleen never seems to have shown much romantic interest in young men. At least one young man, however, showed an interest in her. During this period she was spending time with Bob Francis, a farmer she had met in South Africa, who had traveled back to England on the same boat. Francis tried to attach himself to K, but although she thought him a very nice young man, she also found him a bit dull. Perhaps she found it hard to say no, because she did continue to see him as long as he was in England. They went to lunch and dinner and the theater, but she was relieved when he finally left the country.[7]

Indeed, in the early months of 1930 K seemed more interested in her new black-and-white puppy of uncertain terrier descent than in Bob Francis; Sir Frederic reported that she was "spend[ing] all her time . . . in puppy worship."[8] At Sir Frederic's suggestion the new puppy was named "Solomon," quickly shortened to Solly. K was devoted to him. On some level she probably preferred dogs to people. Throughout her life she certainly displayed an indulgence with dogs she never did with human beings. For example, while K liked children, she never liked bad-manned children; but she had no reservations about bad-mannered dogs. Always adept at managing human beings, K was never very good about disciplining her dogs. As a result, Solly was not especially well behaved; in particular, he had an unpleasant habit of biting people. Unsurprisingly, he was not popular with everyone else in the family, particularly Lady Kenyon. K, who rarely admitted that a dog could do anything wrong, thought this was unreasonable of her mother.[9] Despite Solly's obvious faults, K never hesitated to defend her dog, more than once pleading that he be forgiven for her sake.[10]

The normally self-possessed Kathleen was unquestionably soppy where animals were concerned. The thought of putting down a horse could reduce her to tears.[11] Troublesome mongrels like Solly wrung from her unusual displays of emotion. When, a few years later, the dog vanished on a trip into London, K was frantic. For the week that Solly was missing she was miserable, constantly imagining him wet, cold, and hungry. She was so obsessed with her lost dog that she considered giving up sugar in her tea. It reminded her of Solly because she always took an extra sugar for the dog. So unhappy that even her mother was sympathetic, the normally unflappable Kathleen embarrassed herself by breaking down in front of a total stranger. But when hope was almost gone, Solly turned up. K was overjoyed, writing exuberantly to Nora, "The miraculous has happened, and I have got Solly back."[12] Indeed, K's attachment to her dogs would one day even threaten her professional life.

But in the spring of 1930, lectures and dances and the theater—even the new puppy—were not enough to keep K occupied, for she confided to her sister she was bored in London.[13] She needed something more absorbing; she was no doubt relieved when she finally joined the St. Albans excavation at the end of July. There she found something that would absorb her for the rest of her life.

Kathleen entered archaeology at a critical point in the discipline's development. The method she would learn at St. Albans and spend the rest of her life advocating owed much to General Augustus Henry Lane-Fox Pitt Rivers, who had been part of the general revolution in archaeology at the end of the nineteenth century. After his retirement from the army in 1880 he began excavating on his estate in southern England. Rather than merely burrowing into the ground in order to find interesting or valuable objects, Pitt Rivers recognized that apparently insignificant items like small finds or potsherds could help unravel the chronology of a site if their positions in the archaeological layers were accurately recorded. His military background and sense of order were apparent in the way in which he methodically excavated a site, precisely recording the position of all finds and publishing his results completely and promptly.

Rik Wheeler had been greatly influenced by Pitt Rivers. Having been awarded his D. Litt. by the University of London in 1920, Wheeler became Director of the National Museum of Wales in 1924. He had carefully read the four volumes of Pitt Rivers's *Excavations in Cranborne Chase*, published between 1887 and 1898. The systematic nature of Pitt Rivers's method appealed to Wheeler, who was also a former military officer, and his approach

Thames, and eventually defeated Cassivellaunus, leader of the Belgic kingdom of the Catuvellauni. This victory was not followed up, and the Roman legions quickly withdrew until A.D. 43, when they invaded again. This time the conquest was permanent. Despite the brief rebellion of Queen Boudica in A.D. 60, by the end of the administration of the Roman governor Agricola in A.D. 84, the island as far north as southern Scotland and as far west as Wales was controlled by Rome.

The Wheelers' goal was to examine the development of the Roman city at Verulamium and discern its relationship with the British settlement that had preceded it. The excavations would eventually stretch over five or six miles. The site of the pre-Roman *oppidum*—or fortified settlement with rampart and ditch—did not lie under the Roman town next to the Ver River, as Wheeler had originally supposed. It was located instead in an area called Prae Wood, about three-quarters of a mile from the Roman site. There, the excavators discovered a Belgic *oppidum* dated by the pottery to about 15 B.C. But Wheeler was determined to take the history of Verulamium back to the time of the first Roman incursion under Julius Caesar in 54 B.C., and so he kept searching. He investigated two earthworks, one a mile to the north of the pre-Roman site known as Devil's Dyke, and the other across the Ver River, to the northwest of Verulamium, called Beech Bottom. The Devil's Dyke was likely a boundary marker for the Belgic *oppidum*. Beech Bottom was also a pre-Roman earthwork, which led Wheeler to suspect it was the boundary between the Belgic *oppidum* near the Ver and another close to the nearby Lea River. An investigation revealed such a site nearly six miles northeast of Verulamium, near the town of Wheathampstead, which was satisfactorily dated to the middle of the first century B.C. Triumphant, Wheeler declared that "this *oppidum* is more likely than any other known site to have been the headquarters of Cassivellaunus at the time of Caesar's invasion in 54 B.C."[23]

Much attention, of course, was also focused on the Roman settlement on the Ver. Excavations revealed a town—a *municipium*—which grew up around Watling Street, the Roman artery to London. While the town did not appear to have amounted to much in the first century A.D., the second century was a period of great expansion. Excavation of eleven acres in the southern half of the town revealed an expanding street plan, buildings—shops as well as wealthy townhouses—constructed of flint and brick rather than timber, and a triumphal arch over Watling Street. A more limited examination in the northern part of the town revealed another arch, a theater, and part of a forum. The city wall also dated from the second century. The third century, Wheeler argued, was one of decline, caused no doubt by the crises that shook the Roman Empire in that period. Signs of rebuilding appear with the restoration of peace at the end of the third century, but Verulamium again went into decline in the fourth century. Although Wheeler found no material evidence of Roman life past the fourth century, written sources demonstrated the continued presence of a Romano-British population in the fifth century. Eventually Roman Verulamium would be replaced by the nearby medieval St. Albans, named for the Christian martyr of the third century.

The future Mistress of Stratigraphy began at St. Albans by performing "every task from cleaning the skeleton of a Roman baby to digging a trench with pick and shovel" and was rewarded with the sarcastic compliment of one of the workmen that she would make "a first class navvy."[24] The excavation began with a trial trench dug across the site, which immediately revealed several buildings, including the edge of a tessellated floor, which K was set to clearing with a trowel. She found it thrilling when she came across a fifth-century pot buried under the floor, but uncovering the pavement was hard, tedious work.[25] A picture of Rik Wheeler working on the pavement was published in September 1930 in the *Illustrated London News* and subsequently was much associated with Wheeler, although it was apparently K who did more of the real labor. Of course, Wheeler was well aware of the value of publicity. This was another lesson Kathleen would learn from him.

K returned to St. Albans for five seasons of excavation. In the second season of 1931, having achieved a degree of proficiency, she excavated the northwest gate. Most of the structure itself was gone, but through meticulous excavation K revealed the "ghost" of the walls. Trenches had originally held the foundations of the walls. After the end of the Roman period the stone of the walls was removed for other uses, and the foundation trenches filled with debris. By carefully removing this debris, K was able to show where the walls had been (Figure 3.3). In 1932 she was given responsibility for uncovering the Fosse, an earthwork that extended from the west side of the Roman wall. K found it a tedious job, as it required no real technical skill but was simply a matter of figuring out in which direction the earthwork ran. She didn't actually have much to do much except watch the workmen. Although dull, the Fosse nevertheless managed to cause her endless aggravation, as she chased it one way and another, trying to pin it down. So, bored with the Fosse, K was delighted when, in September 1933, she was also given the job of uncovering

FIGURE 3.3: Verulamium "ghost" walls: excavation of trenches of robbed walls.
Courtesy of the St. Albans Museums.

the theater, which had been discovered earlier that season. Excavating the theater with its missing walls was just the kind of technical challenge Kathleen was coming to relish.[26]

Lord Verulam, the owner of the land on which the theater was located, announced that he would provide the money necessary to clear and preserve the theater, and K was told that she would get to do the job in the final 1934 season. Always eager for independence and responsibility, she wrote excitedly to her sister, "I am to do the whole show . . . and next year I shall be more or less on my own."[27]

She was therefore extremely disappointed when Wheeler decided that she would not do the theater alone as planned, but that Tessa Wheeler would be present. He explained that Lord Verulam might not want K left unsupervised. K did not believe this. She asked Mrs. Wheeler directly whether her husband was unhappy with her work. Mrs. Wheeler assured her that she would be in charge, but K wasn't entirely convinced.[28] In the end, both Rik and Tessa

Wheeler went to excavate the Dorset hill-fort at Maiden Castle, leaving Kathleen happily on her own.

K returned to the excavation of the Verulamium theater in May 1934. Her first major independent project turned out to be an important site: the only Roman theater known in Britain. Located in the northern part of the Roman city, on the western front of Watling Street, it was originally built about the mid-second century A.D. and modified shortly thereafter. A classical Roman theater typically had a semicircular orchestra and a large stage, with seats facing the stage. By contrast, the St. Albans theater was very simple, with a circular orchestra surrounded by a bank, or *cavea*, which no doubt had contained the audience's seats. A small stage was located in the area not occupied by the bank. The orientation of much of the audience toward the central area, rather than toward the stage, was striking. Indeed, the St. Albans theater was very similar to theaters found in northern and central France, and Kathleen suggested that such structures had been used for dances of some kind or possibly animal baiting, perhaps cock fighting (Figure 3.4).

K discovered that about ten years or so after the theater had been built, it had been altered in an attempt to make it more like a typical classical Roman theater. The size of the stage was increased, and almost half of the orchestra was turned into a seating area. Corinthian columns were added at the back of the stage. She concluded that these changes reflected the increasing Romanization of Verulamium. Further additions were made in about A.D. 200, but the theater fell into disrepair during the third century, a time of crisis and civil war for the Roman Empire. When order was restored near the end of the third century, the theater was rebuilt and enlarged as part of a general program of rebuilding that occurred at Verulamium in about A.D. 300. By the second half of the fourth century, however, it had become a garbage dump, bearing witness to the final decline of Roman power in Britain. The walls of the theater were removed by later Saxon and Norman invaders, the earth *cavea* collapsed, and eventually the theater was completely covered up. The robbing of the walls and the collapse of the earth bank made this a difficult site to excavate; K's success at doing so demonstrates her skill as an archaeologist even at this early stage of her career. She promptly published her report on the theater in the journal *Archaeologia* in 1935.[29]

Rik Wheeler was well aware that the general public took a decidedly romantic view of archaeology, and his published reports took account of that

FIGURE: 3.4: Reconstruction of Verulamium theater, ca. A.D. 180. *Painted by Alan Sorrel (1967). Courtesy of St. Albans Museums.*

view. His publication of the Verulamium excavation demonstrated more about his ability as a showman and his sense of what the public wanted than a realistic sense of what the archaeological evidence could support. He interpreted the site in terms of a historical narrative that included such dramatic characters as the Romans Julius Caesar and Agricola, and the British leaders Cassivellaunus, Tasciovanus, and Boudica. The archaeological evidence to support such connections was, however, dubious. Nowell Myres, son of Professor John Myres, published a stinging critique of Wheeler's report, accusing Wheeler of presenting a romantic account based on rather shaky evidence.[30] A heated exchange in the journal *Antiquity* resulted in what Wheeler's biographer Jacquetta Hawkes called "the most bitter and long-lasting feud to rend British archaeology between the two World wars."[31] Kathleen, of course, knew both men. There is no evidence that she took Wheeler's side in this quarrel, probably because her own interpretations were

53

more cautious than his.[32] But in the future she, too, would try to appeal to the public's sense of the dramatic.

ALTHOUGH THE YOUNG KATHLEEN was just learning her trade, St. Albans was not her only excavation of the early 1930s. An opportunity also arose for her to dig in Mandate Palestine, so for most years from 1931 through 1935 she spent the spring in the Near East and the late summer and fall excavating at St. Albans.

The European rediscovery of the lands of the Bible must be reckoned to have been launched by Napoleon's invasion of Egypt in 1799. By the middle of the nineteenth century Western travelers had begun searching Palestine, a mere backwater of the Ottoman Empire, for remnants of the biblical past. Edward Robinson, an American biblical scholar, is sometimes called the father of Biblical Archaeology; he was most certainly a pioneer of the historical geography of the Bible. Robinson was not, of course, the first Western traveler in the Holy Land, but he was the first with sufficient knowledge of modern biblical scholarship to attempt a reconstruction of the historical geography of the region. Comparing Arabic place names to the names of places given in the Bible allowed him to accurately identify dozens of biblical sites.

Robinson's efforts were only the start. One of the great achievements of the Palestine Exploration Fund (PEF) was its reconnaissance of the lands of the Bible. Founded in London in 1865 "for the accurate and systematic investigation of the archaeology, topography, geology and physical geography, natural history, manners and customs of the Holy Land, for biblical illustration,"[33] the new organization quickly began sponsoring historical and geographic surveys. Under the auspices of the PEF Charles Wilson not only undertook the scientific mapping of Jerusalem, but also began a survey of possible excavation sites. His work was carried on in 1867, when Charles Warren arrived in Palestine. The most comprehensive project of the PEF, however, was *The Survey of Western Palestine* (1881), which ran to seven volumes, covering over 10,000 sites and 6,000 square miles.

This greater knowledge of the geography of the Holy Land spurred its archaeological exploration. Explorers began digging in Palestine long before they understood the significance of one of the most characteristic features of its landscape. Neither Robinson nor Warren nor any of the early explorers understood that *tells* (Arabic for "mound") were artificial mounds comprised of the layers of hundreds, even thousands of years of accumulated human settlement. Only after Heinrich Schliemann's excavations at Hissarlik demonstrated that the mound represented different layers of the site's history was their significance realized.

But once it was understood, new excavation techniques could be applied. The few archaeological excavations conducted in Palestine in the nineteenth century did not yield much in the way of results because of the primitiveness of archaeological field techniques. When Charles Warren dug into the tell at Jericho, he completely missed the significance of what he found. Flinders Petrie, with his attention to stratigraphy and insistence on recording all objects, conducted the first excavation with modern field techniques in Palestine at Tell el Hesi. Influenced, like Rik Wheeler, by Augustus Pitt Rivers, Petrie dug according to arbitrary levels rather than the natural layers of the mound, but his 1890 dig was a watershed in the history of Palestinian archaeology. He not only understood what a tell was, but he paid attention to the different occupation layers, which he was able to date according to pottery typology.

Some later excavators also employed these more sophisticated methods. The Palestine Exploration Fund sponsored American archaeologist Frederick Bliss, who understood the importance of stratigraphy. After digging at Tell el Hesi, he joined forces with R.A.S. Macalister in 1898 to search for ancient Gath, the city of the Philistines mentioned in the Old Testament. They dug several different sites in their quest, and attention to stratigraphic layers paid off: at Tell Judeideh they were able to identify three different occupation periods.

Nevertheless, not all subsequent excavations took account of stratigraphy. Some excavators continued to use the trenching method, digging not by layers but simply by cutting a wide trench across the top of the mound, which made it difficult to separate the layers of occupation debris. In the early years of the twentieth century, ancient Gezer, Meggido, Taanach, Jericho, and Shechem were all excavated in this way.

The British School of Archaeology in Jerusalem (BSAJ) had been established in 1919 in the aftermath of the First World War and the establishment of the British Mandate over Palestine. Sir Frederic Kenyon, who was chairman of the original organizing committee (which also included Flinders Petrie), was its first president. The declared purpose of the BSAJ was "the study of the archaeology of Western Asia,"[34] with Palestine and Syria as the main areas of focus. The organizing committee stated that "the emancipation by Great Britain of the Near East [from the Turks] involves exceptional responsibilities in relation to the ancient monuments and antiquities," and noted "the imperious duty of preserving these historical places."[35] Part of its mission was also the training of students in proper methods of excavation. Sir Frederic himself wanted the School to instruct students in scientific excavation techniques, because he knew from his own experience that there were not enough properly trained field archaeologists.[36]

In 1930 Frederic Kenyon was still President, and the Director of the BSAJ was John Winter Crowfoot. J. W. Crowfoot had studied classics at Brasenose College, Oxford, where he had developed a great interest in archaeology. With no way to make a living at it, however, he had embarked on a long career as a civil servant in Egypt and the Sudan. Upon his retirement (with a pension) in 1926 he became Director of the British School of Archaeology and excavated both in Jerusalem and at Jerash, in what would later become Jordan.

The biblical site of Samaria had been excavated by Harvard University in 1908–1910, first under Gottlieb Schumacher, and then on a larger scale by George Reisner and Clarence Fisher. In 1929 Harvard was again interested in Samaria, and Dr. Kirsopp Lake of the Harvard Theological Seminary approached John Crowfoot. Thus was born the Joint Expedition to Samaria, a combined effort of Harvard, the BSAJ, the Hebrew University of Jerusalem, the Palestine Exploration Fund, and the British Academy.

At about the same time, discussions were underway concerning a closer working relationship between the BSAJ and the Palestine Exploration Fund. Although the possibility of amalgamating the two organizations was bandied about, in the end it was decided merely to engage in closer cooperation.[37] In that spirit, in November 1930 Sir Frederic was asked to be on the Executive Committee of the PEF.[38] He subsequently became the Chairman of the Joint Advisory Committee of the two organizations.

Given both her decision to make a career of archaeology and her father's association with the BSAJ and PEF, it is not surprising that in 1931 Kathleen became a student of the British School of Archaeology in Jerusalem and joined the Samaria excavation when it began in the spring of 1931. Thus it was that in early 1931 she arrived for the first time in the Middle East, where so much of her professional life would be spent.

The site of ancient Samaria is thirty-five miles north of Jerusalem, near the modern village of Sebastia.[39] It was at Samaria that, according to the Bible, Omri, king of Israel, established his capital. The city was built on a hill rising 430 meters above sea level. Located at a crossroads near the center of the northern kingdom of Israel, it overlooked the road connecting Egypt and the southern kingdom of Judah with the Jezreel Valley, as well as the routes north to Phoenicia and Damascus. Samaria was destroyed in 108 B.C. by the Hasmoneans, but in the first century B.C. Herod rebuilt the city and renamed it Sebaste in honor of the Emperor Augustus, *Sebastos* being Greek for Augustus.

The makeup of the Joint Expedition to Samaria changed over the four seasons of the dig, but the staff included, at one time or another, in addition to John Crowfoot as the director, Eleazar Sukenik (father of Israeli archaeologist Yigael Yadin) from the Hebrew University as assistant director; Nahman Reiss (later Avigad)[40] as draftsman; and Jacob Pinkerfeld of Tel Aviv as the architect. Professor Lake, Silva New, and Professor Robert Blake represented Harvard. In addition to Kathleen, several students of the BSAJ participated, including Archie Buchanan, a former naval officer who did the surveying; Muriel Bentwich, who drew the small objects; and Elizabeth ("Betty") Murray, who worked in the 1933 season, and was a recent graduate of Somerville College and a friend of the Crowfoots' daughter Dorothy. An Australian, Nancy de Crespigny, K's colleague at St. Albans, was also there in 1933.

The British archaeological world was a small one in the 1930s. At Samaria this was even more the case; it was something of a family affair, as various Crowfoot relatives played a role in the excavations. John Hood, a cousin, worked in 1933 as a volunteer. The Crowfoots' daughter, and K's friend from St. Albans, Joan was present occasionally and ran the first-aid clinic in 1933. In 1935 the youngest daughter Diana served as general camp helper. But most important was John Crowfoot's wife. Grace Mary ("Molly") Crowfoot ran the camp and acted as registrar, recording small finds such as pottery, glass, and coins. A highly competent but unconventional woman, she was known for her disheveled appearance and outbreaks of fierce temper.[41] K was a little put off by her at first, but she came to have a high regard for Mrs. Crowfoot, not only finding her extremely kind[42] but also later writing approvingly that she was "a first class archaeologist [who] was prepared to devote endless time and trouble to the minutiae."[43] Prevented from attending university by a mother who saw no need for it, Molly Crowfoot became, despite the birth of four daughters, recognized as an expert in ancient textiles.

As on most archaeological excavations, living conditions were simple. The dig house, which had been built before their arrival, formed a U-shape around a central courtyard and included a kitchen and dining room, bathroom, pot rooms, drawing office, and darkroom. Although they had a hotel-trained Egyptian cook and Palestinian servants to do the washing, the expedition staff lived in tents, sleeping on camp beds. For furniture K improvised, keeping her clothes in boxes and using a packing case as a dressing table. As usual, she didn't mind the inconveniences of camp life, enduring the mice infesting her tent, grasshoppers that ate holes in her clothes, and a wasp who built a nest on the back of her trunk. She even seems to have gotten over her objection to early rising. Work started at 6 am but could begin even earlier when the weather was especially hot.

At Samaria K was introduced for the first time to the complexities of running a dig in the Middle East, with native labor and local landowners. By the end of the final season John Crowfoot reported that he had signed 150 agreements concerning fees, including payments for rent, wages, and the hire of various relatives.[44] All did not always go smoothly. On one occasion work was held up because the owners of some of the land that needed to be leased demanded to be hired permanently by the excavation. The headman, or *muktar*, of Sebastia suggested to Crowfoot that he agree to the landowners' terms. Later he explained that he meant that they should be hired, the agreement regarding the land signed, and the landowners sacked the next day. K, who was rapidly developing the affection for the Palestinian Arabs that would characterize her career, apparently approved of these tactics, telling her mother that the *muktar* "is a wonderful man!"[45]

The small society of a camp abroad made personality conflicts between the eclectic staff inevitable. The Hebrew University's representative Eleazar Sukenik was a difficult, touchy personality disliked by many although, according to one of his daughters, John Crowfoot had a soft spot for him.[46] K, because of what she had heard about Sukenik, was prepared not to like him but on first acquaintance thought him "rather nice." K and Betty Murray did not care for each other, K finding Murray unbearably earnest,[47] while K struck Murray as superior and aloof.[48]

While archaeology for Kathleen was a serious endeavor, she was not always a serious archaeologist. In letters home Betty Murray criticized the lack of gravity of K and others, decrying their horseplay and lighthearted banter.[49] K and Murray undoubtedly did not sit together at dinner, because K clearly preferred to think of dinner as a social occasion and liked the arrangement whereby the Americans, Sukenik, and Molly Crowfoot sat at one end and what she characterized as the "lighter spirits"—herself included—sat with John Crowfoot at the other.[50] At one time K ended up in the midst of the Americans, whom she accused of talking nothing but shop: "It was more than I could bear, and I hope I succeeded in moving without causing offense."[51]

Other than dinner, the social life of the dig consisted of having cocktails at the end of the day, playing bridge after dinner, and in 1933, listening to jazz records on Nancy de Crespigny's gramophone. Regular Sunday outings, complete with a beer on the way home, provided a welcome break from work. On one of these jaunts Kathleen was able to visit Dorothy Garrod's excavations on Mt. Carmel, the first of several visits over the years of the Samaria dig. On several occasions the Samarian excavators toured the University of Chicago dig at Megiddo, where they were envious of the money the Americans had to spend: all of the rooms of the dig house had hot and cold running water. Sightseeing trips were made to the Sea of Galilee, Mt. Tabor, and Acre. During the 1933 season the Sunday outings shifted away from sightseeing, and usually consisted of trips down to Netanya, to the sea, which was fine with K, who very much enjoyed swimming.[52]

The main focus of attention, of course, was the excavation itself. The Joint Expedition built on the achievements of its predecessors. The excavators began by digging in five different locations, including several of the areas previously explored by the Harvard team. Perhaps the most important of these was the summit of the hill. On the western end the earlier Harvard expedition had found part of Herod's Augusteum, or temple of Augustus, as well as the royal palace of the Israelite kings, and a nearby storehouse called the Ostraca House because of the numerous ostraca—potsherds with writing on them—in it. The Joint Expedition extended the excavations of the royal palace to the east and, in doing so, found a significant collection of ivory carvings. Such carvings were probably used to ornament furniture and walls and, quite possibly, belonged to Ahab's biblical "house of ivory." The royal palace was shown to be part of an upper city on the top of the hill, while a lower city (of which little was excavated) extended down the slope of the hill. Two walls were found on the summit: a smaller, earlier wall, which was attributed to Omri, and a second, later, larger wall. Ten meters thick in places, this was a casemate wall—a wall made up of two walls with partitions in between. In addition, over the four seasons of the dig, the Joint Expedition also uncovered a forum, stadium, Hellenistic fort, a temple dedicated to the goddess Kore (or Persephone), a Roman theater, tombs, and a fifth-century Christian church (Figure 3.5).

FIGURE 3.5: Work on the Roman tombs, Samaria. Possibly K is one of the female figures but they are uncertain.

In 1931 K began supervising the excavation of what the Reisner-Fisher expedition had called the "Hippodrome," which turned out not to be a hippodrome at all, but probably a stadium containing a *palaestra* (or gymnasium). The site was not completely excavated, but K worked on the northern section in 1931. Eventually she was also given charge of site Q—the summit and royal palace. This is important because she introduced to this rather confusing site the techniques she was learning from Rik Wheeler at St. Albans. On the summit there had been much destruction, much robbing of stones, and much rebuilding, all of which had disturbed the deposits. Wheeler's method of very precise three-dimensional recording, while painstaking and time-consuming, was ideal for such complex stratified layers.[53] By digging a north–south trench across the summit and carefully noting the layers and the finds associated with them, K was able to distinguish between the various strata and to determine to which layer each set of building remains belonged. While the joke on the site was that she spent her days excavating walls that weren't there,[54] K wrote her father that she found it "quite interesting disentangling them [i.e., a series of houses built on top of each other]."[55]

Kathleen's work at Samaria may well have been made easier by the presence of six Egyptian *ra'asa*, or foremen, who had been trained by George Reisner. Three of these had actually worked on Reisner's Samarian excavations of twenty years earlier. This was important because Reisner, like Petrie, emphasized "adequate training and staffing . . . close supervision of work in progress, and . . . detailed and accurate recording of finds."[56] Being a good *reis* was not an easy job, and a *reis* who had been trained by Reisner would be better prepared to excavate as K would do.

Excavating as K did, of course, involved extensive work with the pottery. One of Flinders Petrie's major contributions to archaeology had been the introduction of typological sequence dating to the Near East. Using pottery typologies, he had been able to fix a chronology for prehistoric Egypt. Petrie was then able to do the same thing for Palestine by excavating Tell el Hesi, where he noted, for the first time, the precise location of pottery within the stratigraphy of the mound. Thus, he established the foundation for a chronology that allowed any layer associated with a particular form of Palestinian pottery to be dated. Since then, other scholars had worked to refine this ceramic sequence.[57]

So, in order to establish an accurate stratigraphy and to date the various layers precisely, K had to pay close attention to the pottery. Betty Murray, not one of her admirers, was so impressed by K's knowledge that she was convinced that she knew more about the pottery than even Molly Crowfoot, who as registrar was responsible for cataloging it.[58] Since much of the analysis of the pottery was done after the dig ended and there was so much of it to do, K began shipping the pottery home and working on it over the winter.[59]

Kathleen eventually distinguished six different building periods on the summit of the hill at Samaria between the founding of the city by Omri in 876 B.C. and its conquest by the Assyrians in 722 B.C. Arguing that there had been no occupation of the site before Omri (and using the biblical account to support this argument), she dated Period I to the time of Omri (822–871 B.C). Period II she dated to the reign of Ahab (871–852 B.C.), Omri's son and, famously, the husband of the infamous Jezebel, daughter of the king of Tyre. In this period the larger casemate wall had been constructed. K dated Period III to Jehu (842–814 B.C.), who revolted against Joram, son of Ahab, wiping out the remainder of Ahab's family. Period IV was the time of Jeroboam II (784–748 B.C.), under whom Samaria reached its height. Periods V and VI were periods of decline, which culminated in the conquest of Samaria by the Assyrian Sargon II in 722 B.C.

The first Samaria volume, *Early Ivories from Samaria, Samaria-Sebaste*, Volume II, was quickly produced by John and Molly Crowfoot, appearing in 1938. *The Buildings of Samaria, Samaria-Sebaste*, Volume I, with K's stratigraphical analysis of the buildings at the summit, came out in 1942. The final pottery report, however, was not published until 1957, in *The Objects from Samaria, Samaria-Sebaste*, Volume III, because of, among other things, the Second World War. K's work on the pottery generally received favorable reviews and, in fact, quickly became the standard reference work for the chronology of Iron Age Palestine. The American archaeologist William F. Albright praised the publication of the pottery and small finds and described *Samaria-Sebaste III*, along with the publication at about the same time of the Hazor excavation by Yigael Yadin, as "represent[ing] a new high point in the history of Palestinian archaeology."[60] Albright's student G. Ernest Wright was also enthusiastic: "I have no hesitation in affirming that the Kenyon work at Samaria is one of the most remarkable achievements in the history of Palestinian archaeology."[61]

However, K's report also provoked a debate, one rooted in differences in archaeological method. She dated buildings on the basis of pottery found in the foundations of the buildings—that is, pottery that must have been present during the building's construction. Other archaeologists, however, including

Albright and Wright, as well as the Israelis Yohanan Aharoni and Ruth Amiran, argued that pottery from the foundations of a building must predate the building. They instead dated buildings based on pottery found lying directly on the floors.[62] As one scholar has noted, "[b]oth systems had merit; they simply addressed different aspects of the same methodological issue. Kenyon's approach yielded a floor's *terminus post quem* (construction date), whereas Wright's provided its *terminus ante quem* (occupation dates)."[63] On the basis of these differences, Albright, Wright, Aharoni, and Amiran argued that the pottery from K's Periods I and II preceded her Building Phases I and II, and thus concluded that the site at Samaria was occupied before the establishment of Omri's capital in the later ninth century B.C.[64] Not one to change her mind easily, K was unpersuaded. She never accepted the presence of earlier Iron Age material in her Period I pottery, even while acknowledging the presence of even earlier Early Bronze Age pottery.[65]

Another criticism of K's interpretation of Samaria has been that she tried too hard to make the archaeology fit the biblical account of Omri's foundation of the city. A. D. Tushingham, however, has defended her, writing that "K did not herself equate the archaeological evidence with the literary (biblical) record,"[66] and pointing out that, indeed, she herself stated that the excavations at the summit of Samaria

> revealed a series of buildings of the Israelite period, of which the relative chronology could be definitely established by stratification, but of which the absolute dating is much less certain. The various building periods, therefore, are referred to by numbers, which is less misleading than ascribing them to the periods of the various kings, for such ascription can at the moment only be hypothetical.[67]

But despite her desire to be cautious, the attraction of the neat written chronology of the Old Testament was strong. It seems clear that in both her excavation reports and her popular articles, K was influenced by the biblical account more than would be acceptable to some (but by no means all) archaeologists today. She was to tell a student some years later that knowing all about Iron Age pottery was all very well, but it wouldn't get you very far if you didn't also know the First and Second Book of Kings.[68]

Recently Ron Tappy, criticizing the lack of stratigraphical information given in the published volume of *Samaria-Sebaste III*, has gone back to the original field notes to re-examine K's conclusions. He has argued in favor of revising her chronology, arguing, for example, that the pottery clearly demonstrates occupation in the eleventh and tenth centuries B.C., long before Omri, and that it is only K's Pottery Period 3 which can be dated to the ninth century. Nevertheless, he notes approvingly the meticulous nature of the excavation—which he attributes to both Kathleen and Molly Crowfoot—and K's "comprehensive notes . . . [which] attest to her perceptiveness and thoroughness as a field archaeologist."[69]

In addition, it should not be forgotten that when K completed the Samaria excavations in 1935, she was only twenty-nine years old and had been doing archaeology for less than six years. Her work at Samaria, accomplished while she acted essentially as a co-director of the excavation, was a tremendous achievement, given her youth and relative inexperience. Despite Tappy's differing conclusions, it was precisely her ability as a field archaeologist that allowed a productive reexamination of the excavation.[70] So, whatever the merit of these debates, which continue, at Samaria in the early 1930s Kathleen was honing her skills as a field archaeologist and pioneering new field methods. This was the first application of Wheeler's method, sometimes called debris-layer analysis, to the Middle East—the first application of what would come to be known as the Wheeler-Kenyon method.

THIS SUMMARY OF THE EXCAVATIONS at St. Albans, where she learned the Wheeler method, and those at Samaria, where she applied it, may mislead because it disguises the fact that K was bouncing back and forth between England and Palestine from 1930 to 1935. She spent the late summer and fall of 1930 at St. Albans, going out to the Middle East from March to June 1931. She was at St. Albans again in the fall of 1931 and 1932 and out at Samaria again in the spring of 1932 and 1933. The last season at Samaria was supposed to be in 1933, so K was able to go back to St. Albans to excavate the theater in May 1934. But, in fact, there was an additional season at Samaria, and she went out to Palestine again in March 1935.

The Joint Expedition had originally intended only three seasons at Samaria, from 1931 to 1933. Near the end of the 1933 season, however, they discovered a round tower on the summit, as well as some additional walls in relatively good condition. Suspecting that these areas might be able to clear up some remaining questions concerning the topography of Israelite Samaria, John Crowfoot wanted one more season. Up until this point, Harvard University had provided most of the funds, but the final season in 1935 was financed mostly by the British Academy and the Palestine Exploration Fund. The withdrawal of American resources meant a much smaller staff than in previous years. Besides the Crowfoots, Kathleen and Nahman Avigad were the only staff members to participate again. They were joined by Dr. and Mrs. Immanuel Ben-Dor of Jerusalem and Professor A. H. Detweiler of Cornell University, who served as surveyor and architect. In addition, Eleazar Sukenik was able to help out occasionally. Work began in early April, with K continuing excavations at the summit while Dr. Ben-Dor took charge of the tower.

In many ways, K found this the most difficult year of the excavations. For one thing, she was kept very busy supervising a large group of workmen and drawing the sections—that is, recording the stratigraphy of the site as they dug down, layer by layer. She found she was so overwhelmed that she sometimes skipped the traditional Sunday outings, including the trips to the beach of which she was so fond.[71]

Also, and unusually, she did not get on with John Crowfoot that season. She found him uncharacteristically irritable, so much so that she wondered if he was ill, or perhaps unhappy that he was due to retire at the end of the season. K thought that he was particularly short-tempered with her and found him so hostile that, although she tried to be agreeable, she was truly afraid of losing her temper with him.[72]

She did lose her temper with his wife, who was known for her own sudden displays of anger. People generally ignored Molly Crowfoot's outbursts because they never lasted long; she and K usually got along quite well. But at one point near the end of the dig, K had had enough, telling Mrs. Crowfoot point blank that she "disliked being talked to like that." The storm passed, however, and afterward their relations were very amicable.[73]

The big problem K faced, however, in 1935 as well as earlier seasons, was her frustration with others' lack of interest in, and understanding of, stratigraphy. The budding Mistress of Stratigraphy was neither fully appreciated nor understood. And perhaps, as she was not always the most diplomatic person, others found her opinionated and didactic. She was using the method she had learned from Wheeler, digging according to the natural layers of soil and paying careful attention to the levels in which the pottery was found. This method was particularly valuable in digging a complex site such as the summit at Samaria, where many of the walls had been dug out and reused. K reported home that her site on the summit "has many robbed walls and no actual ones."[74] But the other members of the staff were unconverted. For example, in 1935 Ben-Dor was excavating the round tower on the northeast corner of the summit. John Crowfoot had originally dated it to the Israelite period because Reisner had dated a similar round tower to the time of Jeroboam II. However, once a shaft was sunk into the tower and the debris inside cleared out, Hellenistic pottery found at the bottom showed that it could have been built no earlier than the fourth century B.C. Kathleen found this "a marvelous example of the danger of clearing the face of a building and deciding on its dating, without getting the associated levels!"[75] In addition, when Ben-Dor was later excavating south of the tower on a site with many walls, K complained that he did not know how to separate them, being as ignorant as he was of the importance of stratigraphy.[76]

Sukenik, too, was uninterested in her methodology. Although K still found him pleasant enough on occasion, she also thought him exceptionally difficult on the subject of stratification, lamenting that he hated any mention of the subject. She tried to explain the evidence to him but maintained that he refused to show any interest.[77] She found John Crowfoot no help, having told her in an earlier season, "Damn your stratification."[78] K particularly resented Crowfoot's unhappiness with her, because she was able to show on the summit that one of her walls had been built subsequent to the other, but both were in use at the same time; at Ben-Dor's site they had to guess at the dates of the assorted walls because the relationship of the layers to each had been ignored.[79] The young archaeologist could become so obsessed with the problems of her site that once she felt obliged to apologize to her father for writing such a dull letter: "I have been thinking too much about stratification."[80]

In 1935 K may also have been preoccupied with thoughts about her new job at Rik Wheeler's recently established Institute of Archaeology in London. Establishing an institution for the proper training of archaeologists had long been a dream of Wheeler's, and in January 1934 Tessa Wheeler had telephoned Kathleen to ask for her help with the Palestinian section of the projected Institute, presumably on the basis of her experience at Samaria. K was delighted to help: "I gather I am to have charge of it. . . . It sounds great fun."[81] In July 1935 Wheeler wrote to her on behalf of the Management Committee of the Institute of Archaeology (of which her father was a member), offering her the post of Secretary of the new institution. She accepted, but was ambivalent, writing to her mother: "I am a bit mixed in my feelings about it, as I am not at all sure it is the sort of job I want, but I don't see how I could help taking it."[82] Her lack of enthusiasm for an administrative position probably stemmed from her love of fieldwork, her inability to turn it down from her admiration for the Wheelers.

Before K had accepted this position, with its obligation to be back by October 1, she had been planning to go to Japan with a friend and to return to England in November. But in May the friend had backed out of the trip. K decided to compensate by planning an interesting journey home.[83] So, for the homeward journey in 1935, K, Joan Crowfoot, and Diana, the youngest Crowfoot daughter, decided to drive from Palestine to England.

The girls first had to find an affordable car and, although used cars were expensive in Palestine, they managed to find a 1926 Dodge for a mere thirty pounds.[84] There was a reason the car was so affordable; after buying it, K and Joan Crowfoot tried to drive away and the car immediately began to sputter and choke. Once at the garage, the problem took all afternoon to fix. Afterward, they had the car inspected and overhauled by a helpful mechanic who worked for the Department of Antiquities. To be on the safe side, they planned to take enough money to pay for train fare if the car gave out.[85]

Initially the young women also planned to have a man accompany them at least part of the way; the mechanic who worked for the Department of Antiquities was their first choice. In fact, K wrote to reassure her mother that they would not leave without him.[86] But in the end they did go without him, as the Department of Antiquities would not grant him the necessary leave. K was not too disappointed, as she feared he would have taken charge of the expedition and she, clearly, preferred to take charge herself.[87] The three then decided to pick up a driver to accompany them through Turkey when they reached Aleppo, although, as it turned out, this did not happen either.

Where they would have put another person in the fully packed Dodge is something of a mystery anyway. Their suitcases were strapped to the back of the car. Packed into it were the necessities for the journey—food (mostly corned beef and sausages), cooking supplies (including a Primus stove), tents, thin, rolled-up mattresses, and other equipment. On the running boards of the car they carried cans of water, petrol, and oil and paraffin. Neither of the front doors of the car could be opened, which meant that the driver had to climb in through the window, which, as K observed, "was easy enough . . . [but] difficult to do . . . with dignity in front of an admiring crowd"[88] (Figure 3.6).

The 1935 Samaria season ended well. Kathleen believed that she had done what she had set out to do and that, despite struggles over stratigraphy,

FIGURE 3.6: K, Diana Crowfoot, and Joan Crowfoot leaving Samaria.
Courtesy of Sebastian Payne.

John Crowfoot properly appreciated all that she had accomplished on her site. The last weekend of the dig they all went into Jerusalem for a dance at Government House, at which K greatly enjoyed herself, staying until 2:30 am. The next week the girls set off, and most of the village of Sebastia came to say goodbye.[89]

From Samaria they headed west, past Megiddo, and then took the coastal road north to Lebanon. They were behind schedule almost from the start, slowed by problems with the car. It usually chugged along comfortably at about forty miles per hour (although, because of inadequate springs, they had to go more slowly on bad roads), but not only did it run through oil at the rate of about a half gallon a day, it also had frequent brake problems, which had to be attended to in Beirut, Aleppo, and Istanbul.[90]

In Aleppo they contacted the British Consulate about finding a chauffeur to accompany them through Turkey. The vice-consul advised them to wait until they crossed into Turkey so that hiring a driver would be cheaper. When at Adana they again looked into the possibility of hiring someone to accompany them, the agent of the Shell Oil Company there suggested that they could manage on their own. They decided they could.

Turkey was the roughest part of the trip; they did not encounter really good roads again until reaching Italy several weeks later. Furthermore, in Turkey they were required to stop at every police station and register with the authorities, who had to record names, occupations, destinations, and so on. Since they often did not find anyone who spoke English, French, German, or Arabic, and since the Turks had only recently switched to the Roman alphabet from Arabic script, this was an extremely time-consuming process, often taking an hour just to get down their names. But they had little real trouble. As three young women traveling and camping out alone, they encountered more amusement than hostility, setting aside the time they were briefly taken for cattle thieves and woke to find themselves surrounded by men with rifles.[91]

Being mistaken for cattle thieves was not their only adventure. On the drive through the Taurus Mountains, the exceptionally bad roads took a toll on their tires. At one point the girls faced a real problem: when they went to change a flat tire, they discovered that when the spare tire had last been repaired in Aleppo, the rim had been bent so that it would not go on the wheel. They flagged down a passing bus for help and discovered a bus driver who spoke some Arabic and who, although unkempt and scruffy looking, K declared "an angel in disguise."[92] He was able to fit a spare tube into the flat tire so that the car could move. He then directed the girls to a nearby camping spot. There he left them, taking the tire with him, returning—tire mended—the next day. The relieved travelers tried to show their gratitude by offering to pay him for his trouble, but their savior gallantly refused.[93]

Continuing through Anatolia, they stayed in Istanbul briefly but didn't linger because they were already behind schedule. K did, however, make time to visit the local museum to see the ostraca recovered from Samaria by the first Harvard expedition. After leaving Istanbul they were delayed again, when a suitcase strapped to the car fell off and they had to retrace their path to find it. Nightfall was approaching and they were having trouble finding a suitable camping spot when they were invited to stay at an agricultural station guest house that offered rooms to students on holiday. K was allotted one room and the Crowfoot sisters another. K was perturbed the next morning when she told her companions that a young man had come into her room during the night to take the other bed in the room. K had pulled the covers up over her head, pretending, she said, not to be there. Joan and Diana found the incident amusing; K's timid reaction surprised them. The humor of the unorthodox situation apparently did not appeal to her conservative temperament.[94]

To slow their progress even more, K came down with a fever, running a temperature of 102 degrees. She was so miserable bouncing along the bad roads that they spent an unscheduled night or two in Sofia in a hotel. They then continued through what was then Yugoslavia to Dubrovnik (Ragusa), up the coast, through Italy and Austria into Germany.

K made most of the necessary repairs to the car during the trip, but eventually the car trouble worsened, so much so that they despaired of making it over the Alps. Once in Germany they had to take it to a series of garages as they tried to nurse the car home. Their reception in Germany was briefly marred by the fact that their Palestine car decal raised suspicion that they might be Jewish, but proving their British citizenship solved the problem.

Finally, they entered Belgium, crossed the Channel at Ostend, and drove into Kirkstead in time for lunch on August 31. The trip had taken six weeks instead of the month they had anticipated. The three women arrived with about six pounds between them. Indeed, toward the end of the trip they couldn't have afforded train tickets home if the car had died.[95] Nevertheless, Kathleen Kenyon was home, her taste for adventure intact. But a new phase of her life was about to begin.

CHAPTER FOUR

THE INSTITUTE OF
ARCHAEOLOGY

I N 1935 KATHLEEN WAS TWENTY-NINE years old. Pretty as a child, she had
grown into a handsome, if not beautiful young woman. She had a tendency
to stoutness, due at least in part to a healthy appetite; Rik Wheeler's biographer Jacquetta Hawkes, who knew Kathleen, dismissed her as "lacking in grace
in her appearance."[1] But she could be quite attractive when she slimmed down.
Nora Kenyon noted her new trimness after the six-week journey from
Palestine, remarking that K's new figure made her look much prettier. She
hoped her sister would be able to maintain it.[2]

K did not do so. People who knew her even as a relatively young woman
remember her as having a very solid figure. In addition, it must be admitted that
the self-described "dirt archaeologist" was not greatly interested in clothes and
did not display much style, elegance, or even common sense in her dress. Even
her sister thought her sartorial choices could be disastrous.[3] Once when
Wheeler took K to lunch, she showed up with large runs in her stockings, and
he told her that in the future he would not take her to meals unless she dressed
properly.[4]

While she was not universally popular, many described the young
Kathleen as capable, confident, straightforward, kind, and generous. She liked
having a good time, complaining of people who were too serious or earnest.[5]
Although sociable, she was not overly warm and didn't have a real interest in
personal relationships. Diana Crowfoot would later remark that K gave the
impression of liking people's company without being excessively fond of them.[6]
She was so straightforward—perhaps even a bit masculine for the time—that
John Crowfoot advised others to deal with K by treating her like a man; that is,

71

one did not have to worry about her feminine sensibilities.[7] Others would describe her as "a man's woman." People who knew K later in her life often described her as shy, but there is no hint of this in recollections of the young Kathleen.

But, like many people who appear outwardly very sure of themselves, privately K suffered from insecurities which might have surprised the people who knew the older, extremely formidable Kathleen. Only her letters to her sister preserve a trace of this diffidence. She wished, for example, she had more sangfroid in social situations. And she admitted that attractive young women made her very self-conscious.[8] She was aware that she wasn't as self-assured as she appeared, confessing, "I wish I didn't appear so self-sufficient, because I am not in the least, and I hate it when people think I am superior. . . . I do feel very lonely at times."[9] And despite her open sentimentality where animals were concerned, Kathleen also realized she was undemonstrative with people, even those she loved. In this, no doubt, she took after her father (Figure 4.1).

Whatever her insecurities, she was used to associating with people of a certain social prominence. While K was undoubtedly a gifted excavator, her career was definitely enhanced by her social connections. Having a father who was Director of the British Museum, on the Management Committee of the Institute of Archaeology, on the executive committees of both the Palestine Exploration Fund and the British School of Archaeology in Jerusalem, and a member of the British Academy could only help her archaeological career. She ran in elevated circles: she was at Somerville with the daughter of the Speaker of the House of Commons, the granddaughter of Lord Oxford, and a cousin of the king of Siam, among others; she knew a daughter of the Home Secretary, and once lunched at the same club as the Queen, almost getting a citation for blocking Her Majesty's car.[10] Despite this, K wasn't a snob and had a certain sense of humor about her social connections. Once, irritated by a woman who had a tendency to drop names, she confessed to Nora, "I usually retaliate, telling her about people I maybe met once with Daddy!! I should hate anyone who knows me to hear me! But the temptation can't be resisted!"[11]

By 1935 Kathleen had settled into a career in archaeology. She had already learned the cardinal rule of the discipline: when you discover an object for which there is no apparent practical use, label it a "cult object."[12] Women archaeologists in the early part of the twentieth century were not as rare as one might expect. Certainly Sir Frederic had encouraged his daughters to think in terms of a career,[13] and he undoubtedly did what he could to further K's. It is true that

FIGURE 4.1: Kathleen and Sir Frederic Kenyon, 1930s. *Courtesy of Janet Heath.*

some women, like Tessa Wheeler and Molly Crowfoot, became involved in archaeology through their husbands. But it is also true that other women, such as Jacquetta Hawkes and Aileen Fox, met their husbands as a result of doing archaeology. And there were single women, like K, who established independent careers for themselves. Gertrude Caton-Thompson, of course, was one, but there was also Dorothy Garrod, who excavated Paleolithic sites in Iraq and

73

Palestine and became the Disney Professor of Archaeology at Cambridge in 1939. Winifred Lamb excavated Bronze Ages sites in the Aegean in the 1920s. Gertrude Bell helped establish the Antiquities Department in Iraq. Margaret Murray, a student of Petrie's, was a well-known Egyptologist. Joan du Plat Taylor, Veronica Seton Williams, and Olga Tufnell were professional archaeologists of K's own generation. An independent income was certainly a help for some of these women (including K), as it was for male archaeologists: there were relatively few professional positions. Perhaps, as K later pointed out, being a woman was even an asset. Unlike a man, one was not expected to support a family.[14] Certainly K didn't worry about being a woman in a male-dominated field. Years later she told a journalist, "You don't consider whether you are a man or a woman. You are just an archaeologist. That's all there is to it."[15]

Despite taking the administrative position of Secretary at the Institute of Archaeology, Kathleen was most interested in fieldwork. She had excavated the theater at St. Albans more or less on her own and had exercised a fair amount of independence at Samaria. By the mid-1930s she was ready to excavate her own site. On their way out to Palestine in 1933, Kathleen and Nancy de Crespigny had made a stopover at Cyprus and, while touring the island, visited the ancient Greek city of Kourion. K was smitten with a desire to excavate the site, at the same time thinking she was too young and inexperienced to organize her own excavation. But she realized that sooner or later she would have to excavate on her own and comforted herself by noting that a number of young archaeologists were running their own digs in England. In the end the Cyprus project didn't come off, because while K was still looking into sources of funding, an American expedition came along and got permission to excavate the site.[16]

Kathleen was otherwise very active professionally. In addition to scholarly lectures, such as the one she gave to the Society of Antiquaries on the theater at Verulamium in 1934, she was also giving talks on Zimbabwe, Verulamium, and a trip she had made to St. Catherine's Monastery on the Sinai Peninsula, to schools and civic groups.[17] She was also doing a lot of writing. In addition to her contribution to Gertrude Caton-Thompson's Zimbabwe volume and her publication of the theater, she published an article in the Palestine Exploration Fund's *Quarterly Statement* on the temple at Samaria in 1933. But, again, following the example of both Rik Wheeler and her father, she also sought a popular audience, writing several articles on Zimbabwe and South Africa for the *Kodak Magazine*, an account of St. Catherine's Monastery for the *Journal of the Royal Air Force College*, and articles in *Discovery* on the Roman theater and Samaria.

When K joined its staff in the fall of 1935 (her first paying job with a meager salary of £200 a year, not really enough to live on in London), the Institute of Archaeology was just getting off the ground.[18] Rik Wheeler, however, had been incubating the idea for years. Early in his career he had decided on the need for an institution to provide instruction in proper excavation techniques. He had begun agitating for his institution soon after arriving in London in 1926, and in 1934 the Senate of the University of London approved the establishment of the Institute. A management committee was set up, and Wheeler was appointed honorary director. In addition, a donation of £10,000 given to help house Petrie's Palestinian collection made it possible for the Institute to take over St. John's Lodge, a stately but dilapidated eighteenth-century mansion in Regent's Park with a ballroom suitable for the display of the artifacts. Wheeler took responsibility for lectures in British archaeology, and arrangements were made for professors from other institutions to provide instruction in Near Eastern archaeology. In 1935—before even St. John's Lodge was ready—the first students began the Diploma course—Rachel Clay (K's friend from St. Albans) and Barbara Parker.[19]

While Kathleen may have initially worried that she hadn't "the faintest idea how to set about the job [at the Institute] ," [20] she caught on quickly and soon settled down to dealing with the nuts and bolts of establishing a new institution—insurance premiums, finances, and other aspects of taking over St. John's Lodge—as well as the transfer of the Palestinian collection to its new quarters, its unpacking, and arranging.[21]

In much of this, of course, K was assisting Tessa Wheeler, who provided the hard work and attention to detail that went so well with Rik Wheeler's visionary genius. But on April 15, 1936, without any warning, Tessa Wheeler died. While Wheeler was on a tour of the Middle East, she had gone into the hospital for a minor operation and died suddenly of a pulmonary embolism.

There is no record of K's reaction to this tragedy. Unfortunately, few of K's letters from this period survive. She was probably living in London with her sister and going home to Kirkstead frequently, so letters home were unnecessary. Certainly, she liked and admired Tessa Wheeler, and it is not unreasonable to assume that she was hit hard by her death. In a letter to *The Times*, Sir Frederic wrote, "All who worked under her loved her . . . [and] [h]er death is a

... grief to scores of admirers and friends."[22] It does not stretch the bounds of credibility to believe that this reflected his daughter's view.

What is clear, however, is that K quickly filled the gap at the Institute left by Mrs. Wheeler's death. Rik Wheeler himself wrote that K "stepped into the breach with a generous devotion that is beyond gratitude [in such a way that] . . . Tessa would have been proud of her."[23] In October 1936 the Institute finally moved into St. John's Lodge and the next April was officially opened by the Chancellor of the University of London, the Earl of Athlone. In all this K continued to exercise independence from Wheeler. On one occasion, replying to a member of the Management Committee who had informed her that the Institute had more money than expected, she wrote that she would keep that fact to herself until she saw a need for the money: if Wheeler knew, he might spend it.[24]

Tessa Wheeler's death may have been even more of a shock to K because it coincided almost exactly with a very happy occasion: Nora Kenyon's marriage to barrister John Ritchie. Despite her own apparent lack of a romantic life, K never displayed any jealousy of her sister's romance and in the months before the wedding was her sister's main confidant, listening patiently as Nora talked endlessly about her fiancé and their future plans[25] (Figure 4.2).

Kathleen's own love remained fieldwork. The terms of her employment at the Institute of Archaeology allowed her time for digging,[26] and she carried out a series of excavations in the later 1930s. In late summer of 1936 and 1937, K excavated the Roman city of Viroconium, near the village of Wroxeter in Shropshire, about five miles east of Shrewsbury. Although the site had been excavated before, K wanted to use stratigraphic methods to answer certain questions, including that of the date of the city's defenses. Viroconium Cornoviorum—the settlement of the Cornovii tribe—had been the fourth largest city in Roman Britain, and the original headquarters of the Fourteenth and Twentieth Legions. So, for several weeks in 1936 and 1937, K, with student and volunteer assistance, examined the defenses of the city and reexamined the "Bath Building" and "Basilica," both identified when excavated earlier in the nineteenth century. Limited funds and time restricted what she could achieve. Nevertheless, she was able to show that the first defenses dated to about the end of the first century A.D. and were expanded about the middle of the second century. She sketched an outline of the development of the baths, but she herself realized that further excavation of the site was needed.[27]

Perhaps most importantly, Kathleen's work at Viroconium reflected a new approach to Romano-British history, which had developed in the early part of the twentieth century. Archaeologists and historians were more and more inclined to look for the connections between Romans and British natives rather than merely view the two groups as oppositions. A new emphasis on the fusion of Roman and Celtic cultures had emerged which saw Roman Britain as a field of inquiry rather than the brief story of the triumph of civilization over barbarity.[28] At Verulamium, Wheeler had been interested in the relationship between the Belgic hill-fort and the Roman town. At Viroconium Kathleen was interested in the relationship between the Roman city and the original native settlement about three and a half miles away, and in 1939 she spent five weeks excavating the British hill-fort on the Wrekin, about three and a half miles from Viroconium. Her results (which she admitted were provisional) suggested a period of occupation before the earliest fortification. After the initial defenses were constructed, they were allowed to fall into disrepair but were then hurriedly rebuilt, possibly in reaction to the coming of the Romans. Kathleen meant to do a second season's work there, but the Second World War intervened.[29]

FIGURE 4.2: Nora Kenyon's wedding party, 1936. *Courtesy of Janet Heath.*

FIGURE 4.3: K with workmen in front of the Jewry Wall. *Courtesy of S. Spencer.*

But by far the most important of the excavations K conducted in the later 1930s was the Jewry Wall site (Figure 4.3), in Leicester, a city in the English midlands. In the eighteenth century the discovery of a Roman milestone confirmed the tradition that the city of Leicester was indeed the Roman town of Ratae Corieltauvorum, the administrative center of the Corieltauvi.[30] A Roman wall known as the Jewry Wall was one of the largest to survive in England (almost 25 feet tall, 35 feet after excavation), but no one knew what its function had been. The origin of the term "Jewry Wall" was itself unclear. Thus, in the summer of 1935 when the City Council purchased the land on St. Nicholas Street on which the wall was located, with the intention of demolishing the existing buildings and building public baths, plans were made to have the Jewry Wall investigated in the process. Local organizations interested in the site—the Literary and Philosophical Society, the Leicester Archaeological Society, and the Parliamentary and General Purposes Committee of the City Council—established a Leicester Excavation Committee, raised funds for the excavation of the site, and approached Kathleen.

Excavations, under Kathleen's direction, began in May 1936, with K being paid the grand salary of almost six pounds a week.[31] Because the buildings on the site had to be destroyed and removed before the construction of the baths, the city's Sanitary and Baths Committee agreed to pay for the removal of the top layers of the site, requiring the Excavation Committee to pay for only the actual archaeological excavation.[32] But by July K had come to the conclusion that the Jewry Wall was actually part of the Roman basilica abutting the forum.[33] A basilica was a sort of Roman town hall and the forum was the central meeting area of the local citizens. Thus, what K believed she had uncovered in the center of modern Leicester was the center of Roman Leicester. This meant that city officials had to decide whether to build the city baths as planned, or to preserve the archaeological remains. The Baths Committee suspended its financial support of the excavation, and a difficult decision had to be made. This was still a time when sanitary facilities in homes were often very rudimentary. Many people still took a bath once a week in a tin tub in the kitchen or used the public "slipper baths"—individual bathrooms that were part of the public swimming facilities. One city councilman argued that the baths were necessary because there were not enough public bathing facilities in a city that had 53,000 households with no bathroom and 20,000 with no hot water. The city had spent a large sum of money for the site, and some could not see the rationale for preserving what they saw as a few old bricks at the expense of such badly needed bathing facilities. Nevertheless, in February 1937 the Leicester City Council voted—33 to 21—to preserve the remains.[34]

After the Baths Committee withdrew its support in July, a public appeal was made to raise the necessary funds. Enough money was collected that the excavations were able to continue until September, albeit on a reduced scale.[35] K excavated the site with the help of her assistant, Joan du Plat Taylor, a reliable foreman named Sutton with whom she had worked before,[36] forty laborers, and volunteers—locals as well as students from the Institute of Archaeology. One girl, recruited from a local grammar school, had a vivid memory of K on the site, puffing on the ever-present cigarette.[37] K seems to have stayed in a local hotel while the workers were housed in an adult education college, Vaughan College.[38] She must have come to see the Baths Committee's point, because her residence apparently did not have bathing facilities. John Peel was a local schoolmaster who was very enthusiastic about the dig, zealously garnering local support and acting as an unofficial publicity director.[39] Once a week K would have dinner with Peel and his family, and as part of the visit use their bath. K's devotion to her dog Solly remained intact. One of the things Peel's wife and daughter remembered about K was that she would bring her dog into the bathroom with her.[40]

The Leicester excavations illustrate the tensions created by K's desire to excavate and her obligations at the Institute. In addition to her job as Secretary, K was also the curator of the Palestinian collection and was giving lectures at the Institute. Her work at the Institute kept her so busy that she was not able to take a holiday for three years, until April of 1938.[41] In the first two seasons at Leicester some of the topsoil could be removed by workmen—under the supervision of Sutton—with K coming up once or twice a week to keep an eye on things. But once the real work of excavation had begun, K felt she had to be on site daily to properly supervise. This caused some difficulty with the Excavation Committee. In 1938 the committee, led by Colin Ellis, was eager to have the excavations begin as early as possible, in order to have them finished that year. K, however, insisted that they could not possibly begin until mid-June, when the Institute's term was over, although she promised to work until October. Ellis even suggested the possibility that an assistant could be hired to begin supervising the excavations. But K was adamant that anyone she knew of who was qualified would also be occupied until the end of the academic year. The exchange got a bit tense, and at one point a representative of the committee hinted not very subtly that if K would neither supervise the excavations nor suggest someone who could, the committee would find someone on its own.[42]

In the end K prevailed. The excavations of 1938 stretched from mid-June until the beginning of October. This season was notable for what K later described as the only object of intrinsic value she ever discovered—a late second-century engraved gold signet ring.[43] The find was exciting enough that K and the crew—forty workmen and ten students—retired to the local pub to celebrate.[44] But perhaps the most charming discovery that season was a brick, built into the Jewry Wall, with the impression of the footprints of a dog and small child (Figure 4.4).

K identified the Jewry Wall site as a forum and basilica, the civic center of Roman Leicester. Yet in her report of the site, published in 1948, she struggled to account for some odd features of the forum, which she dated to ca. A.D. 125. In the usual arrangement, the basilica formed one edge of the open-air forum; shops surrounded the other sides of the forum. But at Leicester, unusually, the "basilica" was almost eight feet above the ground level of the "forum." Steps would have been necessary to connect the two, although no evidence of steps

FIGURE 4.4: Footprints of dog and child uncovered at Leicester.
Courtesy of the Jewry Wall Museum.

was found. K argued that the normal shops had been built to the north of the "forum," but not to the south. This was most likely due, she explained, to soil subsidence on the south side. In fact, K concluded that the Leicester forum had probably not been used as such for very long, if at all, before the problem of the subsidence made it necessary to build another forum elsewhere. Only then was the area in the center of the old forum used for public baths.[45]

The reason K had to struggle to explain the unusual features of the forum and basilica was that the remains proved not to be that of a forum and basilica at all. This was suggested by some of the earliest reviews soon after publication of the site. In the *Journal of Roman Studies* of December 1949, both M. V. Taylor and Richard Goodchild criticized her analysis. Taylor faulted K for settling on the interpretation of the site early in the excavation and offering no other possible explanation in her final report. Both reviewers suggested the possibility of other interpretations, Goodchild in particular arguing strongly that it made more sense to interpret the remains as public baths and a *palaestra*, or exercise area.[46] If K had been quick to make up her mind, she was slow to change it, and was not persuaded by these arguments.[47] Indeed, her interpretation was not an unreasonable one, even though, as K herself admitted, her "forum" was not where one would have expected it to be, on the main crossing of the Roman town.[48] Subsequent excavations east of the Jewry Wall, however, located the true forum and basilica, and archaeologists now accept that K's "forum" was a public bath and her "basilica" a *palaestra*.[49]

Despite their criticisms of her interpretation, both reviewers also complimented K's final report, calling her a skilled excavator who had carefully and thoroughly published the material. Her pottery report, in particular, was very good. Taylor praised K for publishing all the objects found rather than only selected pieces and lauded her painstaking catalogue of the pottery, calling it "a model of its kind."[50] And, in fact, K's Leicester report was a pioneering effort in the dating of the main sequences of a site using pottery.[51] In the 1990s it would still be called "one of the finest pottery reports ever to appear from Roman Britain."[52]

But this was all in the future. At the time, the Leicester Excavation Committee was simply pleased with the results of the excavations. The Museum Committee wanted to have a public lecture that would both celebrate the accomplishment and maintain public interest in the site. So, the Excavation Committee invited Rik Wheeler to give a celebratory talk. It is to Wheeler's credit and demonstrates his professional respect for K—or "Kath" as he called her—that he hesitated and only agreed once he was assured that she was in on the plans and would not feel he had stolen her thunder.[53] In the end, in fact, Wheeler could not attend the meeting, which was held October 21, 1939, and chaired by the Lord Mayor. Instead, K spoke on "The Roman Forum of Leicester."[54] In gratitude for K's services, the committee had wanted to make a public presentation to her, and Colin Ellis had asked Sir Frederic to suggest an appropriate gift.[55] So, that evening the Excavation Committee presented her with a set of the four volumes of the eighteenth-century *The History and Antiquities of the County of Leicester* by John Nichols.

ASIDE FROM HER ONGOING EXCAVATIONS, the year 1938 was significant for Kathleen in two other ways: her mother died and she met Vivienne Catleugh. Lonely because Nora was married, and Kathleen and Sir Frederic away in London much of the time, Amy Kenyon answered an advertisement in *The Lady*, for a "Companion-Chauffeuse with Domestic Science Training" placed by Vivienne Catleugh. Five years younger than Kathleen, Catleugh was from

Norfolk, the second child of a mayor of King's Lynn. Having studied domestic science at school, she then spent a year at a finishing school in Paris. After spending another year in Berlin, she advertised in *The Lady*, and Lady Kenyon telephoned.

Vivienne Catleugh went to Kirkstead in February 1938, and barely two months later Amy Kenyon had a severe stroke. Catleugh took over, arranging the necessary nursing care. Lady Kenyon was very deaf by this time, but members of the family spent as much time with her as they could, often sitting at her bedside, reading with her from the Bible. She appeared to be getting better when she had another stroke, lived only a few more days, and died on July 16.[56]

The girls took their mother's death hard. Near the end of her own life, Nora remembered that when Amy Kenyon died the entire family was devastated.[57] Several months after her death, in a letter to her sister, Kathleen reflected on what they had lost: "It can't ever be the same without Mummy, as she really hadn't any interests of her own to compare with her interest in us, and she really did devote herself completely to us."[58] On the second anniversary of her death, K was still trying to comfort Nora: "I did wish *very* much you could have been at home yesterday, but I know we were all thinking of Mummy. . . . I do wish I could help you to be less unhappy."[59]

Vivienne Catleugh stayed on. According to her own account, after Lady Kenyon's funeral, Sir Frederic looked at her and said, "Vivienne, you won't leave us now, will you? You can see we can't manage without you."[60] So, Catleugh took over the management of the Kenyon household. While it is unclear how well Kathleen knew her before her mother's death, they seem to have become friends quite quickly, because by October 1938 they traveled together to Oxford, staying with Kathleen's cousin Winifred Williamson.[61] Catleugh also began going into London with K two or three days a week, taking courses at the Institute in photography and surveying. In the late summer of 1939 she ran the excavation camp when K excavated on the Wrekin.

Like her relationship with Rik Wheeler, Kathleen's friendship with Vivienne Catleugh has been the subject of much speculation. Over the years many people, primarily those who did not know them intimately, suspected a romantic attachment. K, after all, had an almost masculine presence, and she and Catleugh lived together for almost forty years. But the weight of the evidence is against anything other than a platonic relationship. As with Wheeler, K's conventional morality would very likely have prevented a physical relationship, whatever her private feelings. Lesbian partnerships were not unknown in the circles K and Catleugh inhabited, but theirs was not known to be among them. Beatrice de Cardi, Wheeler's secretary at the Museum of London, knew of other lesbian archaeologists but did not include K and Vivienne among them.[62] Tom Holland also knew of other lesbian couples in their circle, but when he lived with Kathleen and Catleugh for several years as a graduate student in the 1960s and 1970s, he never saw any evidence of a romantic relationship.[63] Finally, Vivienne Catleugh herself denied the rumors, in later years telling a close mutual friend that such stories were untrue.[64] In fact, Kathleen never seems to have shown much interest in a romantic attachment of any kind,[65] and later rumors about K and Catleugh—or for that matter, about K and the dashing RAF officer who was supposed to have broken her heart—remain that, unsubstantiated gossip, the kind of stories told to explain an unmarried women with a career at a time when most women did not work outside the home.

In the forty years they lived together, Catleugh played a critical role in Kathleen's life. Like Kathleen a determined and capable woman, she had different talents and could run domestic affairs, leaving K free for her professional pursuits. She took great pride both in K's reliance on her and the good care she took of K, boasting to a friend that even during the Second World War, using a two-burner hot plate she made sure K had "meat and two vegs" each evening.[66]

Only in hindsight is it clear that war was coming in the 1930s. It is not evident how seriously K, like many other people in Britain, took the threat at the time. Despite her mother's involvement in Conservative politics, Kathleen herself does not seem to have been greatly interested in national or international politics. She took a three-week holiday to Germany in April 1938 with a friend, only a month after Germany's annexation of Austria. In the only extant letter of that trip, K's primary concerns are sightseeing and viewing Roman material in the museums in Cologne and Bonn. Her only vaguely political observation was that propaganda concerning the upcoming election was everywhere.[67] Certainly, by the end of the war she was referring to "the perverted nationalistic theories from which Europe has suffered,"[68] but there is little direct evidence of how she felt in the 1930s. Like others in her family, she was probably pro-German but not pro-Nazi.[69] Circumstantial evidence of this may be found in a letter Sir Frederic wrote to *The Times* in 1938, appealing for aid for those persecuted by the Nazis.[70]

Many expected war in late 1938 with the German takeover of Czechoslovakia, but Chamberlain's concessions at Munich delayed the military conflict. War finally broke out with the invasion of Poland at the beginning of September 1939. Kathleen and Vivienne Catleugh were in Shropshire on the Wrekin until late August, finishing the five-week-long excavation after K had completed her last season at Leicester earlier in the summer. K seems to have finished at the Wrekin and then crossed over to Hamburg to pick up Sir Frederic, who had attended the recent international archaeological conference in Berlin.[71]

Immediately following the declaration of war was the period of the "Phony War," when nothing appeared to be happening. But when France fell in June 1940 and the possibility of an invasion was quite real, Nora Ritchie, at the insistence of her husband, left for Shropshire with their one year-old daughter—and K's goddaughter—Janet.[72] The Battle of Britain—the fight for air supremacy over Great Britain—began in the late summer of 1940, and on August 15 Sir Frederic and Kathleen watched the battle in the air from the garden at Kirkstead until debris falling from the sky led them to retreat into the house.[73]

In expectation of war, the Institute of Archaeology shut down in August 1939. The collections were packed up and stored in the basement of St. John's Lodge. Nancy Sandars, who had been digging with K earlier in the summer, recalled tossing pots down the stairs to K in the basement.[74] Many members of the staff were called up to active duty, Wheeler rejoined the Army, and K was left in charge of the Institute.

During the war, in addition to overseeing what was left of the Institute of Archaeology and, in fact, keeping the fledgling institution alive, Kathleen worked full-time for the British Red Cross. Even before the threat of war emerged, K had followed her family's tradition of public service and noblesse oblige by joining a Volunteer Aid Detachment in March 1930.[75] VADs were units of the Red Cross whose members were trained in first aid and nursing and could be called up in times of national emergency. K would later say that she went in for the Red Cross because she thought knowledge of first aid would be useful to an archaeologist ("You never know when someone is going to fall into a trench"),[76] but it is likely that her family's tradition of public service had as much to do with it.

Kathleen and Catleugh had both been members of the London Westminster Division of the Red Cross, but soon after war broke out K became the director of the Hammersmith Division.[77] Hammersmith was the area in which St. Paul's Girls' School was located. K's name was known, and meant something, in that area of London. In the 1930s people still took class and status very seriously. So, having the Kenyon name was a real advantage. In addition to commanding the division, Kathleen was also commandant of a detachment within the division—Detachment L/208—while Catleugh commanded Detachment L/304.[78]

The headquarters of the Hammersmith Division was a small, two-room facility on Brook Green Road[79] known as "the Hut." At first, it was so primitive that it did not even have its own toilet, and Red Cross members had to use the facilities of the nearby public library. Over time K and the others worked hard to make the Hut more comfortable, painting and furnishing it, eventually adding an extension which included a bathroom. During the summer K would bring in rhododendrons from Kirkstead to brighten things up.

Hammersmith was a medical supply depot which loaned out such items as wheelchairs and bed pans, but its activities were certainly not limited to this. K quickly began recruiting VAD members and starting courses in first aid and nursing, eventually adding other courses such as Air Raid Precautions. Initially lectures were held in the Hut, but later they were held throughout the borough of Hammersmith. K's duties were many and varied. Not only did she and Vivienne Catleugh do much of the early lecturing and demonstrating, she had to recruit doctors and nurses as demonstrators to train the Red Cross members, raise money, keep track of the accounts, and do the paperwork regarding lectures and examinations. Help was also offered to the relatives of POWs, and foreign-language first-aid classes were offered to refugees. Under Kathleen, Hammersmith was to grow enormously from one small detachment to at least five detachments of about forty members each.[80]

While K was in London both working for the Red Cross and running the Institute of Archaeology, she was actually camped out at St. John's Lodge. Because of the danger posed by incendiary bombs, firewatchers were needed; and K, joined by Catleugh for much of the time, lived at the Institute accompanied only by Manson, the caretaker. They did, in fact, put out their share of fires.[81]

The London Blitz began in September 1940. From September until May, with something of a lull during the winter, London endured heavy bombing by the Luftwaffe. For over seven weeks after the first major assault of September 7, London was subjected to daily raids, and eventually these shifted to mostly night attacks. The Germans indiscriminately bombed industrial and civilian targets, including hospitals, schools, businesses, and historic landmarks. On some nights the combination of high explosive and incendiary bombs, flashing guns, searchlights, and fire almost turned night into day. On the night of May 10–11 the Institute of Archaeology sustained considerable damage from an air raid in which Manson was injured.[82] K herself escaped unscathed.

By this time K had had a chance to build up the Hammersmith Division, and she was able to provide both volunteers and equipment for the local air-raid shelters. One volunteer remembers her fearlessly touring these shelters at night, boosting morale as she did so.[83] During the Blitz some 20,000 people in London, including forty members of the Red Cross, were killed. K and Vivienne Catleugh were there for most of this time. Little other information about K during the Blitz is available. She seems to have remained in London for the most part, except for an Air Raid Protection school she attended for several weeks in January and February 1941.[84] During a late spell of bombing in 1944 K did not want to leave while the raids continued,[85] so it is not unreasonable to suppose that she remained in London during the winter of 1940–1941, working for the Red Cross and fire-watching at the Institute of Archaeology.

When the heavy bombing ended in the spring of 1941, K and Catleugh began going down to Kirkstead most Fridays to spend the weekend with Sir Frederic. They would return on Sundays, often giving a Red Cross lecture to volunteers who had other jobs during the week, and going out for dinner Sunday evening. During these weekends at Kirkstead K could no more bear to remain inactive than she could in London. She and Catleugh would occupy themselves doing chores such as building a new chicken coop, clearing brush, chopping firewood, and working in the garden. But these weekends were also opportunities for relaxation. K and Catleugh would sometimes golf or skate. During the winter K often spent Saturdays hunting. After a long, exhausting week in London, she might well spend ten hours in the saddle, arriving back home in the late afternoon or early evening. After feeding and cleaning her horse, K would bathe and come downstairs dressed for dinner at 8 pm. Even during the war the Kenyons still had formal dinners, for which everyone was expected to dress: Kathleen and Catleugh in long evening gowns and Sir Frederic in black tie.[86]

Even after the intense bombing of the Blitz ended, the war, of course, continued, and there was still much work to be done for the Red Cross. K remained almost frantically busy. The Hut in Hammersmith was a bustling place, with people coming and going constantly. K complained that she had trouble getting any work done because of the constant interruptions.[87] The day-to-day running of the Hammersmith Detachment was not her only obligation;

fundraising was another. One such event was a Flag Day, on which volunteers collected funds, giving donors little paper or silk flags. Although her efforts were quite successful, K found this an immense amount of work, organizing the collection of money, giving out the flags, and hosting distinguished visitors—Lady Limerick, President of the London Branch of the Red Cross; Mrs. Churchill, wife of the Prime Minister; and Lady Mountbatten, wife of Admiral Louis Mountbatten.[88]

Not all of her fundraising efforts were such a success. One function, organized by the mayor of Hammersmith, was to help the Russians. Initially K was asked to provide volunteers to help collect funds, but at the last minute the mayor informed K that one of the speakers had cancelled and asked her to speak in his stead. She thought the event was awful. First, because of insufficient advertising, only 500 people showed up rather than the thousands expected. Next, the main guest, a journalist who had just returned from Russia, was a terrible speaker who went on so long that he had to be asked to stop. He was followed by another verbose orator who also had to be cut off. When K spoke for only two minutes, she "got many thanks afterwards for being brief!" K, still with no leftist sympathies, seemed rather surprised that when they sang the Communist anthem, *The Internationale*, a number of people were able to sing along. The final straw, however, was a photo taken of K as she spoke with a large hammer and sickle behind her. She thought her efforts had been for naught: "an awful waste of a Sunday morning."[89]

In March 1942 Kathleen took a new job with the Red Cross. She became the first Director of Youth with the task of creating Youth Detachments of the Red Cross for those aged sixteen to twenty-one for all of Britain. Starting less than two weeks after first hearing about the post, she began completely from scratch with the rank of colonel, an office in Belgrave Square, a typist, and a couple of ideas.[90] She was not completely abandoning Hammersmith. Vivienne Catleugh took over as divisional director, but K continued as the commandant of Detachment L/208 and as divisional treasurer.[91] Nevertheless, the Hammersmith Division seems to have taken her departure very seriously. At a farewell presentation, she was sent off with a gold wristwatch and a silver cigarette case.[92] K, who could find public displays of emotion embarrassing, found all this leave-taking rather discomforting.[93]

K tackled her new job with the energy she brought to everything she did and quickly came up with plans to recruit new members into the Youth Division. But K did not at first enjoy her new job, in part because the ever-social Kathleen missed the friendly atmosphere at Hammersmith.[94] But the Youth Department job also came with a salary of £300 a year. K had told the Red Cross that she would not do the job without a salary, as she had been doing at Hammersmith. Despite her various investments and income (including Rose Hill), K was not financially well off during the war and in debt much of the time.[95]

IT WAS, IN FACT, A GOOD THING that K and Catleugh and the caretaker Manson were watching for fires at the Institute of Archaeology, because St. John's Lodge was bombed several times, although the damage was mostly superficial.[96] But before the Blitz, during the period of the "Phony War," K was anxious to resume normal activity at the Institute as soon as possible. In a letter to the University of London Senate in May 1940, she reported that the library had been reopened, some work on archaeological material had been resumed, and lectures would begin again in the fall. The start of heavy bombing in September put an end to these plans, but various aspects of the Institute's work were resumed on a limited scale as soon as was practical, even after real fighting began.[97] And it must be remembered that K was running the Institute in addition to her duties at the Red Cross.

K had been left as Secretary to administer the Institute in Wheeler's absence. The Management Committee recommended that she be appointed Acting Director. At first the University of London's Academic Council refused on the grounds that this was unnecessary. But the Management Committee tried again. The chairman of the committee, Sir Charles Peers, wrote to the Academic Council, insisting that in the present circumstances the Institute needed someone with the title and status of Director.[98] So, in April 1942 K was duly appointed Acting Director of the Institute of Archaeology, becoming the first woman to head a major branch of a British university.

Surprisingly enough in light of her many responsibilities at the Red Cross and the Institute of Archaeology, K did manage to continue some of her own archaeological work during the war, mostly at odd hours at night and on the weekends. [99] She published the report on Viroconium in 1940 and the Wrekin in 1942. As part of research for a paper she gave to the Royal Archaeological Institute in March 1942, she made a quick visit to Shropshire in February to check some aspects of the Wrekin site. Staying with her aunt, she borrowed her car and drove out to the site in a snowstorm.[100] She also continued writing for popular magazines, publishing "Archaeology as a Career for a Woman" in *Women's Employment* and "Learning History With a Spade" in *Strand Magazine*.

Under K's direction the Institute of Archaeology continued to function on a limited basis throughout 1942 and 1943. In early 1942 the Institute sponsored an exhibit on the archaeology of Turkey as well as a series of lectures on Turkish archaeology.[101] In March 1943 it put on a photographic exhibition at London Museum, "The Present Discovers the Past," designed to demonstrate the connection between archaeology and the modern world.[102]

One of the most important activities of the Institute must be reckoned to be the conference it sponsored, on a bank holiday weekend in the late summer of 1943, on "The Future of Archaeology." The idea for this conference emerged in December 1942.[103] Now that the end of the war was in sight, many people, including K herself, were affected by what she termed "post-war-itis" and were thinking about what would happen to archaeology after the war. Kathleen believed that the Institute of Archaeology had a vital interest in shaping the future of archaeology in order to attract the students on which the institution depended, and a recent conference she had attended on the planning of science had convinced her that such a conference for archaeologists would be beneficial.[104]

Those who attended the meeting she convened in March included representatives from the Ashmolean Museum and the British School at Athens, Christopher Hawkes (K's old dancing partner) of the British Museum, Joan du Plat Taylor, Veronica Seton Williams, M. V. Taylor, Olga Tufnell, Sir Frederic Kenyon, and others. Agreeing with K that such a conference would be worthwhile, they determined to hold the conference the next August, and a committee was formed to draft a program.

One of the things that becomes clear is that K wanted to treat archaeology as a united whole—not surprising given her background—and expected the conference to address both British and Near Eastern archaeology, writing to Stephen Glanville that "it is such an awful pity we all live in water-tight compartments, and one ought to look at the problem as a whole."[105] The only reason that such a regional scope had even been imposed on the conference was that it had been decided to emphasize those areas for which the most specialists were available.

The "Conference on the Future of Archaeology" was held at the Institute of Archaeology on the weekend of August 6–8, 1943. It was a great success. The over 280 attendees, representing a number of archaeological societies, museums, and universities, included most of the distinguished archaeologists present in Britain at the time, including Christopher Hawkes and his wife Jacquetta, Ian Richmond, V. Gordon Childe, Sir John Myres, Nowell Myres, Sir Cyril Fox and his wife Aileen, John Crowfoot, Gertrude Caton-Thompson, Margaret Murray, and Sir Leonard Woolley.[106]

During the war the government had exercised unprecedented control over many aspects of national life, seemingly successfully. Faith in the state's capacity to solve the nation's problems was on the rise. This would be confirmed in the election of July 1945, when the government of the popular war leader Winston Churchill was thrown out of office and replaced with a Labour government. This attitude had clearly affected the archaeologists of Great Britain, and one of the most important issues addressed at the conference was, as K must have expected, state support, and possibly state control, of postwar archaeology.[107] Serious discussion of the topic occurred in sessions on "Planning and the Independence of Societies" and "Archaeology and the State at Home." While there seems to have been general agreement that the government had an important role in protecting Britain's archaeological resources, and that private funding for archaeology would be more difficult to come by in the future, differences of opinion over the role of government in funding archaeology were apparent. Some participants were concerned that such funding would lead to state control which would stifle individual initiative. One participant, referring to recent events in Europe, worried that state-sponsored research might have baneful consequences. Margaret Murray argued that what archaeology needed were amateurs who did archaeology because they loved it.

Others, however, disagreed, arguing that government money was a necessity, would not lead to stagnation or regimentation, and would allow talented people without independent incomes to do archaeology.[108] Despite her generally conservative political views, K took the side of those arguing for the necessity of state funding: "We can all admit that the Government is not such a devil in disguise as is thought. It allows the British Academy £2000 per annum for research, and it does not attempt to control how it is spent . . . , and what we have to do is persuade the Government, i.e., persuade the Nation, that it is necessary and worth while."[109]

One session was devoted to "The Training of Archaeologists," and, not surprisingly, K gave a paper on "Training for Field Work." Because excavation inevitably destroys evidence which can never be recovered, she argued, it was of paramount importance that students be properly equipped for fieldwork. She called for more genuine training digs, on which students were actually instruct-ed, not just exploited as free labor.

K's paper emphasized the importance of learning about the recording and interpretation of stratification, as well as the recording of objects, and she dif-fered considerably with the following speaker, J. D. Beazley. Beazley, Professor of Classical Archaeology and Art at Oxford, argued that archaeologists need-ed to understand an ancient culture in its entirety and therefore needed knowl-edge not only of its history, but also of its language and literature. K, on the other hand, explicitly maintained that while archaeologists should acquire knowledge of the history and culture of a particular region, they should leave more specialized knowledge to the experts. She denied, for example, that one needed to read Hebrew to excavate biblical sites, because one always had access to experts who could: "[I]t is far more important that [the excavator] should be able to interpret its find spot than the actual inscription."[110] This would be a stand for which some would later reproach her.

The conference was such a success that the Institute sponsored a sequel the following year, September 16–17, 1944, on "Problems and Prospects of European Archaeology." A smaller, more specialized conference, it still drew over 150 attendees, including many foreign archaeologists.[111] But despite all this attention to postwar conditions, the war wasn't yet over. The Allied inva-sion of Normandy had begun on June 6 of that year, and a week later the Germans launched the first of their Vergeltungswaffen—"weapons of revenge"—flying bombs that could be launched from the Continent. The first, the V1, was nicknamed the "buzz bomb" or "doodle bug" for the insect-like droning sound it made. The second, the V2, was even more terrifying. It made no sound, and because it flew so high, could not be intercepted by the RAF. The launching of these new and harrowing rockets seems to have delayed the conference. But the assault on London appeared to have ceased on August 31, and this may have led to the conference being called on short notice. In the early morning on the Saturday of the first day of the meeting, however, flying bombs landed in London, killing several people.

Nonetheless, the conference went ahead as scheduled. Vivienne Catleugh helped K with the catering, providing lunch and a late afternoon tea. When most of the participants had dispersed, several stayed behind to help K and Catleugh clean up, and they all planned to go out to dinner afterward. But about 6 pm, a bomb struck the Institute of Archaeology, shattering the front windows. K and Catleugh threw themselves under a table, and no one was injured.[112] Kathleen seems to have handled this with typical aplomb, writing to Molly Crowfoot a few days later, "We finished up Sunday by having all the windows in the front of the house blown out by a doodle-bug! It made us laugh alot. It would have been a little disturbing if it had been the night before!"[113]

ONE ARCHAEOLOGICAL ENDEAVOR that began before the end of the war, but which did not end so happily, at least from the point of view of K's involvement, was the Council for British Archaeology. The CBA grew out a concern for the course of postwar archaeology. Large parts of cities such as Canterbury, Exeter, Southampton, and London had been destroyed by enemy bombing, and many archaeologists wanted to ensure that proper rescue excavations were undertaken before rebuilding began. In May 1943 Sir Alfred Clapham, the President of the Society of Antiquaries, hosted a meeting of interested archaeologists which included, among others, Kathleen, Gertrude Caton-Thompson, Christopher Hawkes, and Sir Cyril Fox. In March 1944 the Council for British Archaeology was officially proclaimed, with Kathleen on its executive committee as its first Secretary, with the goal of promoting all aspects of British archaeology. This involved the formation of a regional organization representing museums, universities, and national, county, and local archaeological societies, while assuring proper excavation, and the preservation of historic sites, in addition to encouraging public support for archaeology.[114]

Kathleen, as the Secretary of the new organization, was very busy in its first five years. She sat on panels representing the Romano-British period, as well as the Neolithic, Bronze Age, and Iron Age. She helped produce a pamphlet outlining both the archaeological training and jobs that were available, published a summary of the CBA's activities for 1944–1948, and worked on a similar summary of archaeological activities in foreign countries. Responsible for all the correspondence associated with a national organization, she was involved with setting up student exchanges, corresponding with the local societies who were concerned about the implications the CBA had for themselves, helping local societies arrange excavations, as well as conducting some of these excavations herself.

But not everyone was happy with K's execution of her duties. An official complaint by Christopher Hawkes in 1948 suggests perhaps that K's many other obligations were not allowing her as much time to devote to the CBA as the CBA required. Although the executive committee declined to criticize K's job performance in any way,[115] shortly afterward Rik Wheeler and Philip Corder were appointed to conduct an inquiry into the views of the members. Their report demonstrated that many felt the executive committee was out of touch with the views of local societies, that the CBA was too bureaucratic, too professional, and too London-oriented. In response, one of Wheeler and Corder's recommendations was that the CBA have a part-time honorary secretary who could deal with policy issues, and a full-time, paid assistant secretary who would be responsible for day-to-day administration and who would be expected to keep in close touch with archaeologists all over the country.[116]

In 1945 the CBA had received a small grant from the Carnegie Trust, which permitted K to be paid an honorarium of £100 a year.[117] But when the CBA received state recognition, and so state funding, it was in a position to hire a full-time secretary. In 1949 K resigned as honorary secretary to be replaced by W. F. Grimes. Beatrice de Cardi, who had been both Wheeler's student at the University of London and his secretary at the London Museum, was appointed full-time assistant secretary.

After this Kathleen's involvement with the CBA ended. Beatrice de Cardi was surprised that K (who had known her slightly at St. Paul's Girls' School) made no effort to fill her in on the goings-on at the CBA, leaving that to Grimes. K was perhaps too distracted by other things or possibly did not want to prejudice the incoming administration. Or perhaps her departure was not without hard feelings. De Cardi believed that K had not been as tactful as she should have been in her dealings with local societies and had ruffled some feathers. Many felt that the notices she sent out to them had a rather peremptory tone; this did not go over well with the local archaeological societies.[118]

The end of the war brought changes to the Institute of Archaeology. In 1946 K ceased to serve as acting director when V. Gordon Childe, the noted prehistorian, was appointed director, Wheeler having gone to India as Director General of Archaeology. There were also changes in her personal life, as K left the Red Cross (although Vivienne Catleugh was to make a career of it) and they moved into a flat in Hammersmith.

What did not change was K's commitment to fieldwork. She had excavated in 1939 practically until war was declared, and the war in Europe was barely over when, in May 1945, she began excavations in Southwark, in south London on the southern bank of the Thames. As early as 1942 the Surrey Archaeological Society (of which both Kathleen and Sir Frederic were members) had established a Post-war Planning Committee to deal with excavations after the war.[119] Kathleen, A. W. G. Lowther (with whom she had excavated at St. Albans), and Sheppard Frere were among those appointed to the committee. Eventually the committee approached the mayor of Southwark, who was very enthusiastic, and the Southwark Excavation Committee was established. Because of the scarcity of both funds and labor, work was carried out almost entirely by volunteers for three years, mostly from spring to autumn, during the evenings and school holidays.[120]

In addition to Southwark, K was also involved in rescue digs elsewhere. Late in 1945 the Leicestershire Archaeological Society wrote to the CBA about Breedon-on-the-Hill, an isolated Iron Age camp in northwest Leicestershire, which was imminently threatened by quarrying. K arranged with the Ministry of Works, which was responsible for Ancient Monuments, to spend two weeks in July 1946 excavating the 23-acre hill-fort.[121] Based on her two-week excavation, K argued that the Iron Age camp had been inhabited by a tribe called the Coritiani from about the first century B.C. until, possibly, the coming of the Romans. She identified two periods of fortification, tentatively suggesting the first may have been aimed against the Belgae and the second against the Romans.[122] But she felt that further excavations should be done and hoped for a second season, although this did not prove feasible.[123]

The CBA was also contacted in 1947 by local archaeologists about Sutton Walls, an Iron Age hill-fort five miles northeast of Hereford, which was also threatened by quarrying.[124] Again sponsored by the Ministry of Works, K conducted excavations assisted mostly by volunteers, students from the Institute of Archaeology, and enthusiastic locals. These excavations, which took place for an average of four weeks each year, 1948–1951, allowed her to trace the history of the hill-fort from the first century B.C. through its "Romanization" in about the second century, until the abandonment of the site in the third century. The most remarkable discovery, made during the final season, was that of twenty-four skeletons. Some of the bodies had had their heads cut off, and all of them had been flung carelessly into a ditch. Since all were young adult males, K thought they were almost certainly casualties of the defense against the Romans.[125]

The big change in K's tenure at the Institute of Archaeology occurred in January 1948, when she resigned as Secretary to become Lecturer in Palestinian Archaeology and curator of the Petrie Collection. The necessity of a curator-lecturer who would teach and conduct training excavations in Palestine had been discussed at the Institute as early as 1936. Because more

British archaeologists worked in Palestine than in any other area outside of the British Isles, this was seen as a priority.[126] In the spring of 1947 a subcommittee headed by Nimrud excavator Max Mallowan (which included John Crowfoot, Professor Stephen Glanville, and Dorothy Garrod) nominated Kathleen for the post of Lecturer in Palestinian Archaeology. But there was a problem. The original report of the subcommittee stipulated that she would be offered the position on the understanding that she would "equip herself for the linguistic teaching required in the Palestinian syllabus." K, however, had never believed that linguistic proficiency was a necessity for an archaeologist. A field archaeologist simply had to know how to dig properly; the appropriate specialists could always be consulted about the texts. She had made this very clear at the 1943 Conference on the Future of Archaeology. But others disagreed. The letter from the subcommittee, signed by Mallowan, stated that the new appointment *should* be made in Western Asiatic Archaeology, and emphasized the linguistic skills needed for the teaching of that subject. But recognizing that the Management Committee wanted to go ahead and appoint a lecturer, without the delay that asking the university to change the title of the position would entail, the subcommittee recommended that the Lectureship in Palestinian Archaeology be only a five-year position, after which it would be changed to Western Asiatic Archaeology. Mallowan's letter concluded: "The Committee also wish to put it on record that the candidate proposed for the Palestinian Lecturer does not at present possess the requirements of the post. It should be made clear to the candidate that this post may be abolished at the end of five years."[127]

At the Management Committee meeting at which K was nominated, there was considerable debate over her appointment. After the word "epigraphic" was substituted for "linguistic" in the report of the subcommittee, the report was accepted, and the Management Committee nominated K on the condition that "she would use her best endeavors to equip herself with a sufficient knowledge of the scripts for the teaching of Palestinian epigraphy, having regards for the requirements of the syllabus."[128] In fact, K never did any such thing, and the position was only changed to a Lectureship in Western Asiatic Archaeology after her tenure. But the disagreement over what made a competent archaeologist may have played a role in the subsequent tense relationship between Kathleen and Max Mallowan.

It is not unreasonable to suppose, given the requirements of her new job as well as her personal predilections, that K wanted to return to the Middle East.

She had hoped to go abroad again in the late 1930s[129] but was prevented by the outbreak of war. And immediately after the end of the Second World War, the situation in Palestine created by the relinquishing of the British Mandate and the establishment of the state of Israel made excavations there impractical. In the late 1940s, however, K did have the opportunity to go abroad again, this time to North Africa.

The province of Tripolitania ("land of the three cities") in North Africa was named after the three ancient cities on the coast of the Mediterranean: Oea (modern Tripoli), Sabratha, forty-five miles west of Tripoli, and Lepcis Magna, on the other side of Tripoli, fifty-five miles to the east. Occupied by the Italians before the war, this region came under the control of the British from 1943 until 1951, when it became the modern country of Libya. In the 1920s and 1930s, Italian archaeologists had uncovered and restored much of the ancient cities of Lepcis Magna and Sabratha.

Major John Ward Perkins was an archaeologist who had excavated with Rik Wheeler in Brittany, worked on his staff at the London Museum, and served with him in North Africa during the war. When the Eighth Army occupied the area after the fall of Tripoli in 1943, Wheeler and Ward Perkins discovered that the British troops were doing their best to aid in the deterioration and outright destruction of the ancient monuments. Wheeler managed to persuade the military to protect the sites instead.[130] Major Ward Perkins was appointed Antiquities Officer and given the job of determining what measures were needed to preserve the antiquities of Tripolitania and Cyrenaica, a territory to the east of Tripolitania, eventually producing a "Memorandum on the Antiquities of Tripolitania and Cyrenaica and on the Future of Archaeological Research in These Two Countries."

After the war Ward Perkins became Director of the British School at Rome and wanted to continue the work of the Italians. Kathleen was part of the BSR expedition that went to North Africa for three months in the summer of 1948; Vivienne Catleugh went with her to run the camp.

K's commitment to the instruction of students was once again evident, because the expedition was intended as a training dig for students who had not been able to gain experience in Mediterranean archaeology since the 1930s. Consequently, twenty-five students were part of the expedition, most of them working at Sabratha under K's direction. Richard Goodchild, Assistant Director of the BSR and acting Antiquities Officer of Tripolitania, surveyed what had been the Roman frontier zone, locating two previously unknown

Roman frontier stations. A small group under Ward Perkins surveyed the monuments at Lepcis Magna. But most of the work took place at Sabratha, where K endeavored to establish a sequence of pottery types and to date stratigraphically some of the major buildings.

As camp manager Catleugh had a challenging job, feeding the whole crew on a limited budget. Because the local village was inadequate for their needs, once a week an Army driver took her into Tripoli to do the shopping. The British Military Administration was most helpful. K had arranged to borrow as much of their equipment as possible from the Army, only three miles away; large, double-roofed Army tents were delivered the first day. Catleugh, knowing Ward Perkins was an ex-Army officer, asked him to help set up the tents. He laughed and replied, "Good heavens, no. This is where I would say, 'Carry on, Sergeant Major.'"[131]

The military also proved useful in transporting finds back to Britain, the difficulties of which should not be underestimated. At the end of the 1948 season, for example, K had seven tons of pottery to ship home. In 1951 at least six cases of finds were brought back in the baggage of the First Battalion of Grenadier Guards.[132]

Both the excavations and camp were located in a lovely spot next to the Mediterranean, where the excavators could cool off—and clean up—by swimming in the evenings. Catleugh recalled everyone sitting around in the moonlight after dinner, drinking gin and eating peanuts. Sometimes they would go to the Army headquarters to see a film or play tennis, or hang out at the NAAFI,[133] which had a bar and a café. Sometimes they managed to entertain themselves. At an end of the dig party held in the Roman baths in 1948, Olwyn Brogan, wife of Dennis Brogan, Professor of Modern History at Cambridge and an archaeologist in her own right, presided as "Queen of the Potsherds," bestowing upon everyone a farewell gift. K received a divining rod for locating foundation trenches. The evening of drinking and singing and dancing through the ruins was rounded out with a moonlight swim.[134] The liveliness of the crew that first season, with twenty-five students along—and K's sense of fun—is illustrated by a prank pulled by some of the would-be archaeologists. Two students, Nicholas Thomas (later Director of the Bristol Museum) and Leslie Alcock (later Professor of Archaeology at Glasgow), aided and abetted by several others, decided to play a joke on K. Going to the local market, they bought a water jar, which they painted, aged, and smashed. Sneaking down to the ghostly forum in the dead of night—slightly drunk after a party—they planted the fake artifacts in Christian graves K was planning to open soon. K's reaction is not recorded, but she was probably suspicious from the start. Still, the pot, when discovered, was duly recorded in the site notebook. (And, in fact, was published in the final report.[135]) But at some point someone must have confessed and named the culprits, allowing K to show that she, too, had a sense of humor. Some months later, while lecturing to the Oxford University Archaeological Society on Sabratha, and knowing that the two main conspirators were in her audience, she showed (as a slide) a drawing of two suspicious-looking characters in trench coats, with a more than passing resemblance to Thomas and Alcock, stuffing pots in a tomb, and made a vague allusion to the plot. The guilty parties knew the truth was out.[136]

While Ward Perkins continued work at Lepcis Magna, and Richard Goodchild continued his survey of the Roman frontier, the Sabratha excavations covered three seasons: 1948, 1949, and 1951. In 1949, money being tight, K went with a much smaller group to clear up some points that had arisen the previous year. No expedition went out in 1950, but Kathleen spent three months in Rome in early 1950 working on the excavation report, returning to Sabratha for a final season in 1951.[137]

Sabratha's importance stemmed from its role as a center of Mediterranean trade, exporting olive oil as well as gold, ivory, exotic animals, and slaves from across the Sahara. In an article published in the *Illustrated London News* in 1952, K recounted the preliminary results of her three seasons' work. She had been able to trace the development of the central part of the site from the earliest Phoenician trading camps to the first permanent settlement of about the fifth century B.C. In the first century B.C, with the beginning of Roman occupation, Sabratha underwent radical renovation, and a large part of the town was cleared for the building of a Roman forum, basilica, curia, and several temples. By the beginning of the third century, more public buildings had been added, including a theater. By the fourth century, however, Sabratha was showing the effects of the barbarian incursions, and some of the buildings presented evidence of destruction and rebuilding. The Vandal invasions of the fifth century also had a deleterious effect on the city, but there was a short revival in the sixth century with Justinian's reconquest of North Africa. In the seventh century the Arab conquest brought a final end to Sabratha.

Unfortunately, this article in a popular magazine was as close as Kathleen ever got to publishing the results of the excavations. Sabratha marked a turning point in the publication of her fieldwork. K had published the Verulamium theater shortly after finishing the excavation. Samaria-Sebaste III was delayed in large part by events she could not control, namely, the Second World War. Even during the war she was able to publish Viroconium and the Wrekin, in addition to Samaria-Sebaste I, and she was clearly working on Leicester, finally publishing it in 1948. The final report for Breedon-on-the-Hill was published in 1950 and Sutton Walls in 1954. Southwark was not published until 1950, and she apologized for the its tardiness, blaming her heavy workload.[138] But although the Annual Report of the BSR for 1966 optimistically predicted the imminent publication of Sabratha, it was never published by either Kathleen or John Ward Perkins. K worked on the Sabratha excavation report off and on for nearly thirty years, but it was unfinished at her death and was finally completed and published by other scholars in the 1980s and 1990s, after the deaths of both K and Ward Perkins.

Philip Kenrick published the first Sabratha volume in 1986. One problem he ran into was the lack of systematic plans, probably a consequence of organizational problems caused by having two directors. Ward Perkins had become more and more interested in architecture, especially at Lepcis Magna, and K herself was primarily concerned with the drawing of sections. Otherwise, Kenrick was impressed with her meticulous and methodical field notes.[139]

Kenrick found, in fact, that K had written much of the excavation report by the mid-fifties. What delayed the final report was "the immense task of studying the pottery and providing the dating evidence required to correlate the stratigraphic sequences which had been established."[140] Working with relatively unknown pottery, K had to create a typological series, classifying the pots and putting them into a chronological sequence. And Kenrick concluded that "the enormity of the task defeated her."[141] He was able to complete the work in the 1980s because he had access to the knowledge of Mediterranean pottery gained in the previous thirty-five years.

Moreover, such a job really required one's full-time attention, hard to give if one had other duties, such as teaching. In addition, the year after the final Sabratha season K would embark on a demanding project which would put her further and further behind in publication. She would never catch up.

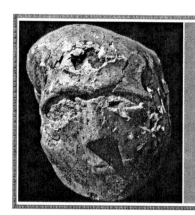

CHAPTER FIVE

WALLS OF JERICHO

IN 1930 PROFESSOR JOHN GARSTANG of Liverpool University announced
that he had found the Jericho conquered by Joshua. Or at least he strongly
implied that he had. His was not the first expedition to the famous biblical site
where, according to the Old Testament, the Israelites made the walls come
tumbling down. In 1868 Captain (later Sir) Charles Warren of the Royal
Engineers, in Palestine at the behest of the Palestine Exploration Fund, dug
into the mound, but he didn't know enough about mud-brick to realize when
he had dug through an Early Bronze Age wall. He declared there to be little of
interest at the site.

The first real archaeologists to investigate the tell were a German-Austrian
team in 1907–1909 and 1911. Carl Watzinger and Ernest Sellin uncovered
two fortification systems, a double wall at the top of the mound and another
wall farther down the slope. Watzinger came to believe that the lower wall
dated to the Middle Bronze Age (ca. 1800 B.C.) and that the upper double wall
dated to the third millennium B.C. He argued that there was no evidence of
significant occupation during the Late Bronze Age, the period agreed to be that
of Joshua. In an article of 1926, Watzinger wrote that "in the time of Joshua,
Jericho was a heap of ruins on which stood perhaps a few isolated huts."[1]

In the early twentieth century, archaeologists and historians of the Bible
took the Old Testament account of Hebrew history much more literally than
many do today, when the historicity of the Hebrew Bible is hotly debated.
Even archaeologists like Kathleen Kenyon who were not out to "prove" the
Bible accepted the story of the Hebrew conquest of Canaan as a more or less
historical account. At the time the generally accepted view was that the

101

Israelite conquest had occurred in the Late Bronze Age (ca. 1580–1200 B.C.), although there was quibbling about precise dates. Thus, Watzinger's view that there had been no city to conquer provoked controversy.

John Garstang launched a new series of excavations in 1930–1936. While he agreed that the lower wall dated to the Middle Bronze Age, Garstang placed the upper double wall in the Late Bronze Age, ca. 1400, arguing that confusion had been caused by the fact that it was built over an earlier, Early Bronze Age wall. Since it showed signs of destruction and burning, this fit nicely into the accepted biblical chronology. Even more importantly, however, Garstang's excavations revealed Neolithic and Mesolithic levels, taking the history of the site back to ca. 4000 B.C. At the time, this received less attention than the Joshua question but in the long run would prove much more significant.

Enter Kathleen. Professor Garstang and Kathleen Kenyon knew each other through the Palestine Exploration Fund and British School of Archaeology in Jerusalem. By about 1950 Garstang realized that much had been learned in the last fifteen years about Palestinian archaeology, including pottery chronology. Accordingly, he asked Kathleen to review his material and evaluate it in light of current knowledge

It is interesting to speculate as to what role Sir Frederic played in all this. Only a few years earlier, in 1948, he had noted that controversy over the dates of the destruction of Jericho would be solved by the accurate dating of the pottery.[2] At any rate, Kathleen examined Garstang's findings and published her results in an article in the *Palestine Exploration Quarterly* in 1951. While agreeing with his date for the Middle Bronze Age walls, K questioned, as delicately as she could, his other conclusions. In particular, K argued that Garstang had not, in fact, found any Late Bronze Age I (ca. 1500–1400 B.C.) pottery in his excavations, and so there was no evidence of a town destroyed in the fifteenth century B.C. There was, she argued, evidence for some occupation of the site in the succeeding century, a time during which Garstang had declared the site abandoned. K concluded her evaluation with the suggestion that a relatively small excavation might resolve these questions.[3] Kathleen would get her excavation, but in the end it would definitely not be a small one.

The chance to excavate at Jericho may have been just the opportunity she was waiting for. K was no doubt eager to return to Palestine after an absence of fifteen years. Despite her extensive experience in British archaeology, Palestine was central to her interests. Since the 1930s she had been working on the final Samaria report. In the late 1930s she and J. H. Iliffe, Curator of the Palestine

Archaeological Museum in Jerusalem, had discussed co-authoring a book on Palestinian archaeology. Although nothing had come of that plan, in the mid-1940s she still considered the possibility of writing such a book, perhaps with John Crowfoot.[4] Since 1948 she had been Lecturer in Palestinian Archaeology and Curator of the Petrie Palestinian Collection at the Institute of Archaeology. Active in the Palestine Exploration Fund, K served on the executive committee and had been elected treasurer in 1948.

The Second World War had frustrated whatever plans she may have had to go back to Palestine in the late 1930s. After the war the political upheaval that accompanied the British withdrawal from Palestine and the subsequent Israeli War of Independence in 1948–49 prevented the immediate resumption of archaeological work in the region. In fact, conditions were such that in 1947 the BSAJ was officially suspended, and in 1949 a member of the executive committee of the PEF even suggested that the organization change its name, since it would probably no longer be able to excavate there.[5] The outlook looked bleak for Palestinian archaeology.

But in 1949 the fighting ended with an uneasy truce between the new state of Israel and the surrounding Arab nations, including the Hashemite Kingdom of Jordan, which at the time included the West Bank and East Jerusalem. By the end of 1950, both the American School of Oriental Research and the French École Biblique et Archéologique de St. Etienne had resumed operations in East Jerusalem. The British School wanted to do likewise, provided it could get a government grant to support its work. Possibly acting on the advice of Rik Wheeler, then Honorary Secretary of the British Academy and on the Council of the BSAJ, K suggested that the best way to reopen the School was to recommence excavations.

In December 1950 the eighty-seven-year-old Sir Frederic Kenyon resigned as Chairman of the Council of the BSAJ for health reasons (although he remained as President), and K was elected to serve in his place. At the same time it was decided she should go to Palestine and investigate the possibility of excavation. Given the group's limited funds, Kathleen thought Jericho would be the place to start, as the United Nations might be willing to supply refugee labor, and she thought that a limited excavation would be all that was necessary to answer some of the questions Garstang's expedition had raised. All of this was done with Garstang's full approval.[6]

Flying out to Jerusalem in January 1951 to inspect the situation on the ground, K reported optimistically back to the BSAJ executive committee in

February. Her trip had confirmed the suitability of Jericho as a place for the BSAJ to resume excavations. The site was located in the new Hashemite Kingdom of Jordan, and while K thought the British School should strive to maintain good relations with both the new states of Israel and Jordan, labor was much cheaper in Jordan. The BSAJ no longer had a building in Jerusalem, but most of its equipment had been safely stored by the Dominicans in the École Biblique; she had ascertained that the expedition could also borrow equipment from the Jordanian Department of Antiquities. At Jericho itself, she found that Garstang's trenches were still in reasonably good shape and could serve as starting points for an exploration of the Neolithic and Bronze Age levels. Although K herself was more interested in the earliest levels than in proving or disproving the Bible, she thought that working on the "biblical" layers would make it easier to raise money. Garstang, however, warned against making promises about finding biblical material that might not be fulfilled. Shortly thereafter, K resigned as chairman (to be replaced by John Crowfoot) and was elected the new Director of the British School of Archaeology in Jerusalem, the first active field director since 1939.[7]

K returned to Jerusalem in late December 1951 to begin fieldwork. One of her first stops was the American School of Oriental Research (ASOR) in Jerusalem (now the Albright Institute). Traditionally, relations between the American and British Schools had been very friendly. When the BSAJ lost its building in the 1920s, for instance, the American School had taken in its library. K hoped for collaboration and financial support from the American School and thought this might be facilitated if she asked them to provide an assistant director for the dig.[8] At the American School she was introduced to A. Douglas Tushingham and his wife Maggie. Doug Tushingham was then the Annual Professor of ASOR. An easy-going, tactful, gentlemanly Canadian who spoke Arabic, he was the perfect counterpart for the more aggressive, much less diplomatic Kathleen. Although not very experienced as an archaeologist, he readily agreed to serve as assistant director at Jericho. Maggie Tushingham would come along as a registrar of finds. Previously, the American School, overrun with Protestant ministers, had tended toward teetotalism, which couldn't have appealed to Kathleen. The Tushinghams made an agreeable impression when, at their first meeting, they offered her a gin. It was the start of a friendship that would last the rest of her life[9] (Figure 5.1).

One of K's objectives in restarting the BSAJ was, of course, the training of students in proper field methodology. What K considered "proper field

FIGURE 5.1: Kathleen and Doug Tushingham at Jericho.
Courtesy of Stuart Laidlaw, Institute of Archaeology, UCL.

methodology" for Palestinian archaeology was still relatively unknown. In 1939 she had delivered a paper and then published an article in the Palestine Exploration Fund's *Quarterly Statement* on "Excavation Methods in Palestine," but it made little impression on the archaeological world. Her volume on the Samaria pottery had not yet appeared. *Beginning in Archaeology*, which expounded her methods, appeared only in 1952; Wheeler's own discussion of field technique, *Archaeology from the Earth*, wasn't published until 1954. Rik Wheeler would famously say that it was in Palestine "where more sins have probably been committed in the name of archaeology than on any commensurate portion of the earth's surface."[10] K no doubt agreed with this assessment and was determined to do something about it.

The older approach to Palestinian archaeology, the method familiar to John Crowfoot and Eleazar Sukenik, was basically architectural, emphasizing the exposure of entire buildings, in the words of an eminent modern archaeologist, "almost to the exclusion of everything else, often ignoring stratigraphy and ceramic typology, so that precise dating and interpretation of complex architectural phases was impossible."[11] This was the approach K had complained about so vociferously at Samaria. In fact, in the first Harvard excavations at Samaria,

George Reisner had introduced techniques quite similar to those K would employ. But Reisner had not continued in Palestinian archaeology; he had returned to Egypt to excavate, and K does not seem to have been aware of how similar his method was to the one she advocated.[12]

The approach K used at Jericho, based on Wheeler's debris analysis techniques, consisted of digging in (usually) five by five meter squares, leaving baulks between the squares so that the stratigraphy would be apparent. Neither at Jericho nor in Jerusalem would she stick to a rigid grid system of extended squares, because topography did not allow for it. Rather, she was forced to adapt the squares to circumstances. Section drawings of the stratigraphy recorded in the baulks nonetheless preserved a record of the depositional history of the site. Because digging was done according to the natural layers of the soil, which were distinguished by color and texture, it was possible to separate each layer and the artifacts in it from other layers, and so provide relative dates for all structures and finds.[13] K's goal was to have at the end of the season "a complete record of the site."

> [The excavator] has plans of walls which he can prove are contemporary by their association with the same floors. He has pottery and objects from the various levels, with measured sections to prove to which of the various building periods they belong. . . . He is therefore able to classify his material, and to date the unknown by association with the known.[14]

Perhaps the most significant long-term aspect of the Jericho excavations would be the spread of the chronologically precise Wheeler-Kenyon method to Middle Eastern archaeology.

JERICHO IS LOCATED IN the rift of the Jordan Valley (part of the Great Rift Valley, which extends from northern Syria to East Africa). Thirty miles from Jerusalem, 900 feet below sea level, it is on the plain through which the Jordan River flows from the Sea of Galilee south to the Dead Sea. The Dead Sea shimmers in the distance, eight miles to the south; the Mountains of Moab and Gilead are off to the east, and the Mount of Temptation (where, according to tradition, Jesus was tempted by Satan) towers over the site to the west. Located in the midst of an otherwise barren desert, Jericho is a lovely sight, a lush oasis of date palms, banana trees, and orange groves. K enjoyed working in such a picturesque site, writing that "[t]he view to the east from Jericho in the late afternoon, with the palm trees and banana groves of the oasis in the fore-ground, is one of the most beautiful I know."[15]

Old Testament Jericho—Tell es-Sultan—is about a mile from Ariha, modern Jericho (Figure 5.2). The tell, created by the accumulation of thousands of years of human occupation as generations of inhabitants built and rebuilt, is a roughly oval-shaped mound covering about ten acres, 65 to 70 feet high and 300 yards long. The oasis was created by the spring, whose waters, according to the Second Book of Kings, were miraculously made drinkable by the prophet Elisha. The spring itself is now buried under the mound but seeps up at the foot of the tell into a reservoir, from which it flows out into several streams.

In January 1952 K began to dig at Jericho for what everyone believed would be a one-or perhaps two-season expedition. The excavations instead would last for seven field seasons and involve fifty-eight field supervisors, six surveyors, three draftsmen, three photographers, five conservators, five camp managers, a handful of other assistants and advisors, and hundreds of laborers.

FIGURE 5.2: The tell of Jericho.
Courtesy of Stuart Laidlaw, Institute of Archaeology, UCL.

K had twenty-one staff members that first year, not including Doug Tushingham. Of fourteen site supervisors, six were from the American School, and two, Awni Dajani and Abdul Karim Gharreybeh, from the Jordanian Department of Antiquities. The expedition members would change over the years; in particular, site supervisors, who were often graduate students or young professors, would come and go. There was less turnover among the more specialized personnel. Cecil Western, who had worked with K at Sabratha, was there for several seasons; Nancy Lord was one of the expedition's photographers. Diana Kirkbride was in charge of the tombs for several seasons, a job eventually taken on by Kim Wheeler, Rik Wheeler's third wife. Kathleen Bowman served as camp supervisor in 1952, although in several later seasons Vivienne Catleugh would run the camp. One of the most important and constant members of the expedition was Dorothy Marshall, who K had known through the Council for British Archaeology. A tough and likable Scot, Marshall was the registrar of finds and the "medicine man" of the camp, doling out relief to the crew for the ubiquitous "gippy tummy" and to the Arab workmen for various ailments. K liked this particular group very much, writing to her sister, "The party is first rate, both archaeologically and as persons."[16]

Luckily, K did not have the kinds of problems leasing land that John Crowfoot had had at Samaria. The tell itself was government property, and a permit to dig sufficed as permission. Most helpfully, site supervisor Awni Dajani was both Inspector of Antiquities for Western Jordan and a Jericho landowner. This made him extremely useful to K in helping to lease the needed accommodations.

A two-story, nineteenth-century mill house located beside one of the canals flowing out of the reservoir at the base of the tell became the headquarters of the dig. The dig house was lit by paraffin pressure lamps but, eventually, courtesy of the American School, it was equipped with an electric generator. The cook produced meals on three primus stoves in the first-floor kitchen. Arab servants then carried the food upstairs by way of an outside staircase to the dining room, a long narrow room with a long narrow table around which, when necessary, as many as sixteen could be squeezed. When more were present (and often more were), some ate in the adjoining, smaller room, which also served as a common room. The drawing and dark rooms were also upstairs, while the pottery room was downstairs next to the kitchen. A smaller house next door served as the women's dormitory, while the men camped out in the banana grove next to the mill house.

The actual digging was done by local Arab workmen, who called K "The Great Sitt"—the Great Lady. The title was given sincerely because she provided employment and, as it turned out, for some of them, a profession. The people of Jericho were, for the most part, extremely poor and chronically unemployed. Hundreds were desperate to sign up to be paid what was a pittance by American or British standards. The first year K selected laborers more or less arbitrarily, but over time she developed a core of experienced and capable workmen. The most skilled of these would go on to careers as professional diggers, in high demand for their expertise (Figure 5.3).

Kathleen had no difficulty as a woman in the Arab world. Despite the fact that her Arabic was still "dig" Arabic and she could easily get out of her depth in conversation,[17] one native Arabic speaker insisted that she understood everything.[18] Doug Tushingham always said that despite her tentative grasp of grammar, she always gave the workmen instructions with such complete authority they assumed she must be correct.[19] As an Englishwoman of her class, someone born and bred to exercise authority, she was highly regarded by Arabs of all social classes, who regarded her as a sort of "honorary man." With the power to hire and fire, she was certainly greatly respected by her workers, who would sometimes even ask her to mediate quarrels among themselves. Occasionally, on paydays there would be squabbling over who had worked and who had taken a day off, but K's word was law. She herself was to note later, "There is much to be said for a dictatorship."[20]

K's workers admired her not only for her authority but because she also looked out for them and, in some cases, protected them from the local authorities. In 1953 one of the site supervisors reported the theft of some of her belongings. The local police response was to round up any of the workmen who had ever been in trouble with the law, cart them off, and beat them up. Kathleen had something of the colonial administrator in her and wasn't afraid to tell the local police how to do their jobs. Upon learning of these events, she angrily stormed into the office of the District Inspector and, in her own words, "went round and round and round" without making him quite understand that she thoroughly disapproved of such heavy-handed methods. She was able to take home most of the workers, having made the police promise not to harm those left in custody. When she returned the next day to find they had been beaten anyway, she was furious.[21] Not surprisingly, on a later occasion, she wouldn't let the police take one of her workman away at all. Two policemen turned up to arrest a foreman because of three pounds owed in back taxes.

Figure 5.3: K hiring Jericho workers. *Courtesy of David Spurgeon.*

Kathleen offered to pay the three pounds that day and deduct it from his wages.[22] A good foreman wasn't to be parted with easily.

The day at Jericho began at 6:30 am with a light snack of "tea and a wad"—hot tea and bread with jam, butter, or sometimes Vivienne Catleugh's home-made marmalade. Work began at 7 am. A hot breakfast was served about 9:30, with a lunch break from 12:30 to 1:30. Work ended at 4:30, followed by after-noon tea. After tea, K held sessions in which recent pottery finds were dis-cussed. For baths before dinner one had the choice of hot water in a pan heat-ed on a primus stove, or rather more water from the very cold spring. Dinner was at about 7 pm, and after an evening of canasta or bridge, most of the very tired crew went to bed by 10 or 11 pm.

The Wheeler-Kenyon method required the field assistants to supervise their crews very closely. Each site supervisor had a pick man and several shov-el men to dig, and basket boys to carry away the refuse. The idea was to shave off the soil, layer by layer. As the workmen removed the soil, the supervisor recorded in his or her site notebook the finds from each soil layer, paying close attention to changes in soil color or texture. All of this is more easily described than accomplished. Being a good site supervisor required patience and diligence. Because of the nature of excavation, everything was found in reverse, the debris from a building's occupation before the foundation trench-es of the walls. One had to anticipate, as far as possible, what could be expect-ed next, and had to proceed slowly, stopping the workmen and investigating very carefully when anything usual or unknown was encountered. ("Dig there" and "stop" were the most important words in a site supervisor's Arabic vocabulary.) In addition, as one dug downward in the square, the sides of the five by five meter squares had to be kept perfectly straight so that the stratig-raphy could be clearly seen. Although K taught the site supervisors to draw sections—that is, the sides of the squares showing the stratigraphy—she usually drew the final sections herself, even though she was not, by her own admission, a good draftsman.

As the site supervisors and workmen dug down, all the potsherds were placed in a basket marked with the level in which they were found. The pottery was then taken to dig headquarters, where it was sorted, washed, and laid out on mats to dry. K then chose the specimens she wanted, mainly those sherds with diagnostic features like rims, bases, and handles, or distinctive decora-tions. These would be used to create the type series, the classification of pot-tery based on forms and features that would permit the Jericho pots to be com-pared with those found elsewhere. The chosen pottery was then sent to the reg-istrars, who marked each sherd with the identifying number of the level from whence it came. While some pieces were selected to be drawn immediately, most of the sherds were bagged and set aside to await long-term analysis.

In the late afternoon, after tea, K held pottery sessions. She would point to a pile of the washed pottery lying on the mats and ask, "What can you tell me about this lot?" as a way of beginning a discussion about which sherds came from which level. A thorough understanding of the pottery sequences found in the occupation layers was essential to the methodology K was trying to teach the young archaeologists. She herself had an extraordinary command of the pottery sequences, able to recognize instantly if one coarse lump of pottery was found where it didn't belong.

The Kathleen Kenyon who became a modern archaeological legend—even a myth—originated at Jericho in the 1950s. She was in her mid-forties when the dig began, so this legendary figure is a confident, stout, middle-aged woman with intense blue eyes, a low-pitched throaty voice, striding manfully up and down the mound in the battered trench coat she would wear throughout the Jericho excavations, a cigarette ever-present in her nicotine-stained hand or mouth, alerting the loafing basket boys to her imminent presence by her rattling smokers' cough. This is the woman who could consume frightening quantities of gin without showing its effects and who was reputed, quite wrongly, to carry a flask of the stuff around with her. And the woman who could bend over at the waist and pick up and examine pieces of pottery without bending her knees.

While some of the site supervisors remember that at the beginning of the season she would give an introductory lecture on what to do, others recall being dumped on the site with a gang of Arab laborers and being told to get on with it. Many no doubt had an experience similar to that of the site supervisor at Sabratha who was abandoned to two Arab workers whose entire command of English consisted of "Yes," "No," and "Okay, Johnny," or the twenty-year-old at Jericho who protested that he didn't know any Arabic and to whom K replied, "You will, you will." In these circumstances, one young field assistant at Jericho, given an experienced and competent foreman, thought it best to limit his activities to observing him. The real training was given when K visited each site supervisor once or twice a day to see how he or she was getting on. As she walked up to the site, her greeting was always, "What are you doing? Where are you?" She would also give talks in the evening, explaining the developments on the various sites on the mound, occasionally taking the group around the tell (Figure 5.4) so all could get a sense of the dig as a whole.

FIGURE 5.4: Weekly tour of the Jericho site.
Courtesy of Stuart Laidlaw, Institute of Archaeology, UCL.

Everybody called her "K," with the exception of one or two who could not bring themselves to do so and insisted on referring to her formally as "Miss Kenyon." Although she could be brusque, many believed this was a cover for an underlying shyness. She may have still recalled the terrifying Caton-Thompson, for Kathleen was extremely patient with novices who didn't know quite what they were doing, mildly pointing out to one site supervisor that she had inadvertently cut through a mud-brick wall. One of the traits that made her such a good teacher was her ability to let people work out problems for themselves. When Phillip Hammond felt he had gotten lost in his square, K reassured him, "Don't worry. You'll find the floor level." And he did. She also listened to her assistants. Although she had a reputation for never changing her mind once it was made up, several site supervisors recall arguing her over to their side in disputes over interpretation of stratigraphy. When James Mellaart believed he had not yet reached bedrock, and K thought he had, she let him dig down another five meters to find three stone walls.[23] Nevertheless, she did not

113

give praise easily, so Lawrence Toombs felt she had paid him the ultimate compliment when she finally looked at him and said, "I think you'll get along Larry. You can cope."

No one would have taken K for a saint. She had no patience with those she believed were lazy, stupid, or not trying. If someone asked a question that showed he or she was just not paying attention, she would growl "Nonsense." She was jealous of her own authority, always making clear who was in charge of the expedition. Years later one of the servants, Dahoud Jibrin, told interviewer Minna Lönnqvist of the time he neglected to wake everyone at the usual time because of the weather. K didn't like this at all, asking him, "Are you the Director of the excavation?" When he protested that it was raining, she declared in no uncertain terms, "I decide when we work and when we do not work."[24] And she could be out of sorts and uncharacteristically rude on occasion. But at least K knew when she had behaved badly. On one occasion, when she snapped at a site supervisor who had been ill and unable to work for several days, she went to him several hours later and apologized.

Overall, people remember K's good humor and common sense, which seems to have inspired extraordinary loyalty. People liked working for her, and as she expected the best out of people, she often got it. Because she worked such long hours—sometimes eighteen hours a day—no one complained about the hard work. Often, long after others had gone to bed, she would stay up, working on the reports of other excavations by the light of a lamp, getting perhaps four or five hours of sleep a night after a long, arduous day.

The experience at Jericho was one of learning a rigorous methodology from a demanding but kindly teacher. Those being trained by K knew they would become better archaeologists. But nobody, least of all K, suspected that they were on the verge of one of the great archaeological discoveries of the century.

ONE OF THE EXPEDITION'S aims was to solve the Joshua question. Doug Tushingham remembered sitting with K at the top of one of Garstang's old trenches, discussing what had been found twenty years earlier. Had he really located the walls that surrounded the city at the time of the Israelite invasion? K didn't think so. She suspected the wall Garstang had dated to the time of Joshua in fact dated to some thousand years earlier.[25] To find out meant examining the Bronze Age defenses. To do this K began by digging a trench through the middle of the mound on the west side, sensibly if not imaginatively called Trench 1[26] (Figures 5.5 and 5.6). They found a number of mud-brick Early

Bronze Age walls—seven that first season and seventeen altogether. K believed earthquakes to be a common cause of destruction and, in fact, the walls were

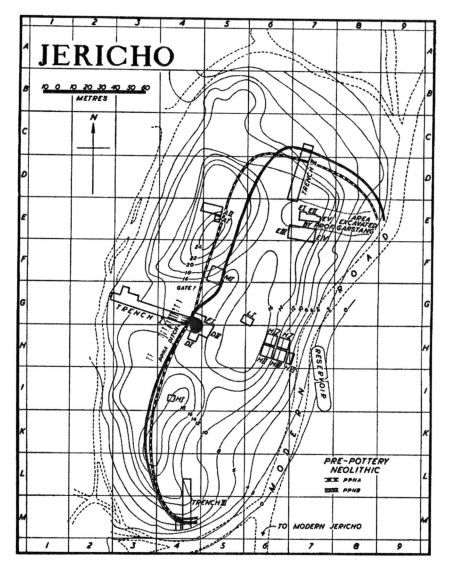

FIGURE 5.5: Plan of K's excavations on the Jericho tell and of the pre-Pottery Neolithic town walls. *Reproduced by permission of the Council for British Research in the Levant, London.*

FIGURE 5.6: Main trench at Jericho. *Courtesy of David Spurgeon.*

built in independent sections in an effort to localize earthquake damage. The final wall, marking the end of the Early Bronze Age at Jericho, had clearly been built in a rush, without proper foundations, with whatever materials were at hand. But despite the desperate attempts of the townspeople to protect themselves, it had been destroyed before completion, probably, K thought, by the nomadic invaders she termed Amorites, who most scholars at the time believed had destroyed the Early Bronze Age civilization.

The impoverished villagers, thought at the time to have been nomads who destroyed the Early Bronze Age civilization, left only slight traces on the tell. This was in contrast to the people, often termed Canaanites, of the next period, the Middle Bronze Age (ca. 1900–1580 B.C.). On account of their pottery, architecture, and burial customs, K concluded that a new, more sophisticated culture had come to inhabit Jericho. This sophistication could be seen in their town's defenses. Evidence was found of a steep, artificial, plastered slope, sometimes called a glacis but more properly referred to as an escarp (because of its steepness), with a mud-brick wall at the top. In 1952 K suggested that since this was the period of invaders known as the "Hyksos," and because they were believed to have introduced the use of war chariots, this steep slope was intended as a defense against chariots. Later, however, she seems to have reconsidered and suggested other possible explanations, such as a defense against battering rams.

Finally, in that first season K discovered that overlying the Middle Bronze Age defenses was Iron Age material, dating to about the seventh century B.C. Thus, no evidence for defenses from the Late Bronze Age, the period of Joshua, was found. The excavations clearly showed that Garstang had been wrong. The pottery that went with Garstang's walls was clearly Early Bronze Age, dating to the third millennium B.C., not the period associated with Joshua.

Despite her own sincere Christian beliefs, K was not worried about "proving" the Bible. She did emphasize biblical associations, mostly for fundraising purposes. But she was not unduly upset when her discoveries did not match the Bible's account, influenced, no doubt, by her father's view of the progressive nature of divine revelation.[27] She, in fact, had once argued that "Palestinian archaeology has suffered to some extent in the past from a too exclusive association with the Bible. We should have obtained a far truer picture if in the last fifty years excavators had been able to visualize the life of the country as part of a whole, and not primarily as a means of proving Biblical accuracy."[28] Nevertheless, her finds troubled her: she didn't want to offend Professor Garstang. While K could flippantly write to Nora that so far she hadn't seen a sign of Joshua,[29] she was very worried about hurting the old man's feelings.

While finding a "Joshua" wall would have been a public relations coup, given her previous reevaluation of Garstang's results, *not* finding walls associated with the biblical story probably wasn't much of a surprise or disappointment to her. Kathleen would always suggest the possibility that the Late Bronze Age city had eroded away. In fact, little evidence was ever uncovered that there had even been much of a Late Bronze Age city for Joshua to conquer. The date of Jericho's undoubted destruction, about the middle of the fourteenth century B.C., accorded with none of the accepted scholarly theories. But she also maintained that as an archaeologist she had no obligation to reconcile the archaeological evidence with the work of biblical scholars.[30]

If Joshua was nowhere to be found, the group's discoveries when they reinvestigated Garstang's Neolithic levels went far beyond anyone's wildest dreams. Instead of a one- or two-season dig, Jericho would become one of the major archaeological sites of the decade, if not the century.

"Neolithic" means the "new stone age" that began with the invention of agriculture and the domestication of animals. Humans no longer had to wander as hunters and gatherers and could settle in one spot, creating villages and eventually cities, and so "civilization." Previously, archaeologists had believed that such settlements emerged in the Near East ca. 5000 B.C., with "civilization" emerging ca. 3000 B.C. When the Jericho excavations began, the earliest known permanent settlement was at Jarmo, a village in northern Iraq which covered about three acres and had been dated to ca. 4800 B.C. But at Jericho K was to show that settled life went back thousands of years before that. Indeed, she would claim to demonstrate that urban life, and arguably "civilization," went back to the eighth millennium.

On the tell, Garstang had identified both a Neolithic level with pottery, and one without. Underneath these two levels he had also found traces of a Mesolithic ("Middle Stone Age") layer, a transitional stage between the Paleolithic ("Old Stone Age") and Neolithic, dating to perhaps 10,000 years ago. In Garstang's old trench at the northeast end of the tell, K's Jericho team found more examples of the type of pre-pottery Neolithic houses he had uncovered. Older than the earliest surviving pottery on the site, these houses were built of oblong, cigar-shaped bricks impressed with a herringbone pattern with the brick maker's thumb (so as to form indentations which would allow the mortar to grip more firmly) (Figure 5.7). The houses had large, well-constructed rooms centered on courtyards, and plaster floors polished to a smooth and glossy finish that was nearly waterproof for easy cleaning. They were in such good shape that that the archaeologists could still wash and scrub them in preparation for photographs (Figure 5.8).

FIGURE 5.7:
Herringbone brick.
*Courtesy of Stuart
Laidlaw, Institute of
Archaeology, UCL.*

FIGURE 5.8: Jericho
Neolithic houses.
*Courtesy of Stuart
Laidlaw, Institute of
Archaeology, UCL.*

119

From Kathleen's point of view, the really exciting discovery was the evidence that Neolithic Jericho, dating to *at least* the fourth millennium B.C. (carbon-14 dating would push this back an additional 3000 years)—a Jericho without the technology to make pottery—was surrounded by a large defensive wall. According to K, this indicated, an organized community, possessing what Tushingham would call a "civic consciousness."[31] At the end of the 1952 season, K was willing to claim Jericho as the "oldest town in the world." By 1956 the large area of Neolithic settlement—at least eight acres—was clear.

Other surprises awaited.

Part of K's plan included tomb exploration. This was important for two reasons. First, excavations have a tendency to turn up mostly small and broken finds, such as smashed pottery. K believed that intact artifacts were necessary to provide as complete a view of the culture as possible. Such items were most likely to be found in tombs. Second, and perhaps just as important, the unbroken, often valuable objects in tombs were more likely to be wanted by museums as compensation for financial support. K always became concerned when such tomb artifacts were not forthcoming.[32]

Garstang had found a cemetery to the west of the tell, and although K began by searching there, she soon located an even more productive area—in the middle of a local refugee camp. During the 1948 war many Palestinian Arabs had fled what was in the process of becoming the state of Israel. Perhaps 500,000 to 1,000,000 (depending on whose account you believe) took refuge in Jordan. Three refugee camps had been established near Jericho, including one of about 12,000 to the north of the mound. The refugees, some of whom had left land or businesses behind, were often even poorer than the Jerichoans. But in some sense, they were also better off because the United Nations Relief and Works Agency dispensed monthly supplies to them. Not unnaturally, tensions had grown up between the native Jerichoans and the newcomers. K dealt with the situation by decreeing that since refugees were helped by the UN, she would hire only locals to work on the tell.

Then the tombs were discovered. Initially, the refugees had been housed in tents, but by 1952 many were in the process of building themselves small, mud-brick houses. One day one of the women, digging for material with which to make plaster and bricks, stumbled into a Middle Bronze Age tomb. A scarab from the tomb was taken to the Great Sitt, thus alerting her to an area rich in finds. Latrine-diggers and brickmakers began regularly to report the discovery of tombs. By offering both monetary rewards and jobs working in the tombs,

K was able to persuade the refugees to let the archaeologists excavate in their camp, in their backyards and, occasionally, in their houses.

She also hired refugees for tomb hunting. Actively looking for the tombs—as opposed to waiting for them to be discovered accidentally—was a matter of locating a spot of soft soil in the rock, which often indicated that a shaft had been cut into the limestone. The size of the tombs varied according to date and burial customs, but typically, a round, vertical shaft led down for several meters to a chamber door usually sealed with a large rock or rocks in mud mortar (Figure 5.9). The chambers themselves ranged from 1.5 to 4.5 meters in diameter. The discovery of the tombs in their midst caused quite a stir in the refugee village. The crowds that flocked around after the initial discovery made it necessary to call in the police for crowd control. Much of the work in the tombs was, in fact, done with curious onlookers hanging around outside. Night watchmen were hired to keep an eye on the tombs, but, fortunately for the archaeologists, little gold, which would have been sure to attract unwelcome interest, was found.

The first season tombs ranging from the Early Bronze Age (ca. 3000–2100 B.C.) to the Middle Bronze Age (ca. 1900–1580 B.C.) were found. In

FIGURE 5.9: Jericho tomb entrance.
Courtesy of Stuart Laidlaw, Institute of Archaeology, UCL.

121

subsequent seasons Late Chalcolithic (ca. 3200 B.C.) and the odd Iron Age and Roman tomb would be uncovered. The most impressive, and richest, burials came from the Middle Bronze Age. The deceased had been placed in the rock-cut tomb, accompanied by such necessities as food and drink, plates and jugs, toilet articles, and furniture. When the next body came to be placed in the tomb, the previous remains were shoved aside, so that bones and grave goods came eventually to be pushed to the back and sides of the chamber. With growing excitement, K realized that much of the organic material was in an unusually good state of preservation. For example, not only did the excavators discover a tiny wooden box delicately carved to look like a pomegranate, but they also found the remains of actual pomegranates nearby. Raisins, platters of meat, skin from a long-disappeared liquid, and even a human brain were preserved. This extraordinary preservation was a mystery that would not be solved until a later season. So numerous were the discoveries that K reported to Nora that everyone was getting rather blasé about tombs with as many as ten skeletons in them[33] (Figure 5.10).

The tombs produced some of the most exciting finds that season and others. One of the most memorable tombs of the first season was discovered at the end of the working day. Impatiently—and K thought unwisely—the tomb was opened just before quitting time. Immediately inside its entrance was the principal burial, although other burials were found, pushed to the side. This consisted of a male skeleton on a wooden bed, covered with a rush mat. The bed was the only one of its kind found. Next to the bed was a large wooden table, at over five feet long the largest they had ever found, covered with food. Surrounding the body was an array of objects: small inlaid boxes, jugs, plates, cups, and toilet articles.

FIGURE 5.10: Tomb interior. *Courtesy of Stuart Laidlaw, Institute of Archaeology, UCL.*

But right away, the excavators realized their mistake. Some of the tomb's most interesting finds, including the numerous wooden objects and a joint of mutton with meat still on it, began to deteriorate in front of their eyes as soon as exposed to the air; K graphically described the objects as beginning to "ooze." Kathleen, Nancy Lord, and three others worked in shifts until 2 am squeezed uncomfortably into the tomb, processing its contents before the organic materials deteriorated completely.[34] Before the wooden objects could be moved, they had to be cleaned with a camel-hair brush and coated with paraffin wax heated on a small primus stove outside the tomb's entrance in the entrance chamber. Other organic objects—baskets, textiles, or bones—had to be coated with a strengthening substance—liquid plastic—applied very carefully so that it would not collapse the material. Since a handful of excavators, including K, spent most of the night clearing the tomb—cleaning, preserving, planning, and photographing—Doug and Maggie Tushingham thoughtfully brought out hot chocolate to keep the excavators warm during the chilly night.

Impressive as the long wooden table was, it was also represented something of a puzzle. Like other tables found in the tombs, it had only three legs, two at one end and one at the other. This mystery was eventually solved by none other than the king of Sweden. On seeing such a table at the Institute of Archaeology, he suggested that the principle was the same as the three-legged milking stool—three legs were better than four on uneven ground.

Working in cramped spaces among dead bodies several feet below ground level was bound to produce a certain number of entertaining—and perhaps scary—stories. Nancy Lord, who had to photograph the tomb assemblages before anything could be moved, had more than her share of tomb adventures. Tests later showed that the tombs contained an unusually high concentration of carbon dioxide, and in fact people who worked in them for any length of time often became drowsy.[35] But before anyone was aware of this, Lord and another woman did in fact pass out because of a lack of oxygen. In another, more frightening incident, Lord and one of her assistants were almost electrocuted. K had borrowed an electric generator from the Department of Antiquities to provide better lighting in the tombs. Lord was squeezed into an undisturbed burial attempting to photograph it when, because of faulty insulation between the generator and her lamp, she was badly shocked and could not free herself. Ahmed Shistawi—a basket boy rapidly promoted to foreman when his talent became obvious—was just outside the tomb entrance. Hearing Lord's distress, he grabbed her and also became stuck. No one could hear their cries over the noise of the generator. Hopping around violently—Lord later claimed that they didn't damage anything—Shistawi was finally freed to turn off the electric current.

Near-electrocution did not deter Lord, but she did, briefly, consider giving up tomb duty for good when a skull seemed to try to speak to her. She was in the process of adjusting the lighting in a tomb of multiple burials when, as she leaned forward, one of the skulls' jaws snapped shut. Understandably startled, she sat back. The jaw dropped open. With admirable self-control she did not flee, but repeated her action, leaning forward again. The jaw again clicked shut. She was greatly relieved to eventually discover that a bone she was leaning against in the crowded tomb was responsible for levering another bone, which in turn moved the jaw up and down.

Given her trials in the tombs, it almost seems unfair that Nancy Lord was not the one to discover the 4000-year-old graffiti in what was thought to be an "Amorite" (Early Bronze IV) tomb. That discovery fell to one of the artists who found himself, his drawings finished, stuck in a tomb waiting for someone to fetch a ladder. As he impatiently waited, he noticed sketches on the wall: doodles of goats, trees, and two men holding spears and shields. The graffiti so accidentally discovered were the first evidence of any creative tendency on the part of the Early Bronze IV villagers.

EARLY IN THE FIRST SEASON, people understood the importance of what they were finding and that they were changing the world's understanding of prehistory. But the gravity of what they were doing and the long hours of work did not stop them from having fun in their little free time, either that season or later. After a long day people needed some relaxation. Everyone had his or her bottle of alcohol, purchased on their behalf by the housekeeper. The local arak was a favorite of other excavators, but for K it was gin before dinner and whisky after. Dinner was a lively, cheerful affair, without the formality of some European digs. K presided at one end of the long table, with Doug Tushingham at her right, Cecil Western and Nancy Lord at the other end, and the rest of the staff packed in between (Figure 5.11). Conversation was lively and wide-ranging, covering everything in general and nothing in particular.

After dinner most remained in the dig house, playing bridge or canasta or just drinking and talking. Although K often spent the evenings working late into the night, she didn't always do so. One evening, for example, Sarnia Butcher, Kim Wheeler, Nancy Lord, and Cecil Western got into an animated

FIGURE 5.11: The Jericho dinner table.
Courtesy of Stuart Laidlaw, Institute of Archaeology, UCL.

discussion with her about the right to question authority, and they stayed up arguing until midnight.

The occasional party blew off steam. Any national holiday was an excuse for a party. Australia Day, for example, was celebrated in honor of the Australians present. George Washington's birthday was celebrated in honor of the Americans. And, then, just to be fair, they had to have a party for King George III, even though no one could actually remember his birth date. And, of course, there was Jordanian Independence Day. For Dorothy Marshall's birthday, one year some of the young men, in an attempt to provide a Scottish theme, wore kilts made out of bath towels. Sometimes these celebrations turned into sing-alongs, leading to an evening of "Green Grow the Rushes Oh" and "The Vicar of Brae." One year a young American taught them the rather appropriate old spiritual "Joshua Fit the Battle of Jericho," which later K would use to introduce her popular lectures.[36] K sang loudly and enthusiastically, if not particularly well. Sometimes the festivities involved dancing, and K would surprise the young men, proving that she was still quite light on her feet. When a visiting European scholar complained that the atmosphere of the dig wasn't sufficiently serious, K just laughed at him.

Sundays were a day of rest, or at least relaxation. The crew could decide to sleep in, write letters, go sightseeing or for long walks in the nearby hills. K frequently took groups to nearby archaeological sites, including Jerash, Khirbet Mefjar, and Shechem. At Samaria that first year, she showed around not only a contingent from Jericho, but also a group that had come from the American School in Jerusalem.[37] In a later season they went to Dhiban (biblical Dibon) where the American School was digging, and K could see how her excavating techniques were being learned and passed on to others.[38] At Khirbet Qumran, Père Roland de Vaux, the Director of the École Biblique, was excavating near where the Dead Sea Scrolls had been found. On one of these trips, a tragedy was narrowly avoided when K managed to smash up the car loaned to them by the American School. No one was seriously hurt, and K, unflustered, crawled out through the car window, looked around, and demanded, "Where is my trowel?"[39]

Each season was finished off by what was ominously known as "The Division." The Director of Jordan's Department of Antiquities—Gerald Lankester Harding for most of the Jericho dig—came at the end of the season to decide which of the finds would stay in Jordan and which Kathleen would be allowed to either keep or allocate to various supporting institutions. This led to something of a frenzy at the end of the season, because nothing could be packed up until the finds had been divided up, they couldn't be divided until the digging stopped, and K wanted to dig as long as possible. In order to make his choice, Harding needed a complete record for each object, including drawings and photographs, so the crew spent a frantic few days at the end of the dig preparing the material for Harding's arrival. After he had made his choice, there was another frantic scramble to pack up all the finds to be shipped to various parts of the world. One year the rush resulted in some pottery being packed in a crate with stone querns, with foreseeable results for the pottery.

Harding wanted a sample of the typical finds and all of the unique ones to stay in Jordan. For purposes of scholarship this did not present a problem. To interpret the site K needed diagnostic features like jar handles and jug rims rather than unusual or unique items. But she did need fairly impressive objects to reward the various museums and universities for their support. She worried constantly about obtaining such artifacts, even complaining when too many interesting or unusual items were being found. If the finds were unique, the Department of Antiquities was likely to demand them. But she usually got on quite well with Harding, finding him quite fair, and she rarely protested his division of the spoils.[40]

Kathleen was quite concerned at the end of the 1952 season about having to return to London and tell John Garstang he was wrong about Joshua's walls. And in June, at a joint meeting of the BSAJ and PEF, she reported on her first season at Jericho.[41] She prepared carefully for the event, having her hair done and paying more attention than usual to her dress. A handful of the excavators who had been at Jericho were in attendance. Garstang was in his late seventies by this time, a bent-over figure with a cane. Word had been circulating about the dig's results, and he probably had more than an inkling of what was coming. Nevertheless, as tactfully as she could, K explained why she did not believe Garstang had earlier found the walls of Joshua's time, diplomatically adding that the work was in its early stages and that further excavation might alter her conclusions. Garstang, thankfully, seemed to take it all in the right spirit, and K, relieved, went out with her Jericho friends for an evening of celebration.

CHAPTER SIX

"THE OLDEST TOWN IN THE WORLD"

A SAD, BUT NOT UNEXPECTED, EVENT overshadowed the triumph of Jericho at the end of that summer of 1952. In August Sir Frederic died. At eighty-nine, he had been in poor health for the last several years, and K may well have considered his death a mercy.

Kathleen and Sir Frederic were alike in many ways (even their handwriting was similar), and although neither was emotionally demonstrative, their similar interests and the amount of time they spent in each other's company suggest that they got along quite well. K certainly showed her father great affection during his decline, trying to make his final days as pleasant and comfortable as possible.[1] They had served together in the PEF, BSAJ, and Surrey Archaeological Society; now in her forties, K still went down to Kirkstead on the weekends. Nevertheless, she stoutly maintained in later years that she did not become an archaeologist because of her father. When asked some years later if her father's biblical interests played a role in her becoming an archaeologist of the Holy Land, she replied rather testily, "Absolutely not!"[2] Still, she must have realized how intertwined were her interests and those of Sir Frederic. Certainly others did. At the meeting of the BSAJ Executive Committee during which his death was announced and a vote of sympathy passed for K, the minutes noted that she "was continuing her father's work."[3]

Kirkstead was left to Nora, and Rose Hill, the estate in Wales, to Kathleen. Since Rose Hill was hardly a convenient weekend retreat, and K's idea of real living was country living, once Nora moved into Kirkstead with her family, K looked around for another weekend cottage. She found Old Brands Lodge near

High Wycombe, in Buckinghamshire, about -fifteen miles northwest of London. A small cottage, suitable for her and Vivienne Catleugh, it was on a couple of acres, which permitted her to have a garden. She turned an unheated outbuilding into an office where she could work undisturbed on the accumulating Jericho material. The cottage could also bring in some needed extra income by being rented out during those months when Catleugh was also out at Jericho.

THE RESULTS OF THE FIRST season's excavation led K to label Jericho "the oldest town in the world," and subsequent seasons would show how truly old community life there was. Nevertheless, the 1953 season got off to a rocky start. K didn't find the excavation team as agreeable as the previous year's, primarily because of some Americans she found irksome, both personally and professionally. In particular, she had to set straight one disagreeable individual who had boasted that he could get away with faking his site notebook and that no mere woman was a match for him. Kathleen was. Almost wearily, she wrote to her sister, "I am freely putting him through it, and I don't think he has any illusions on the subject now."[4]

Despite K's disappointment over the group's lack of congeniality, the 1953 season was a great success, renowned in the annals of excavations for two things, one social and one archaeological. The former was the Great Jericho Boat Race, aka "The Lowest Boat Race in the World." It wasn't unusual once or twice a season for the crew to travel the eight miles to the Dead Sea to swim or picnic. In March of 1953 one of these outings was the scene of a dramatic reenactment of the traditional Oxford-Cambridge boat race on the Thames. The upcoming race had been a major focus of discussion among the British members of the expedition. Then someone proposed a contest with paper boats on one of the local streams. But why not a real boat race? As the Jordan was in flood, the race could not actually be on a river. The Dead Sea would have to do.

Arranging a boat race in the middle of the Judean desert was not easy. Inconveniently for the would-be athletes, fish do not live in the Dead Sea, and the absence of fisherman made appropriate boats scarce. But the archaeologists overcame these difficulties, renting boats from fishermen elsewhere and transporting them to the race site. Politics then complicated matters: as the Dead Sea was on the Jordanian-Israeli border, boats were banned. Everyone arrived on the designated day to discover that the boats had been confiscated by the

Jordanian army. But the determined excavators managed to get the boats returned when they persuaded a local army official that they weren't up to any mischief.

Teams then had to be chosen. Only K herself and Peter Parr actually had attended Oxford; no one present had gone to Cambridge. Nevertheless, sides were picked (sometimes on the most whimsical of grounds such as the ownership of an Oxford suit), and to accommodate everyone, it was decided to run the race as a relay of three laps along the shore, each crew of four rowing one lap. By the time all the arrangements were finished the sun had gone down, but it made no difference to the outcome: Cambridge easily won because Oxford never finished. Due to a broken oar-lock, the Oxford boat ended up going round and round in circles. K charged sabotage by the opposing team. The Cambridge side claimed that the broken oar-lock was "due to poor maintenance, only to be expected of a university which specializes in the humanities."[5] K would not have been comforted by the genuine Oxford-Cambridge boat race that year, for the result was the same—Cambridge won handily. Despite her chagrin over the loss to Cambridge, K thought the whole episode uproariously funny and hooted with laughter throughout.[6]

The other notable event of the 1953 season occurred on what was meant to be the last day of the dig: the discovery of the Neolithic portrait skulls. One of K's strict rules was that the sides of the baulks had to be kept perfectly straight and clean so the stratigraphy could be seen clearly. Digging holes in the sides, even to retrieve a promising-looking artifact, was strictly forbidden. One site supervisor, Father Robert North, once had a pot sticking out of the side of his trench. Since most of the vessel was sticking out with only a small bit still in the soil, he decided to take it out. As he was working, K came silently up behind him and said suddenly, "Father North, you're making a hole!" Her message was clear.[7]

Toward the end of the 1953 season, Peter Parr was supervising a site in the middle of the tell, on the west side. About ten feet down into the mound he had noticed the top of a skull visible in the side of his trench. Naturally, he left it there for several weeks as the sections were drawn. But he persuaded K to allow him to remove it before they departed for the summer, arguing that otherwise some of the local boys would just dig it out after they were gone.

The camp was already packed up, the finds boxed for shipment home, and the Arab workmen dismissed. Most of the staff had gone and the rest were ready to leave, rushing around completing all the necessary last-minute tasks.

On the last day before they were finally to depart, K somewhat grudgingly gave Parr permission to remove the skull. Naturally, it took him some time to do it properly, working slowly and carefully with a penknife and small brush, and during the course of the day he reported that something was unusual about the skull: it appeared to be covered with a layer of clay. And that evening at dinner he presented her with his astonishing find. It was a remarkable object: a human skull modeled with plaster to resemble an actual, living human being, complete with eyes made out of shells[8] (Figure 6.1).

This was a staggering discovery. Nothing like it had ever been seen before from so early a date—probably, K thought at the time, 7000 years ago. The surprise and excitement was exacerbated by the fact that two more such skulls had immediately become visible. Awni Dajani was sent to alert Père de Vaux, excavating at Qumran. De Vaux was so excited that he jumped into the car, drove pell-mell to Jericho, and abandoned his car dangling over the edge of the ramp leading down to the camp as he rushed up the tell to see the skulls.

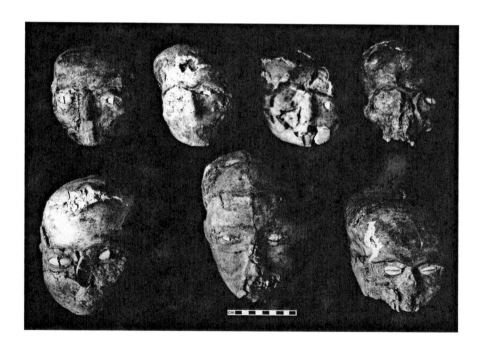

FIGURE 6.1: The Neolithic portrait skulls.
Courtesy of Stuart Laidlaw, Institute of Archaeology, UCL.

Although no one liked it, plans to leave were immediately abandoned. For five more days a small crew, which included K, Vivienne Catleugh, Peter Parr, Cecil Western, Nancy Lord, and Diana Kirkbride, camping out uncomfortably with no furniture and no cook, slowly extracted these two skulls, then three more, and then a final, seventh skull.

The skulls, which K initially dated to ca. 5000 B.C. but later revised to ca. 6000 B.C. (the period of the Pre-Pottery Neolithic) in light of carbon-14 dating, were, she argued, the first known examples of realistic human portraiture and, as such, "the earliest human portraits directly ancestral to modern art."[9] Although Garstang had earlier found a human head made of clay, it was flat, highly stylized and not at all lifelike. All male, K's skulls had been packed with clay, and facial features sculpted to produce realistic-looking, if somewhat chubby, individuals. They all had eyes, six made of two fragments of shell with an opening representing a pupil, and one with eyes made of whole cowrie shells. Only one, the most striking example, was complete with a lower jawbone. In the others a jaw had been fashioned out of clay. Brown paint on one might have represented hair or some sort of headdress.

K speculated as to the purpose of these heads. The people who had discarded the skulls clearly had no use for them, for they were found in a disorganized heap, dumped between two walls. Conversely, the artist or artists who had created them clearly took much effort to portray individual human beings. Searching for clues, K invoked anthropological models such as those found in New Guinea where heads can represent venerated ancestors or trophies taken from enemies. K herself preferred the ancestor theory: "I have personally always been convinced that they are the heads of venerated ancestors, largely owing to the impression they give of being portraits, and to the loving care which the skillful modelling of the features suggests."[10] Subsequent discoveries were, in K's view, to confirm this interpretation.

These priceless but fragile treasures then had to be taken to London for study and conservation before being dispersed to various museums. The skulls were flown back to England, some carefully packed in boxes under the seats of BOAC airliners (the predecessor of British Airways), others in the laps of cautious excavators. Despite all precautions, the most striking skull, the one with the jawbone, was broken in transit, and Cecil Western had to reconstruct it in London.

The Neolithic portrait skulls made not only *The Times* of London (and all the British papers) but the front page of *The New York Times*. While the discovery of "the world's oldest town" had elicited a good deal of newspaper coverage around the world, the discovery of the portrait skulls solidified Jericho's position as one of the most important—and renowned—archaeological digs of the century. Until then, K had been reasonably well-known and widely respected in British archaeological circles, but now she became genuinely famous, a minor celebrity, to be lumped with such other widely known archaeologists as Wheeler, the American biblical scholar W. F. Albright, and, later, Yigael Yadin, the excavator of Masada. Kathleen was the only woman in the group. The Jericho excavations, which Wheeler called the most important since the end of the war, were covered in major newspapers around the world. K wrote articles on Jericho which appeared in *The Times*, the *Sunday Times*, the *Daily Telegraph*, *Illustrated London News*, *Scientific American*, and *National Geographic Magazine* (with Doug Tushingham), as well as more staid academic journals such as *Antiquity* and the *Palestine Exploration Quarterly*.

DESPITE JERICHO'S IMPORTANCE to her life and career, we should not forget that Kathleen had an existence apart from the three or four months she spent in Jordan each year. Her academic career was the focus of this other life. She had been awarded a Doctor of Literature in May 1951 from the University of London on the basis of her earlier publications, and so was entitled to be called "Dr. Kenyon" although to most she remained "Miss Kenyon." Her duties at the Institute of Archaeology kept her extremely busy. At that time the Institute offered only postgraduate degrees—a two-year Diploma and a doctorate—but her teaching duties were many and varied. She gave lectures in introductory archaeology, offered seminars on more advanced topics, contributed to courses on the "practical" aspects of archaeology such as excavation technique, and advised Ph.D. candidates. She lectured in Palestinian archaeology, of course, and on occasion, at least, gave lectures on the British Iron Age. Kathleen was a good lecturer, organized and clear. One former student remembers her lecturing with slides but no notes. Certainly whatever notes she might have used were minimal.[11] And, as with everything else, she didn't waste anyone's time. One year, three weeks before the scheduled end of her course on the archaeology of Palestine, she announced that she had covered all the material she had meant to cover, and so dismissed the class for the remainder of the term.

Her students, like the site supervisors at Jericho, represented an array of countries. One year her small research seminar consisted of an American, a

Canadian, an Israeli, and a Jordanian. Her Ph.D. students at the Institute included Americans such as Joe Callaway, Jordanians such as Awni Dajani, and Israelis such as Claire Epstein, all of whom would go on to successful archaeological careers.

Ros Henry, K's assistant in 1956–1957, remembers that their day at the Institute began at 10 am with K, cigarette in hand, dealing with her correspondence, while students and colleagues would drop by throughout the morning. After lunch K would lecture or go to the unheated Palestine Gallery—a ballroom in a previous incarnation—to work on her pottery. Late in the afternoon she had tea in her office and then a short nap at her desk. Sometimes Rik Wheeler would come by in the evening and share a pitcher of martinis. She usually stayed well after Henry left at 6 pm, working late into the night, before going home to the flat she shared with Vivienne Catleugh in Hammersmith.

At the Institute K worked not only with Wheeler (who had returned in 1948 as a part-time professor), but with the well-known prehistorian Gordon Childe (who was Director of the Institute), Olga Tufnell, Margaret Murray, and Rachel Maxwell-Hyslop (née Clay). Possibly her least favorite colleague was Max Mallowan, excavator of Nimrud and husband of Agatha Christie. In his autobiography Mallowan claimed that he and K always got along quite well because he always let her have her way,[12] but this does not fit the recollection of those who knew them. Conflict between the two was perhaps inevitable, as they were both assertive individuals who liked getting their own way. Moreover, K disapproved of Mallowan as an archaeologist, finding him old-fashioned and "unscientific." Naturally, they were very professional and civil to each other in public and served together on a number of committees. Mallowan, at least, could be quite gracious about K in print.[13] However, they must have had some unpleasant conflicts, because after K's death Catleugh burned letters to K from Mallowan which she claimed were so nasty she didn't want other archaeologists to see them.[14]

Kathleen, however, got along quite well with Agatha Christie, a shy woman very different from her husband. On one occasion Christie took K as her guest to a Crime Club dinner with other mystery writers.[15] And K could be very protective of her friend. She wasn't a great novel-reader, but K read Christie's mysteries and defended her against criticism. When one of the Jericho field assistants opined at dinner one night that Christie was often unfair to her readers by concealing the motive for the crime, K jumped all over him. Loyalty to friends, even in the matter of mystery writing, was important.

K and Vivienne Catleugh lived in Brook Green, Hammersmith, Catleugh continuing to work for the Hammersmith Red Cross, and K driving to the Institute most days in her 1927 Rolls Royce. They would retreat to High Wycombe on the weekends. At Christmas, Catleugh went to Norfolk to visit relatives, and K (if she wasn't in Jordan) visited Nora and her family. By this time Nora had three children: Janet, Jeremy, and Elspeth. Usually arriving on Christmas Eve, K would leave on Boxing Day, the day after Christmas. The children saw these as "duty" visits, but K enjoyed being with her family during the holidays. She wrote to her sister after one such visit, "It was lovely being with you for Christmas. . . . It is a pity it always has to be such a rush."[16]

Despite the excitement of Jericho, K wasn't quite finished with British archaeology. She had another season at Wroxeter after returning from Jordan in 1952. In September, less than three weeks after Sir Frederic's death, she began a training dig, as she put it, "with a howling mob of 70 students, all complete beginners, in pouring rain."[17] A final two-week season here in 1953 was her last excavation in Roman Britain, but one that gave her yet another final report to complete.[18] Henceforth her efforts both at excavation and training students in excavation methods would be in the Middle East.

Merely contemplating Kathleen's many activities in the 1950s is exhausting. In addition to the excavations every year at Jericho (and the organization that required), she was busy with the administration of the BSAJ and PEF, teaching duties, producing popular articles and books, and the writing up of Sabratha and various British digs. On top of all that, she somehow found time to help arrange the 1953 centenary celebration of Petrie's birth, "The Archaeology of Palestine" (and write the catalogue), as well as to organize a visiting exhibit from Israel, "The Land of the Bible," at the British Museum in 1954. She was active in the Royal Archaeological Society, served on the Roman and Mediaeval London Excavation Council, helped establish the Society for Roman Pottery in 1957, and was a Trustee of the Palestine Archaeological Museum. Even her great rival Max Mallowan acknowledged her multitude of responsibilities.[19]

K was away from the Institute a good deal, lecturing in order to draw attention to, and raise money for, Jericho. She appeared with Rik Wheeler in November 1955 on "Animal, Vegetable or Mineral," a kind of archaeological quiz show consisting of experts trying to identify mysterious objects submitted by various museums. She frequently gave radio broadcasts, not only on Jericho but on Sabratha, Wroxeter, and topics such as "Palestine in the Time of the New Testament," "Palestine in the Time of the Old Testament," and "Archaeology and the Bible."[20] She even lectured on a Swan's Hellenic Cruise in 1959, as her father had done in the 1930s. The main reason for these lectures and broadcasts was fundraising, and often the check wasn't even made out to her, but to the "Jericho Excavation Fund."[21] Most, if not all, of the money she earned from writing articles also went into the excavation fund.[22] Her fundraising efforts, however, were not always enough, and sometimes K had to spend her own money. Rik Wheeler acknowledged this fact in his history of the British Academy, when he noted that the BSAJ was able to reopen in the 1950s primarily because of "the availability of a scholar of first-class quality, fortified by a small but useful domestic bank-balance and other accessible outside resources" who could spend some of her own funds on her excavations.[23]

She probably wrote her popular account of the Jericho excavations to raise money for the dig, publishing it even before the excavation was complete. She had published *Beginning in Archaeology* in 1952 as a way of conveying her methodology and encouraging young people to go into archaeology. It had begun as an Occasional Paper to be published by the Institute of Archaeology,[24] but it was eventually published as a book, probably to attract more readers. (In fact, one of K's future students, Tom Holland, decided to study archaeology as a result of reading this book.) *Digging Up Jericho* was published in 1957 and *Archaeology in the Holy Land* in 1960. Her popular works generally got good reviews, but some thought her style stilted; one reviewer referred to her "predilection for long, rather Germanic sentences."[25] Although her popular works were certainly accessible to general readers, Kathleen's style lacked Wheeler's elegance, and she admitted that writing for a popular audience was difficult for her.[26] Why this might have been so was perhaps at least partly explained when she mentioned to some of the Jericho team that, after she wrote something, she could not bear to look at it again.[27]

Some criticized *Archaeology in the Holy Land* for relying too much on the sites K dug herself,[28] and for not following her own advice to delay drawing conclusions before all the evidence could be carefully considered.[29] Yet the book was revolutionary at the time, both because it introduced some of her new terminology (e.g., Pre-Pottery Neolithic A and B, Proto Urban) and because it contained the most up-to-date material from the Jericho excavations, which included much completely new material, particularly for the prehistoric periods. Indeed, in the 1960s it was the only major textbook suitable for graduate students available on the archaeology of Palestine. Père de Vaux told her it was a good book for students, valuable for professional archaeologists, and appealing to the general public.[30] K would, in fact, later advise one of her own students to write for the general public, always being sure to include lots of pictures, in order to raise money.[31]

BACK AT JERICHO, THE 1954 season got off to an encouraging start. First, K felt the personnel were a vast improvement over the previous year's group, both socially and professionally.[32] Presumably the tiresome Americans had stayed home. Second, the Queen's New Year's Honours List which included K's CBE—Commander of the Order of the British Empire—was announced in January, just after the beginning of the dig. With her usual modesty, K did not mention her award, but a member of the staff heard about it in a letter from home. Naturally the team held a party to celebrate. K reported to Nora that she had, so far, received ninety-two letters of congratulation, some from people she barely knew. And she had already "answered them all, except one whose signature the united efforts of the party couldn't read!"[33]

K tried to remain realistic, acknowledging that they couldn't always make the kind of spectacular find they had made at the end of the previous season.[34] But the spectacular finds did not run out. Before the season was half over, they came across the bodies likely to belong to the portrait skulls. As they dug farther down below where the skulls had been discovered, they found skeletons under the floor of a house. A number of these skeletons were missing skulls, but not the lower jaws. It appeared that the skulls had been kept in the house while the bodies were buried underneath, and were carelessly thrown away when the house was abandoned.

These skeletons presented something of a puzzle. They represented a large number of individuals—perhaps thirty—and they were, as K confided to her sister, "disjointed in a most mysterious way." They appeared to have been buried after some, but not complete, decomposition. Clearly, K felt, this pointed to some sort of disaster. In her letter to Nora soon after their discovery, K suggested a massacre but later acknowledged there was no evidence of violence. Her immediate problem was that the bones were so fragile that they were very difficult to clean, and impossible to retrieve without breaking. So she sent a telegram off to Rik Wheeler, asking for a physical anthropologist who could measure the bodies in situ, and he immediately sent out Ian Cornwall of the Institute of Archaeology.[35]

As they continued to dig down, layer after layer, it became clear that bodies were commonly buried under the house floors, the skulls often missing. Three more portrait skulls were eventually located: two in 1956 underneath the same house as the original seven, and another one in 1958 some distance away at the north end of the mound. K concluded that "the removal of crania from burials was a regular practice; it is possible that they were removed to some central repository or shrine, which has not been located. It is therefore clear that the Jericho skulls are those of venerated ancestors and are not trophies."[36]

Another interesting find that season was what K described as "the largest Neolithic room . . . found."[37] While it was being uncovered, she confided to her sister "a sneaking suspicion we are going to get the oldest temple in the world!"[38] It turned out to be a large room (at least six meters in one direction), with a plaster basin in the middle and dome-like ends. Aware of the dangers of labeling any unusual building a temple, K nevertheless opined that because it was so unlike the other structures found, it probably was a public building of some kind.

Perhaps an even more significant discovery that season was that the Pre-Pottery Neolithic levels went down even farther than expected, once again adding centuries to the history of the site as an organized community. An even earlier town wall, dated by K to ca. 7000 B.C.,[39] was uncovered. The "oldest town in the world" was getting older and older.

They did, finally, find some trace of the Late Bronze Age town, the town to be associated with Joshua and the Israelites. Diplomatically, K noted that "[t]he remains were not spectacular,"[40] consisting as they did of the foundations of a house wall, a small oven, and a small jug. Some part of the settlement had evidently eroded away, but K had no idea how big that settlement would have been or if there had been a later one on top of it which had also been washed away. In fact, the excavations that year didn't do much to clarify the Joshua question one way or the other. Trying to maintain public interest in the biblical aspects of the site, K did the best she could with the scant material found, attempting in *The Sunday Times* to conjure the image of a frightened Canaanite housewife fleeing her kitchen in the face of Joshua's assault.[41]

Frederick Zeuner, Professor of Environmental Archaeology at the Institute of Archaeology, came out late in the season to try to explain why decay in the tombs had been slowed down to such a remarkable extent. Sniffing the limestone rock of the tombs, he developed a theory about the atmosphere of the tombs and went to work. His experiments got off to a slow start, as the first one was ruined when the workmen, against orders, opened a tomb prematurely—just to make sure it was good enough for such an important experiment—allowing whatever gases were in the tomb to escape. Although they immediately resealed the tomb, their ploy was obvious, and Diana Kirkbride and Kim Wheeler had to stand guard as the shaft of another tomb was cleared so that Zeuner could investigate. Conducting homemade experiments with borrowed equipment, he announced that the tombs contained unusually high levels of carbon dioxide. He returned in 1955 with more elaborate equipment and conducted further experiments, requiring the tomb staff to take air samples from selected areas of each tomb as it was opened. Although Zeuner seems never to have definitively solved this problem, he did suggest a likely answer. Quite probably, high levels of gases present in the tombs slowed down natural decay despite the high humidity in the tombs. These gases were either the result of organic material decomposing in the alkaline conditions of the tombs and producing carbon dioxide and methane, or they were gases occurring naturally below ground and diffusing through the faults of the Jordan Rift valley.[42]

This kind of environmental analysis was new in the 1950s and shows K's willingness to embrace the most recent methods of scientific analysis in archaeology. But it could lead to some awkward moments: according to one story that circulated in later years, one of the Jericho staff, transporting some of the bottles of air back to London for analysis, had difficulty explaining to Her Majesty's Customs why they could not inspect a bottle containing nothing but air.[43] On another occasion Customs agents were, understandably, "rather suspicious of a sample of the local water misguidedly sent back in a gin bottle."[44]

Kathleen also had another, brand-new tool in her archaeological kit. Previously, archaeologists had relied on relative sequence dating, that is, dating objects in relation to one another; creating pottery sequences based on the presence of a pottery type in successive layers is an example of this. But the discovery of radiocarbon, or carbon-14, dating in the late 1940s had provided the possibility of obtaining more-or-less absolute dates. Discovered by Willard Libby of the University of Chicago, radiocarbon dating was based on the fact that all living matter absorbs carbon dioxide. When an organism dies, a particular type of carbon, a radioactive isotope known as carbon-14, is lost at a known rate. Thus, the date when, for example, a tree was cut down can be determined with relative precision. The process was complicated and expensive, but since charcoal and pieces of wood were recovered at Jericho, this was a means of providing relatively precise dates.

The excitement of their discoveries did not make the expedition's financial worries disappear. Maggie Tushingham remembered Kathleen and Doug, during the first seasons of the dig, poring over the accounts in the evenings to see how much longer they could afford to go on, often relieved that they were assured of at least another few weeks. The situation did not improve much over time. Even after the astonishing finds of the first two years, K still had to worry constantly about scraping together the funds to complete each additional season. Inevitably she ran into unexpected expenditures, such as having to rent a new house for the women in 1954 because the old one was needed for work-space, or spending more than usual on labor.[45] Once K seriously considered buying a refugee mud-brick house in order to excavate a tomb under it. Particularly irritating was the time she spent an additional seventy pounds to lease a plot of agricultural land in order to look for tombs on it, but then found nothing.

In 1954, the year after the breathtaking discovery of the skulls, by the middle of the excavation season K had already gone through all the money she had brought out; still, she hoped to scrape by until the end. She expected to get an additional £200 from the British Museum for one of the portrait skulls, but the head of the Department of Western Asiatic Antiquities had managed to offend her even while agreeing to buy a skull. C. J. Gadd told her that the skulls didn't really belong in his department because they were "anthropological," not "archaeological," but he would condescend to take one off her hands if he could also get some objects from the tombs as well.[46] In February 1955 she wrote, "I am just getting to my usual seasonal scare about finance."[47] And in the final season she again confided that money was her major concern, since she needed an additional £1500 pounds to finish the excavations. Fortunately one member of the expedition had the means to lend it; K doesn't say who.[48]

Despite her almost desperate need for money to keep the excavations going, K was exceptionally honest when it came to finances. Not only did she actually publish her financial accounts each year in the PEQ, but in 1954 she asked to be replaced as treasurer of the PEF. She had decided it was not proper for her to hold the position at the same time that she was responsible for most of the expenses the organization was incurring at Jericho.[49]

As much as Kathleen loved excavating, she missed her dogs terribly when she was away. By this time she had two, Sammy and Jo-Jo, strays from the Battersea Dogs' Home. She coped by adopting local strays and tending to local animals. One year a member of the expedition described the camp as "a sort of animal welfare center,"[50] with K treating the sores of local horses and the director of antiquities dropping off birds to be cared for.[51] The uncharitable said that she treated the dogs better than she did her Arab workers. The workmen were so fond of her that the charge is to be doubted, but certainly dogs could get away with things that no worker—or student—could. Maggie Tushingham recalled a stray running across one of the pottery mats, scattering sherds in all directions. A student who had done that would probably have been fired on the spot. K just laughed. No dog ever did anything wrong as far as she was concerned.

One season K adopted Rahab—named for the famous harlot of Jericho—and her puppies. She must have arranged for Rahab to be cared for during the rest of the year, because she was still the dig dog two years later when she suddenly became ill. As Rahab's condition progressively worsened, K, who must have had others things to do in the middle of the dig season, insisted on tracking down a doctor. Veterinarians were scarce in Jordan, but she managed to get hold of an Egyptian physician who knew something about animals. He thought the dog had been poisoned and tried to treat her, to no avail. K was understandably upset when Rahab died, but her workmen were determined that she not be unhappy for long, almost immediately beginning to deliver new puppies to her.[52]

K may have realized she was getting a bit spoiled as far as exciting finds went. Halfway through the 1955 season she wrote to Nora that "we haven't reached the sensation of the season which we have come to expect."[53] There were some interesting discoveries that year, such as the rush mats on some of the Neolithic floors. About 3.5 by 2.5 feet, the remains were sometimes so well preserved that one could see the weave of the reeds. On one, the track of a several-thousand-year-old white ant could still be seen. But the most exciting find, made toward the end of the season, was that of a great, circular, solid stone Neolithic tower, the full extent of which would not be clear until the next year.

For a while it seemed possible that the next season might not happen, for political troubles threatened the excavation. Jordan, historically, had very strong ties to Great Britain. Arab nationalists, however, were agitating to strengthen ties with other Arab nations at the expense of those with the West. In 1955 Britain, Iran, Iraq, and Turkey agreed to the pro-Western, anti-Soviet Baghdad Pact. It looked very much like Jordan would also join and receive the financial and military aid that would go with it. But the nationalists were in favor of a policy of neutrality between the West and the Soviets, and provoked violent anti-government —and anti-Western—riots in December 1955.

141

Undeterred, Kathleen, along with Doug Tushingham and Dorothy Marshall, arrived in Jerusalem on January 3, expecting to begin the excavations on time. Accompanied by Stewart Perowne, a former colonial officer and expert in local affairs who spoke fluent Arabic, they inspected the site and made a social call on the local authorities. Everything seemed quiet. But they returned to Jerusalem to find that more rioting was expected because the recent dissolution of Parliament—desired by the agitators—had been declared illegal by the courts. The British consul general advised K that going to Jericho, which had been a center of the recent unrest because of its large refugee population, would be foolhardy under the circumstances.

Rioting against British and American targets broke out several days later. K and the members of the expedition who were in Jerusalem were sheltered in the American School, while a number of the others en route had been stranded in Damascus. In the course of the demonstrations, the American Consulate was attacked. Despite a guard of the Arab Legion, the rioters almost broke into the consulate and were only driven away when the Marines guarding it let off a few shots. The American School, not far from the consulate, was attacked by a few rock-throwers, inducing their Arab Legion guard to set off tear gas. But the only real damage was suffered a few days later by one of the Arab Legion guards who managed to shoot himself through the hand. There were, however, serious disturbances in Jericho, where many of the refugees rioted.

The Jordanian government imposed a round-the-clock curfew, and the situation soon calmed down. As the curfew was gradually relaxed so people could go outside for a few hours every day, K found the locals perfectly friendly. After two weeks K was hopeful that they would soon be able to leave for the site, but the Arab Legion delayed them another week because of continued concerns about the refugees at Jericho. Finally, after almost a month's delay, the dig began at the end of January. K had found some small consolation for being stuck in Jerusalem in the fact that at the time they should have originally been setting up, it poured rain. As bad luck would have it, they still ended up setting up in a downpour. Nevertheless, K was undoubtedly relieved to get there and get started.

Despite the recent unrest, the expedition was given a warm welcome at Jericho, especially by those who would once again have their jobs. K and Doug Tushingham did take the precaution of meeting with the leaders of the three local refugee camps,[54] but K reported to her sister that she had seen no signs of trouble.[55] They were offered an Arab Legion guard, but as local officials thought it unnecessary, turned it down.[56]

While things were quiet at first, they heated up again later. In March King Hussein of Jordan abruptly dismissed General Sir John Glubb—known as Glubb Pasha—who had commanded the Arab Legion since 1939. Riots broke out again as Arab nationalists celebrated. Palestinians, in particular, had viewed Glubb as representing Western imperialism. Some of the demonstrators threatened, at least implicitly, the foreign excavators. On a least one occasion demonstrators milled about near the Jericho dig house, throwing the occasional stone, making the excavators nervous, but with no more dramatic consequences.

The recent political troubles, however, had not quelled the fondness of the Arab workmen for the Great Sitt; they had also not quelled her affection for the Arabs. K, like many of the people who worked for her at Jericho and Jerusalem, came to feel a real attachment to the Arabs—Jordanian and Palestinian—they came to know. In traditional dress, inhabitants of Jericho often looked like something straight out of the Bible, the men watering donkeys at the spring, the women carrying heavy jars of water gracefully on their heads. Even when extremely poor, the Arabs, including the refugees, were exceptionally hospitable, willing to share what little they had with guests. As an excavator walked through the town of Jericho, she might be pulled inside a house or shop for coffee or tea. The expedition staff was invited to dinner and even to weddings in the modest homes of their workers. If a shopkeeper in Jericho knew someone, he didn't have to have money on hand to make a purchase. The shopkeeper would say simply "Ma'lish bukra!"—"It doesn't matter, tomorrow!"[57]

Because of her experience with them, K, like many others who have lived and worked among the Arabs, became sympathetic to their grievances. It was hard not to feel sorry for often desperately poor refugees, some of whom wore the key to their old homes, now in Israel, around their neck and referred longingly to their homes "on the other side." In an article she wrote soon after the disturbances of 1956 (which may or may not have been published), K tried to explain the Arab position, pointing out that the refugee problem was at the heart of the Arab world's problems with Britain.[58] It was a position that, especially later, would not win her admirers in all quarters.

A grand public relations coup occurred that season of 1956 with the arrival, at the end of February, of Rik (by then Sir Mortimer) Wheeler and a BBC camera crew. K had gotten to know the BBC producer Paul Johnstone the previous year when she appeared on "Animal, Vegetable, Mineral?" Since then he had wanted to produce a program on Jericho for another popular, archaeologically themed series, "Buried Treasure." While K worried about the effects of a television crew on her ability to get work done, she was delighted that they, especially Wheeler, were there.[59] K was to note later that Wheeler's television fame in the 1950s alienated him to some extent from his old friends,[60] but it must have been very satisfying to have her mentor visit her at the site of so much success. It was also wonderful publicity for the dig. The show, "The Walls of Jericho," was shown on the BBC July 31, 1956. Copies were made for various people who requested them, and K asked for a copy to show in Jericho, as she thought her workmen would enjoy it.[61]

That season also did not disappoint; K thought it the most successful yet. The occupation of Neolithic Jericho was pushed even further back into the past, providing more evidence of early communal organization and town life. Work continued on the stone tower located the previous season. A sturdily constructed stone staircase leading from the top twenty-five feet down into the tower was uncovered. At the bottom of the staircase was a horizontal passageway leading to the east, in which excavators found twelve skeletons, clearly disposed of there when the passageway was no longer in use. Up until this point Egypt had provided the world's oldest stone structures, but this stone staircase predated anything Egyptian by thousands of years. K was tempted to suspect that this remarkable engineering feat might be part of a water-shaft leading all the way down to the spring, similar to those of a later period found at Jerusalem, Gezer, and Megiddo. In the end, however, the staircase appeared to have simply been a way of manning the tower. Nevertheless, the ancient tower and stairs (dated by K to ca. 6000 B.C., although now dated to ca. 8500 B.C.) were impressive, whatever their functions (Figure 6.2).

In addition, Trench 1, cutting through the middle of the west side of the mound, now finally excavated to bedrock, exposed a large ditch cut into the rock in front of the Neolithic wall. Although thirty feet wide and eight feet deep, the ditch had been constructed with only the simplest of stone tools. Again, K was impressed most by what this demonstrated about the nature of the early community on the site, the extraordinary planning and cooperation required to built such a defensive work.

By the end of the 1956 season, K realized that the tower and ditch were built not by the Neolithic people of whose existence she had been aware since the first season, but by an even earlier, different Neolithic group. These people—who came to be known as Pre-Pottery Neolithic A (PPNA)—had a building style different from the later group—Pre-Pottery Neolithic B (PPNB). Instead of plaster floors and cigar-shaped bricks, the PPNA people

FIGURE 6.2: The main trench, with the Neolithic tower at right.
Courtesy of Stuart Laidlaw, Institute of Archaeology, UCL.

built round houses, with mud floors using what K called "hog-backed" bricks—one side was flat and the other curved. She concluded that these two pre-pottery Neolithic groups inhabited Jericho one after the other, with a period of abandonment in between.

The one disappointment, again, concerned Joshua and the Late Bronze Age. K hoped to find more Late Bronze Age remains near where slight traces had been found earlier on the east side of the mound. She hired a local contractor to remove a large dump over the area, only to discover previous excavators had already dug there, destroying whatever evidence that might have existed. There was one spot not disturbed by previous excavations, and she hoped, eventually, to find Late Bronze Age remains in that area; that hope, too, would be dashed.

International politics intervened once again in the Jericho excavations. The Suez Crisis of 1956–1957, and the collusion of Britain and France with Israel, left the British very unpopular in the Arab world. The excavation could not begin until March 1957 and lasted only four weeks. But again, K found little of the antipathy toward the West directed at her or her team: "The atmosphere is completely friendly as far as we have been concerned. . . . Our men . . . are delighted to have us back . . . and the shopkeepers welcome us with open arms."[62]

And despite the curtailed digging season, K celebrated a great triumph in 1957: the opening of a building for the British School of Archaeology in Jerusalem. In 1956 the efforts of Rik Wheeler had led the government finally to give the BSAJ a grant that would allow them to acquire an actual building. K had returned to Jerusalem at the end of June in 1956 and had arranged the lease of what was known as the Husseini building, after its owner. The BSAJ did not have the building to itself—the top floor and the basement were both occupied—but it was a permanent base in Jerusalem. Near the American School and St. George's Cathedral, it was a pleasant spot with a garden, providing a place for the BSAJ's library of some 20,000 books, as well as accommodations for students and visiting scholars.[63]

The 1957 season was supposed to be the final one at Jericho, but because it had been cut short, K went back one more time, from October 1957 to February 1958. Because some areas were more complicated to dig than others, and because the more experienced site supervisors tended to excavate more quickly than the less experienced, excavation of some areas of the tell made greater progress than others. When Wheeler visited he had urged K to make haste, in order to finish what she needed to do. During the last season she was trying to do just that, which she admitted led to "very rapid and rather schematic digging in order to get to bedrock."[64] The final season lived up to the dramatic expectations created in previous years. The excavators found evidence of what K termed a "proto-Neolithic" stage—rudimentary shelters used over a long period of time, which K suggested was evidence of a period of transition between the nomadic way of life and permanent settlement at the oasis. More startling, they found remains from the Mesolithic period, almost 10,000 years ago. This odd structure was a rectangular clay platform revetted by a stone wall with sockets for the erection of what might have been totem poles. Possibly, K suggested, it was a shrine built to honor the spring as the source of fertility, a type of shrine known elsewhere in the East, although in the final report Peter Dorrell proposed that the "sockets" were in fact limestone mortars.[65]

Some believed there was more work to be done at Jericho. In fact, Peter Parr had two short additional seasons there in 1959 and 1960 to tie up some loose ends. But K thought it was time to go. She had answered the questions she had set out to answer and in so doing had rewritten the prehistory of the Near East. She had the final excavation report to write. And she believed "it is ill-advised for any one generation of archaeologists to undertake the complete excavation of a *key* site. Archaeological technique improves with each generation of archaeologists. . . . [O]ne should hope that one's successors will have improved techniques and more accumulated experience at their disposal."[66] She suggested that excavation at Jericho be suspended for the time being. In another twenty-five years, perhaps, another expedition, with additional knowledge and employing new techniques, could take up where she left off.

AFTER SEVEN SEASONS OF excavation and reaching bedrock in five areas of the mound, Jericho stood, and still stands, as a unique achievement in the history of archaeology: the only excavated site to yield a complete sequence of occupation from the earliest nomadic hunter-gatherers to a fully developed urban society. The story of Jericho was not one of the steady upward progress of civilization. There were breaks in occupation and occasional retrogressions when more sophisticated cultures were replaced by less sophisticated ones. Nevertheless, the site encapsulated the development of community life over a period of 12,000 years. K's own summary of the history of the site at the end of the excavations is as follows:

The first people at Jericho were Mesolithic hunters who built a sanctuary next to the spring in the tenth millennium B.C. During the ninth-millennium "proto-Neolithic" phase, nomadic or semi-nomadic groups camped on the site on a part-time but regular basis. By about the middle of the ninth millennium B.C., a permanent settlement consisting of single-roomed, round houses built of "hog-backed" mud-bricks had grown up around the spring. K designated this Pre-Pottery Neolithic A (ca. 8500–7000 B.C.). This settlement expanded to a good size—about ten acres—before it was finally surrounded by a wall, with a stone tower attached. Eventually a defensive ditch was also cut into the rock in front of the wall.

While this PPNA culture had local origins, it ended suddenly, to be replaced by a culture that did not appear to be indigenous. The Pre-Pottery Neolithic B (ca. 7500–6000 B.C.) appeared fully developed, probably imported from elsewhere. These houses were more sophisticated than those of the PPNA, with large, rectangular rooms made of elongated, herringbone-patterned bricks clustered around courtyards, and polished plaster floors. Bodies were buried under the houses; this was the period of the plastered skull ancestor cult. While this settlement was originally undefended, eventually a large town wall was built. This culture, too, came to a sudden end at Jericho in the early sixth millennium B.C.

Finally, cultures with the technology to make pottery arrived at Jericho. These Pottery Neolithic A and B peoples (ca. 5200–4000 B.C.) were otherwise unimpressive. The first group lived in pits cut into the ruins of the earlier town, and the second eventually began to build huts and simple houses. A gap in occupation then preceded what K called the Proto-Urban Period (ca. 3300–3150 B.C.) but most other archaeologists designated Early Bronze Age I. In the fourth millennium, newcomers arrived whom K divided into groups A and B on the basis of their pottery. They were the first inhabitants of Jericho to bury their dead in rock-cut tombs.

Around the end of the fourth millennium, the Proto-Urban culture evolved into what K called the Early Bronze Age I–III (ca. 3050–2300 B.C.). Jericho at this time was a fully developed urban center, with town walls that were built, repaired, and rebuilt seventeen times. The final wall of the Early Bronze Age had been hurriedly constructed before the town was sacked by the Amorites ca. 2300 B.C. These nomadic invaders inhabited Jericho during K's Intermediate Early Bronze–Middle Bronze period (ca. 2300–1950 B.C.).[67]

Newcomers, who became the Canaanites, again created an urban community at Jericho in the Middle Bronze Age (ca. 1900–1580 B.C.). While they initially defended themselves with mud-brick walls, eventually they built a steep bank, or escarp, with a wall at the summit. While little of the Middle Bronze Age town itself survived, much is known about the material culture of the period because of the vast amount of material surviving in the tombs. This culture came to a violent end in the sixteenth century B.C., an end possibly connected to the expulsion of the Hyksos from Egypt, and Jericho was abandoned.

For those looking for evidence of Joshua's conquest, the succeeding Late Bronze Age (ca. 1500–1200 B.C.) settlement would have been a great disappointment. Although the site showed signs of reoccupation in the fourteenth century B.C., most of the remains had been washed away by erosion, and what little evidence there was suggested a small and poor settlement. K never uncovered any archaeological evidence of town walls from this period. The site was deserted again toward the end of the fourteenth century B.C. According to the First Book of Kings, it was reoccupied in the ninth century B.C. during the reign of Ahab, but there is no archaeological evidence of such occupation until the seventh century B.C. This period of occupation lasted until the Babylonian Exile of the sixth century B.C. Evidence on the mound of the Persian, Roman, and Early Arab periods is slight, as the site of the town had shifted to elsewhere within the oasis.

When Kathleen made her startling claims for the antiquity of "urban" life, or even "civilization," at Jericho in the early 1950s, not everyone was convinced. Robert Braidwood of the Oriental Institute of the University of Chicago, who had begun excavating Jarmo in Iraq in 1948, did not want to accept that Jericho was an urban center as early as the eighth millennium B.C. Their disagreement was played out in a well-known exchange in *Antiquity*. He argued that there was no evidence of the kind of "full-time technical specialists" or "economic differentiation of labour" which would characterize "urbanization" or "civilization." He also questioned the validity of the radiocarbon dates that gave Jericho a claim to such antiquity.

Braidwood himself recognized that the differences between his position and K's (as well as that of Rik Wheeler who supported her) might simply be one of terminology, that although K and Wheeler used the terms "civilization" and "urban," they were really referring to the emergence of "an effective village-farming community way of life."[68] In that sense Braidwood won the argument. K seems to have been willing to designate any settlement a "city" or "town" or "urban center" (using the terms interchangeably) if it possessed the organization and technical skills necessary to construct walls. More recent archaeologists, however, influenced (as was Braidwood) by anthropological models, would define "city" and "urbanism" in terms of the complexity of social organization. In these terms, while Jericho might be referred to colloquially as a walled town, its "urban" status is in considerable doubt. K's reply to Braidwood in 1957 indicates that this state of affairs would not much disappoint her:

> I simply maintain that I cannot personally class Jericho with the
> early villages of which we have evidence elsewhere. Even Professor

149

> Braidwood goes so far as to call it an "incipient town."... But even
> if future evidence proves that I have overstated the case, and early
> Jericho is lowered to a mere 5000 B.C.... and even if it may only
> be called an incipient town, an incipient town of 5000 B.C. would
> still be a remarkable development.[69]

Certainly K's findings represent a turning point in archaeology. For one thing, she was right about the site's great antiquity. Village life at Jarmo itself is now known to go back to 8000 B.C. In addition, before Jericho, no Neolithic site of its size, or with such walls, was known. Since the 1950s a number of sophisticated Neolithic sites, some with walls and some without, have been discovered. Çatal Hüyük in Turkey, excavated in the 1960s by James Mellaart (one of K's trainees at Jericho), an even larger and more sophisticated site than Neolithic Jericho, is dated to the seventh millennium B.C. Pre-Pottery Neolithic A settlements have been found at Nahal Oren in Israel, Gilgal and Netiv Hagedud in the Jordan Valley, Mureybet and Abu Hureyra in Syria, and Qermez Dere and Nemrik in Iraq. Examples of Pre-Pottery Neolithic B culture have been discovered at Tuleilat el-Ghassul, Beidha, and Basta in Jordan, and Nahal Oren and Munhata in the Jordan Valley. Even the practice of creating portrait skulls was not limited to Jericho, as examples have since been found at Ain Ghazal, northeast of Amman, and Tell Ramad in Syria. Jericho, while no longer indisputably "the oldest town in the world," nevertheless remains the largest and most impressive Neolithic settlement in Palestine.

Not all of K's other conclusions have gone unchallenged. Subsequent generations of archaeologists, including her own students, have disputed her findings. Peter Parr, for example, has suggested that, contrary to K's view, the Proto-Urban settlement at Jericho may have been much more substantial than she thought, even including a defensive wall.[70] While K believed that the steep escarp of the Middle Bronze Age defended the town, more recently it has been argued that it served more as propaganda than as a practical defense: the escarp demonstrated the power of the local ruler rather than actually protecting against enemy attack.[71] Ethnoarchaeological research into population density disputes K's estimate of perhaps 3000 residents for Neolithic Jericho and suggests a population of less than 1000. Ofer Bar-Yosef believes that the tower and wall of the PPNA town were not intended for defense against human enemies but against winter floods.[72] Bryant Wood has even contended, based on a reevaluation of pottery evidence, that K did indeed find the town Joshua conquered.[73]

In particular, K's propensity (and that of her generation) for equating new pots with new peoples and cultures has come under attack in recent years. The tendency now is to look for more indigenous explanations for change rather than attribute new developments to invaders. For example, while K believed that Pre-Pottery Neolithic B culture was brought in fully developed by immigrants from the north, modern scholars argue that "this culture essentially developed from its predecessor while acquiring some innovations from the northern Levant."[74] K attributed the great defensive walls of the Early Bronze period to the need for protection against intruders, but some archaeologists now maintain "that the walled settlements . . . were not the result of new peoples coming into the area, but of internal . . . [social and economic] processes."[75] K also believed that nomadic invaders from the north caused a sharp break between the Early and Middle Bronze ages—her Intermediate Early Bronze–Middle Bronze period. Many modern archaeologists, however, point out that while Jericho and a few other towns were clearly sacked about this time, most other towns, although abandoned, do not show signs of violent destruction. Thus, many argue that this period is more complex than previously thought, and several different models are needed to explain the variety of evidence.[76]

Likewise, K argued that the Middle Bronze Age began when invaders from the north brought to Jericho, and Palestine, a new urban culture which would come to be recognized as Canaanite. But recent scholars have suggested that this new urban culture was, as Jonathan Tubb puts it, an "indigenous development of the population in response to a resumption of more favorable conditions, both climatic and economic, which allowed the return to urban settlement."[77] Still others have suggested that the culture of the Middle Bronze Age was the result of a combination of internal and external factors.[78]

Unhappily, K did not live to publish the final Jericho report in its entirety. While she produced a good deal on Jericho in the 1950s—interim excavation reports as well as popular articles and a popular book—much of the final excavation report did not appear until after her death in 1978. P. R. S. Moorey has pointed out that "[i]t is no exaggeration to say that each day of excavation may require months of study to present the information obtained for proper publication."[79] She did get the tomb volumes out reasonably quickly in 1960 and 1965, and they were extremely well received. Reviewing Volume 1, W. F. Albright enthused that as a result of this "splendid volume," the Jericho excavations promised "to be a landmark in the history of Palestinian archaeology."[80] They were excellent volumes, setting a new standard in the excavation and publication of tombs. The position of every bone, every pot, and every artifact had been meticulously recorded—drawn and photographed—in situ before being moved. They remain a model of their kind.

The tomb volumes, however, could not be the final test of the application of the stratigraphic technique K had employed on the mound. The ultimate test would be whether the principles she brought to bear could be translated into a final report that would clearly explicate her conclusions, providing all the necessary supporting evidence. And in this, many found it sadly lacking.

The final volumes of the Jericho report—those detailing the stratigraphy of the tell, the pottery, and other artifacts—were published from 1981 to 1983. K herself was primarily responsible for the text of the first volume—*Excavations at Jericho, Volume 3: The Architecture and Stratigraphy of the Tell*—but did not live to write a final synthesis in which she pulled together the evidence and interpretation of the site. Two other volumes—*Excavations at Jericho, Volume 4: The Pottery Type Series and Other Finds* (1982) and *Excavations at Jericho, Volume 5: The Pottery Phases of the Tell and Other Finds* (1983)—were published by K's research assistant Tom Holland. Many archaeologists have complained that these Jericho volumes are such a mass of raw, undigested data that they are hopelessly complex and difficult to use.[81] One reviewer summed it up when he wrote: "These tomes are works of reference, quarries or mines in which the enquiring reader can dig and hew unheedingly and with slow profit."[82]

If, however, in one sense the Jericho excavation was a failure, nevertheless in another sense it was an astonishing success. The real triumph of Jericho was the spread of the Wheeler-Kenyon method. The excavations at Jericho marked a revolution in Palestinian archaeology. Whatever the flaws of the final report, K had demonstrated for all to see at Jericho what could be accomplished "with precise stratigraphic control and systematic layer-by-layer recording."[83]

Certainly, her methodology, with its precise examination of relatively small areas, has been criticized as being "so tedious and demanding in application that scarcely ever is a single building completely cleared, let alone a building complex large enough to give us an adequate exposure on which to base our understanding of the material culture of the period."[84] And she undoubtedly met with resistance. According to Henk Franken, some Americans were even discouraged from participating in the Jericho excavations.[85] But spreading what would be known as the Wheeler-Kenyon method was one of K's primary goals. Training students at Jericho was one of the best ways of doing that. At one point she suggested to Peter Parr that he work on an American dig for the express purpose of spreading "the gospel of Digging Method."[86] She could see the results early on. After a visit to Dhiban where the American School was excavating, she noted the difference in the excavation after the Americans had seen what was being done at Jericho.[87]

A turning point was G. Ernest Wright's excavations at biblical Shechem (Tel Balatah) which began in 1956 and at which he adopted important aspects of the Wheeler-Kenyon approach. In fact, some of the Arab workmen who worked for K at Jericho were deliberately hired at Shechem, experienced as they were in her precise methods. American archaeologists trained at Shechem went on to employ this methodology at such sites as Gezer, Ai, and Taanach. To be sure, it was refined and adapted, often, for example, being combined with the opening of wider horizontal exposures. Although the Israelis were slower to be influenced by K's stratigraphic methods—in part for the simple reason that they could not participate in the Jericho excavations—and maintained the architectural tradition to a greater extent, by the 1960s and 1970s they too were being influenced by the basic principles of her stratigraphic method.

Along with a concern with broader horizontal exposures, one of the most important modifications made to the Wheeler-Kenyon method by American and Israeli archaeologists was a greater reliance on teams, rather than a single individual, to direct excavations and shoulder all the responsibilities. At Jericho, Kathleen was the commander-in-chief. She was ultimately responsible for everything, from raising money to drawing the sections to publishing the final report. While this had the advantage, as one scholar has noted, of "singularity of purpose, firm control of strategy and decisive tactics,"[88] it also placed great demands on a single individual. At Jerusalem these demands would be even greater—perhaps too great.

IN MARCH 1959, HAVING BEEN NAMED the Norton Lecturer, an honor bestowed upon a distinguished archaeologist from abroad by the Archaeological Institute of America, K set out on a lecture tour of the United States. Arriving in Boston on March 1, her first two weeks were a whirlwind of lectures given to "large and enthusiastic" audiences—thirteen in as many days, from Boston to Philadelphia, Baltimore, Washington, D.C., Virginia, North Carolina, and Florida. She reported with some relief that things slowed down a bit when she got down south and the distances became greater.[89]

K enjoyed her first visit to the United States, although it was not always what she had expected. She was surprised, for example, by how much woodland

153

existed on the east coast. Her interest in the country and country life is clearly apparent. Only in the south did the countryside look to her like farmland, and she was surprised to see mules still being used for plowing. And much of the south did not look quite as she had expected; Virginia looked like northern England and North Carolina like Surrey.[90] Her hosts in North Carolina may have thought she didn't think America quite civilized when, not being aware of the differences between British and American plumbing, she asked if the water was safe to drink.[91]

K found Florida positively exotic, with its azaleas and dogwoods, mysterious rivers, alligators and turtles. Leaving Florida, she visited Emory University in Atlanta before going on to Oxford, Mississippi, where she spoke to the Mississippi Archaeological Society. Garner James, the husband of her student Frances James, took her down to the Mississippi Gulf Coast to stay with his parents, where she was "well indoctrinated about the sins of the north." After a visit to New Orleans and a swing through the midwest, K returned to the east coast and experienced the shock of going from pleasant spring weather in the south to a snowstorm in Boston.[92] She stayed with her old friend from Samaria, Nancy de Crespigne, with whom she spent Easter. After lectures in Cambridge, Princeton, New York, and Toronto, K's tour culminated at Kenyon College in Ohio.

On April 17, at the college founded in 1824 and named after the second Lord Kenyon—her father's great-uncle—K received an honorary doctorate in humane letters in a special convocation in her honor. She took the honor bestowed on her seriously, in later years filling out alumni questionnaires and even making the occasional donation to the college. At the ceremony K spoke on "Excavations at Jericho from the Beginning of Settlement to the Biblical Period." The citation noted her distinguished family and her contribution to pushing back knowledge of human settlement, adding that "in your trench, a thousand feet below the level of the sea, [you] have proved what we on this hill have long suspected, that if men dig down to the very beginnings of our culture they will find *KENYON* at the bottom."[93]

Kathleen probably enjoyed the joke.

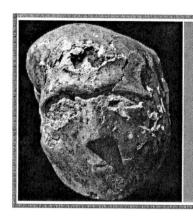

CHAPTER SEVEN

SEARCHING FOR THE CITY OF DAVID

WHY DID KATHLEEN GO to Jerusalem in 1961? She had completed the Jericho excavations a mere three years before. Years of writing up the results lay ahead; only the first Jericho volume had seen the light of day. She still had the final report on Sabratha to finish. Even her great friend Doug Tushingham conceded that many thought her decision to move on to Jerusalem "foolhardy, perhaps even quixotic."[1] She herself admitted it might have been wiser to have waited at least seven years after Jericho rather than only three.[2] Why then, so soon after finishing one large excavation, did she begin work at what has been described as "undoubtedly the most difficult site in [Palestine] to excavate"?[3]

In fact, K didn't begin by assuming that her next site would be in Jerusalem. Initially she thought another Neolithic site would be the best follow-up to Jericho, and she considered sites in the Jordan valley, or perhaps Tell Ta'anak, the biblical Taanach, an ancient Canaanite city near Megiddo.[4] Upon reflection, however, she changed her mind, realizing how difficult it would be to find a Neolithic site that would compare to Jericho. She worried that such sites, while archaeologically important, would be unimpressive after Jericho, and concluded that their excavation, while suitable for small-scale work, would not suffice as the British School's main project. Indeed, such small-scale digging, like the work of Diana Kirkbride at Beihda, near Petra, was already being sponsored by the BSAJ.[5]

Excavations at Jerusalem, however, would be anything but small scale. According to the biblical account, the city had been captured by the Israelite King David from the Canaanite Jebusites ca. 1000 B.C. Control of Jerusalem, located in a critical spot overseeing the route up the backbone of the hill country, allowed David to forge the northern and southern Israelite tribes into a single kingdom. The center of David's united kingdom, Jerusalem has been in spirit, if not in fact, the capital of the Jewish people ever since. Of course, as the site of Christ's trial, suffering, and crucifixion, it was also holy to Christians. And as the site of the Dome of the Rock from which the prophet Mohammed ascended to heaven, the city was sacred to Moslems as well. Jerusalem, K believed, was the only site that could "excel even Jericho in interest and which even more than Jericho offers a challenge to modern archaeological techniques. Few people in the Western world can fail to be interested in the central site of the Old and New Testament and as the third holy city in Islam it is of almost equal importance to the Moslems of the Eastern world."[6] Recent events also helped. Large sections of the city had not been rebuilt since the destruction caused by the fighting in 1948, and like the Jewry Wall site at Leicester and London after the Blitz, could be excavated before rebuilding. At the same time, the rapid growth of the city would soon make some of the most desirable sites inaccessible. (In fact, K would be frantically working ahead of development the entire time.) Moreover, as Tushingham also pointed out, "K was enough of a sentimentalist to believe that the centennial of Britain's involvement in Jerusalem, to be celebrated in 1965, could most worthily be marked by a new, definitive expedition which would solve many of the problems still remaining."[7] She had long thought that Jerusalem, because of the many unsolved questions concerning the period of the Israelite monarchy, would be the most interesting place in Palestine to dig.[8] In the end, she simply could not resist the temptation to try to solve the problems posed by the city with the methods that had proved so successful at Jericho.

And so, in February 1959 K proposed to the BSAJ that the School's next major project be excavations in Jerusalem; her plan was to focus on a site in the Jewish Quarter of the Old City to find the Israelite town, and on another outside the walls of the Old City to look for the original Jebusite settlement.[9] The expedition to Jerusalem was officially announced at the annual meeting of the British School of Archaeology in Jerusalem in July 1960.

But if it made sense that the British School's next big project be in Jerusalem, why did K have to direct the excavations herself? She was, after all, in her mid-50s and had the publication of Sabratha and Jericho still hanging over her head. At Jericho she had trained a number of promising young archaeologists, including Peter Parr, Diana Kirkbride, and Basil Hennessy, any one of whom could have directed these excavations. Indeed, these individuals, and others, went on to make significant contributions to the archaeology of Jordan and Palestine. Why could not one of them have taken over the direction of the British School, leaving K to spend her time writing up her previous digs?

The most likely answer is very simple: Kathleen loved to dig. She always thought of herself as a field archaeologist, and, despite her homesickness when she was abroad,[10] she was happiest while actually excavating. Working in the dirt gave her a real thrill. No one could rival her for unraveling the stratigraphy of a site, and this exercise—of observing the layers, carefully recording the stratigraphy, and using it to interpret the history of a site—was the part of archaeology she liked best.[11] K herself admitted that publication was only a necessary chore.[12] She may well have realized that by the time she finished writing up all her extant reports for publication, it would be too late for her to undertake any more major projects. In addition, the argument could easily be made that association of her name with Jericho would make it easier to raise the vast sums needed for Jerusalem.

Jerusalem would be one of the last great imperial digs, with hundreds of hired laborers under the overall direction of a single authority. It was meant to be the climax of K's archaeological career, the perfect follow-up to Jericho, the ultimate demonstration of what the Wheeler-Kenyon method could accomplish in the ancient Near East. And, of course, it meant staying in the field. As Kathleen herself said, "The King is dead. Long live the King."[13]

JERUSALEM IS ONLY FIFTEEN MILES from Jericho as the crow flies, but unlike Jericho, which is 900 feet below sea level, Jerusalem is 2500 feet above sea level. Consequently, the climate is colder in winter and milder in summer. Thirty-six miles east of the Mediterranean, the city is situated on the spine of the Judean hills, occupying a crest between valleys to the east and west. The walls of what is known as the Old City were built by Suleiman the Magnificent only in the sixteenth century; its outlines were determined by the Roman foundation of Aelia Capitolina, constructed in A.D. 135 after yet another rebellion by the Jews. It is flanked on the east by the Kidron (or Silwan) Valley and to the west by the Hinnon Valley. A third valley, the Tyropoeon—Josephus's Valley of the Cheesemakers—actually cuts through the Old City, dividing it into two parts: the Upper City or western hill, and the Lower City or southeastern hill. This valley, however, has silted up considerably over the centuries. South of the old city, the Hinnon Valley curves to the east to meet the Kidron, forming a kind of V. Two ridges, or spurs, extend south of the Old City, also forming a sort of V. The westernmost ridge is known as Mount Zion, and the eastern ridge is called the hill of Ophel (meaning "bulge").[14] It was here, to the south of the present Old City on Ophel, protected by deep valleys on three sides, that the original Jebusite city captured by David would turn out to be located (Figure 7.1). When Kathleen began excavating in 1961, Jerusalem was still a divided city, as it had been since 1948. East Jerusalem, which included the Old City and the area to the south, was under the control of the Jordanians. West Jerusalem and the newer sections of the city fell in the Israeli sector.

Not surprisingly, given its importance to Christianity, Judaism, and Islam, Jerusalem was one of the first objectives of the nineteenth-century European explorers of the Holy Land. Edward Robinson conducted the earliest modern survey of biblical sites in Palestine in 1838, during the course of which in Jerusalem he explored Hezekiah's tunnel, identified the remains of the so-called Third Wall of Herod Agrippa, and found "Robinson's Arch," part of an arch located near the Temple platform. In 1860 Félicien de Saulcy investigated tombs north of the Old City. The Palestine Exploration Fund, founded in 1865, sent its first expedition to Jerusalem. In 1867 on behalf of the PEF, Captain Charles Warren (the same Warren who burrowed into the mound at Jericho a few years later) began excavating in the city. The Ottoman authorities refused him permission to dig in the city sacred to Islam, but Warren, a military engineer, ingeniously evaded the restrictions. Exploring by means of secret shafts and tunnels, he investigated the foundations of the Temple Mount (in Arabic, Haram esh-Sherif, or Noble Sanctuary). This sacred precinct had been built on the Temple Mount, the site of Herod's Temple, which in turn had, according to tradition, been built on the site of Solomon's Temple. Warren was able to show that the foundations of Herod's Temple went almost 100 feet below ground level.

Warren also explored Ophel, the hill south of the Temple Mount. By means of tunneling, he found and followed a wall that extended from the southeast corner of the Haram esh-Sherif along the top of the ridge of Ophel. Although this wall dated only to the Byzantine period, it turned out to be the successor of a much earlier wall. Warren himself never quite realized that he had stumbled upon parts of biblical Jerusalem, but he had shown that significant ancient remains were to be found south of the Old City.

In the late nineteenth century other expeditions uncovered more ancient remains south of the Old City. One such expedition was directed by Frederick

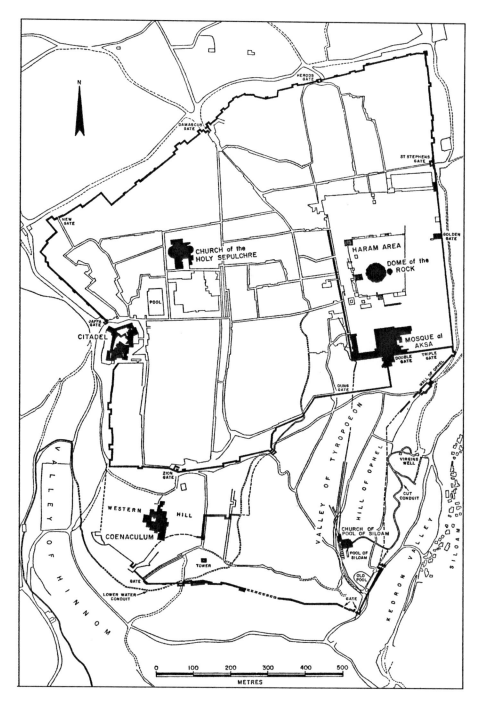

FIGURE 7.1: Bliss and Dickie's 1898 plan of Jerusalem.
Courtesy of the Palestine Exploration Fund.

Bliss and Archibald Dickie. Sponsored by the PEF, in 1894 they began work on Ophel. Like Warren, their method was tunneling. They discovered a massive wall that ran south from the Old City and across the Tyropoeon Valley, linking the tops of the eastern and western ridges. While deploring their primitive archaeological techniques, which caused her much aggravation when she came to apply her own methods, Kathleen acknowledged the achievements of the earlier excavators: "In the history of the exploration of Jerusalem, nothing was on the scale, or of the importance, of the work of Bliss . . . and Warren."[15]

In the early part of the next century, exploration of the area south of the Old City continued. A somewhat mysterious expedition was led in 1911 by Montague Parker. Rumored to be searching for the hidden treasures of the Temple Mount, the party fled Jerusalem when they were caught digging under the Dome of the Rock, the central shrine of the Haram, in the dead of night. Excavations on the Ophel ridge continued in 1913–1914 with Raymond Weill's work on the eastern ridge. In 1923–1925 R.A.S. Macalister and J. Garrow Duncan, sponsored by the PEF, continued work on Ophel, uncovering part of a defense system including what Macalister called David's Tower. In 1927–1929 John Crowfoot and Gerald M. FitzGerald, also supported by the PEF, continued Macalister's work on Ophel. Crowfoot investigated the western side of Ophel, trenching down into the Tyropoeon Valley; here he uncovered a line of fortifications, including the Valley Gate which he assigned to the Jebusite period.

In the 1930s the first attempts to employ stratigraphical analysis to study the ancient city were implemented by two officers of the Department of Antiquities, which had been set up during the British Mandate. R. W. Hamilton excavated north of the Damascus Gate, just outside of the Old City, where he discovered a Roman gate dating to the second century A.D. C. N. Johns excavated in the courtyard of the Citadel, the medieval tower on the western ridge, and exposed the Hellenistic and Herodian phases of the tower. He was able to show that the tower had been built into a preexisting wall and identified four different building phases for the wall.

Such was the history of the exploration in Jerusalem by the time K turned her attention to the city. No excavations had taken place in East Jerusalem since it had become part of the Kingdom of Jordan in 1948. The fact that Kathleen was allowed to excavate in the city holy to Islam shows the regard and respect the Jordanians had for her. As a field archaeologist committed to using precise stratigraphic methods to untangle the past, Kathleen had been interested in the problems posed by Jerusalem for some time, and was determined to demonstrate what her stratigraphical methods could achieve in a complex urban site. The previous excavations had left a number of specific problems for her to solve. While K managed to answer some of these questions, she also ended up raising new ones.

BUT BEFORE SHE BEGAN excavations in the spring of 1961, and for much of the time she was excavating in Jerusalem, K was, rather surprisingly, entangled with another problem—the search for the Dead Sea Scrolls.

The scrolls were discovered in a now-famous incident in 1947. A young Bedouin chasing a runaway goat stumbled across them in a limestone cave in the bleak cliffs overlooking the northwest shore of the Dead Sea. Eventually the scrolls found their way into the hands of a Syrian Christian in Bethlehem, Khalil Iskander Shahin, a.k.a. Kando, who realized they might have real value. In fact, they were manuscripts of the Hebrew Bible that were almost 1000 years older than the earliest known manuscripts of the Old Testament. Amid the chaos of the end of the British Mandate, these first seven scrolls eventually ended up the hands of the Israelis through the efforts of Eleazar Sukenik, K's old colleague from Samaria.

But since they had been found in what was after 1948 part of the Hashemite Kingdom of Jordan, the search for more ancient manuscripts was most easily pursued from the Jordanian side. In 1949 Gerald Harding, Director of Antiquities, sent the Arab Legion looking for the original scrolls cave (which the Bedouin and Kando had tried to keep secret) and eventually found it near Ain Feshka on the Dead Sea, thirteen miles east of Jerusalem. Shortly thereafter, Harding and Roland de Vaux began excavations in the cave, which would be designated Cave 1.

When the antiquity—and value—of the manuscripts became clear, the search intensified, both on the part of the Bedouin eager to sell them and on the part of scholars anxious to save them. Within a few short years, more scrolls and many more fragments of scrolls had been discovered, some by the scholars, many more by the Bedouin. Although the first seven scrolls had ended up in Israel, subsequent searches produced a number of manuscripts and fragments which were sent to the Palestine Archaeological Museum. Harding, as Director of Antiquities, put Père de Vaux, President of the Board of Trustees of the Palestine Archaeological Museum, in charge of the task of editing and publishing the Scrolls.

The Palestine Archaeological Museum (PAM), built and endowed by John D. Rockefeller, had opened in 1938. When the British Mandate came to an end and the museum ended up in the new Hashemite Kingdom of Jordan, the PAM was administered by an international board of trustees, representing academic bodies in the United States, Britain, France, and Sweden. In 1957, on Rik Wheeler's recommendation, Kathleen became the British Academy's representative on the Board of Trustees.[16] Initially she didn't make a particularly favorable impression, because she usually failed to show up. When the Board met on November 28, 1959, her continued absence became an issue, and it was agreed that Père de Vaux, as President of the Board, would bring the matter not to K's, but to Wheeler's, attention. This must have worked; K was at the next meeting.[17] And in the next several years, while she was fully occupied with the Jerusalem dig, she would more than make up for her early neglect of her duties. Certainly, she took her role of trustee seriously and in the 1960s while excavating in Jerusalem was much preoccupied with the PAM's affairs.

John Allegro and the treasure of the Copper Scroll was one source of much aggravation for Kathleen. Allegro was a gifted philologist and a controversial, even eccentric scholar. In 1953 he had become part of the international team working on the Dead Sea Scrolls. A Methodist who had lost his faith, he produced some (to say the least) idiosyncratic interpretations. Over time he became impatient, perhaps rightly, with the slowness with which some of the other scholars were working on their material. Allegro also insisted, quite wrongly, that this slow pace was due to a conspiracy to suppress scroll material embarrassing to Christianity. Because of his outspokenness (which some saw as simply a desire for publicity) and arguably bad judgment, he generated a good deal of controversy and not a little ill will among his fellow Scroll scholars, especially de Vaux. After he gave a series of interviews on BBC radio in which he suggested that a "Teacher of Righteousness" mentioned in the Scrolls had been crucified (and thus implying that the Christian version of Christ's death was merely a rehash of the Dead Sea Scroll story), de Vaux and four other colleagues felt obliged to reply with a letter to *The Times* disavowing Allegro's interpretation.

All of this, of course, was only scholarly infighting and very likely of little interest to K except insofar as Allegro questioned the integrity of Père de Vaux, whom she quite liked. But that would change.

In 1952, in what would come to be called Cave 3, a rather different kind of scroll was found. Called the Copper Scroll, it was made of up two rolls of copper, and so brittle that it had to be sent to the Manchester College of Technology in England to be opened. The task of publishing the contents of this scroll was assigned to Father J. T. Milik, whose official edition did not appear until 1962. In the meantime Allegro, who was a Lecturer at Manchester University, published his own edition in 1960. Written in an unusual form of Hebrew, the Copper Scroll contained a list of sixty-four locations where treasure had been hidden. Allegro romantically concluded that this was the missing treasure of the Jewish Temple, razed by the Romans in A.D. 70.[18] Some scholars, including de Vaux and Milik, believed the treasure was imaginary, an ancient folktale, while others suggested it described real treasure which had long disappeared. But not only did Allegro believe the Copper Scroll described real treasure, he went looking for it.

If there was anything more calculated to infuriate Kathleen—an amateur archaeologist digging "unscientific" holes in ancient sites looking for buried treasure—it is hard to imagine what that might be. K ran into Allegro in January 1960, when she was in Jerusalem making arrangements for her upcoming dig. She and Peter Parr spotted some sort of activity at the complex of tombs at the bottom of the Mount of Olives in the Kidron Valley and went to investigate.[19] After seeing what he was up to, she wrote Allegro quite bluntly:

> You are no more qualified to dig for antiquities than I should be to edit a fragment of the Dead Sea Scrolls. What you are doing is exactly comparable as regards the destruction of evidence as if I were to cut up a manuscript with a pair of scissors without any proper record of its contents. Whether or not you find anything, you are destroying evidence with your rabbit burrows. It will be more especially disastrous if you do find anything, as only proper stratigraphical excavation could establish how and when it was deposited.[20]

Allegro was unrepentant. He claimed that the excavations were under the direct supervision of the Jordanian Department of Antiquities, and her accusations amounted to a lack of respect for the Director, Awni Dajani, and his staff.[21] Kathleen then turned on Dajani and let him know in no uncertain terms exactly what she thought of his having given a permit to Allegro. Dajani had worked for K at Jericho and had completed a Ph.D. with her in London. Although having a former student as Director of Antiquities in Jordan was undoubtedly useful to her, K could be very critical of Dajani, especially when he did not take the stands she thought he should. In addition, she had found out that Allegro had also been digging at Qumran, where Père de Vaux had excavated earlier. She spent an entire afternoon with Dajani, pointing out to him his numerous sins. He denied that his Department of Antiquities was involved with Allegro's activities but maintained that since Allegro had made a favorable impression on King Hussein, he found it difficult not to give him a permit. And Dajani pointed out—with some justice, K admitted—that if she was going to insist that Allegro be allowed to dig only with a properly trained archaeologist, the BSAJ should provide one. He said that if she would agree to do this, he would tell Allegro that he could work only under the supervision of the BSAJ.[22] While K did not like the idea of being associated with Allegro in any way, she consoled herself: "It would really be comparable with Père Vincent's rescue of some archaeology from the work of the Parker Expedition."[23]

But her troubles with Allegro were just beginning. K returned to London, only to read a piece by Allegro in the *Daily Telegraph* that said funds were needed to buy more scrolls from the Bedouin. While K couldn't argue with that, she did take exception to, among other things, his view that it was wrong for the Jordanian government to have raised money to purchase material from Cave 4 by agreeing to allow foreign institutions to have scroll materials in return for a contribution. Allegro's public complaint prompted K's public rebuttal, and in her letter to the newspaper she also challenged Allegro's accusation that the material from Cave 11 was being deliberately delayed.[24]

Although Kathleen thought Allegro had worsened the situation by driving up the price of scrolls,[25] he was right about money being needed to rescue scrolls still in the hands of the Bedouin. The Jordanian government could not come up with the necessary funds and, moreover, had decreed that scrolls could no longer be sold out of the country. The Palestine Archaeological Museum was short of money because it had had to spend a good deal of its endowment in 1957 to purchase some of the Cave 11 material for fear it would disappear or be smuggled abroad for sale.[26] In the short term an American offer to buy part of the Cave 11 cache, while allowing the material to remain in Jordan, helped relieve some of the financial pressure on the PAM. But Kathleen, Wheeler, and others decided to continue to approach the British Treasury in hopes of obtaining funds to purchase additional scrolls from the Bedouin. In May 1960 Her Majesty's Treasury offered to give £25, 000 to help the PAM recoup capital and buy more scrolls on the condition that the other countries represented on the Board of Trustees—the United States, France, and Sweden—also come up with £25,000. The scrolls would then be lent to these countries in rotation. K went to work trying to make the necessary arrangements, meeting with King Hussein, the king of Sweden, and official bodies of the United States and France. Efforts to get funds for this scheme from these countries failed. Other offers from the United States and Holland did materialize, however, and in the end money was raised from private sources in the U.S. and from the Royal Academy of Holland to purchase scrolls from Cave 11.[27] The British Academy funds could be used to purchase additional scrolls from the Bedouin.

But the plan to rescue more scrolls from the Bedouin was badly compromised in the summer of 1961 by Sherif Nasser, King Hussein's uncle. Trying to buy scrolls himself, he was told by the Bedouin, who did not trust him, that none were to be had. Subsequently, when approached by the Jordanian government, the Bedouin, afraid of Nasser's retribution, again said they had none. In fact, there was solid evidence that they did have others. K suggested that the attempt to buy more scrolls be put on hold until things settled down.[28]

In the meantime, despite Dajani's promises, Allegro's treasure-hunting continued. In March of 1960, supported by the London tabloid *The Daily Mail*, he was back in Jordan. Despite all the fanfare—such as a series of articles in *The Daily Mail* under the heading, "Gold Hunt in the Holy Land"—the expedition accomplished very little, much to the disgust of the reporter accompanying him.[29] In December 1960 Allegro returned to Jordan again, sponsored by *The Sunday Times*, looking this time, so he said, for additional scrolls rather than treasure. This expedition turned up a few scraps of leather and papyrus, but no scrolls and certainly no treasure.[30] Allegro was back again in the fall of 1961, still causing Wheeler and K concern over both his unscientific digging and his talk of his own "Dead Sea Scrolls Fund," which had the effect of driving up the price of scrolls. At Wheeler's request, K asked Peter Parr to keep a close eye on Allegro and to work to prevent him "from sticking his beastly spade in."[31] Parr did his best, offering Allegro the official cooperation of the BSAJ, but Allegro seems to have done *his* best to evade him, successfully.[32]

K herself made an effort to do something about Allegro, first approaching Sir Frank Francis, Director of the British Museum, about the possibility of establishing some sort of vetting body for archaeologists wishing to excavate in Jordan, and later (on the suggestion of Rik Wheeler) attempting to get the Foreign Office to refuse Allegro a visa.[33]

Allegro's troublemaking (as far as K was concerned) was not limited to wandering about in the desert, looking for scrolls or treasure. He also tried to use his friendly relations with Dajani and King Hussein to organize his own exhibition of scrolls in England, much to the annoyance of, among others, the Director of the British Museum. An announcement came from Amman that an agreement had been reached for an exhibit of scrolls at the British Museum. This surprised the director of the museum, Sir Frank Francis, who knew nothing about it. In principle Sir Frank had no objection to putting on such an exhibit, but he felt that Allegro's proposal—to exhibit only the Copper Scroll and material from Cave 4—wouldn't be sufficiently impressive. K, on the other hand, was sensitive to the need to manage the scrolls' presentation so as to raise more money for more scrolls. She wanted them exhibited in Britain *after* the £25,000 given by the British government had been spent. That, she argued, would be the time to try to raise more funds for additional scrolls.[34]

The whole problem was resolved quite satisfactorily, from Kathleen's point of view, when Dr. Harold Plenderleith, a UNESCO expert invited to Jordan by the Jordanian government, examined the scrolls and reported that they should not travel in their present condition.[35] Allegro reacted badly, questioning the integrity of Dr. Plenderleith, accusing Père de Vaux of trying to prevent the exhibition because he was a priest, and attempting to bully the American and British ambassadors, who were Trustees of the Palestine Archaeological Museum.[36]

In the meantime K was still trying to spend the British government's money on scrolls. In April 1962 she wrenched herself away from the dig in Jerusalem when she heard from Père de Vaux that additional scrolls had been located and were for sale through Kando. Known as the Jericho Papyri, these appeared to be legal documents in Aramaic dated to ca. 380 B.C. Despite the fact that they were not, strictly speaking, biblical, K decided that they pertained to the "biblical background" and wanted to stretch the terms of the Treasury grant to buy them.[37]

Kando, the middleman, brought the scroll material to the Palestine Archaeological Museum on April 25, 1962, to be met by Kathleen, Père de Vaux, Yosef Saad, Curator of the PAM, and Professor G. R. Driver, an expert from the Oriental Institute at Oxford sent by the British Academy to examine the scrolls. Kando produced an assortment of documents in extremely bad condition. Professor Driver confirmed that these appeared to be official documents of ca. fourth century B.C., and of historical, if not biblical, importance.

Previously Kando had mentioned to Saad a document with seven intact seals. But when de Vaux asked Kando about such a scroll, he insisted these were all he had. Now was the time for bargaining. K, de Vaux, and Driver excused themselves to confer privately. Professor Driver didn't think the badly preserved documents were worth the asking price of £25,000. He wasn't sure they were worth buying at all. At first, K only wanted to offer £1,000 for the lot, but eventually they agreed to the inflated price of £5,000, in hopes of getting negotiations for scroll material started again. But when Kando heard this offer, he then pulled out of his pocket the scroll with seven intact seals and said that if what he had shown them was worth £5,000, this was worth £10,000. This was a mistake. Père de Vaux, in particular, was taken aback because he had had dealings with Kando before and had never seen him do anything like this. They offered £5,000 for the entire collection. Kando refused. He then wanted to accept the original offer of £5000 for the original documents. He was refused and there negotiations ended. That evening K had second thoughts about whether or not they should have offered more money, but the next day Driver reassured her that they had made the right decision.[38]

A few months later the Jericho Papyri surfaced again when Kando showed them to two of Père de Vaux's colleagues at the École Biblique. Since they reported that the name Nehemiah appeared in the scroll and so it might have biblical import, efforts were made to reopen negotiations.[39] But before matters got very far, the Jericho scrolls were bought by the American Schools of Oriental Research for the Palestine Archaeological Museum. Because the scrolls turned out to be contracts of the fifth and fourth centuries B.C. and had nothing to do with the biblical Nehemiah, they would have been hard to justify to the British Treasury anyway.[40] While K admitted she was slightly disappointed that the British hadn't got hold of them, she remained convinced they had done the right thing not to buy the scrolls at the price Kando had asked. She was content that the documents had been purchased. And, there was an additional consolation: she found it "highly satisfactory that the deal was carried through just before Allegro arrived on his present jaunt."[41]

After much protracted negotiations and more annoyance with Allegro, the Dead Sea Scrolls arrived in London in November 1965 after a sojourn in the United States and Canada. But their arrival provided yet another occasion for a public exchange between K and Allegro. An article appeared in *The Sunday Times* on November 21, 1965, outlining Allegro's eccentric view of a Christlike leader of the Essenes, criticizing the Palestine Archaeological Museum for selling publication rights to the Scrolls, calling for another expedition to look for scrolls, and blaming Roland de Vaux for the slowness with which the Scrolls were being released. K wrote a lengthy response and was furious with *The Sunday Times* for not publishing her letter in full. While she had no objection to the deletion of her description of Allegro's activities as "so-called archaeological expeditions"—*The Sunday Times* feared an action for libel—she did object to the cutting of her point that Allegro's adventures had driven up the price of scrolls.[42]

The Scrolls exhibit in the United States had been a triumph, with long lines outside the Smithsonian Institution, and K was worried that such success would not be repeated in Great Britain.[43] She need not have been anxious. They were displayed in London, Manchester, Edinburgh, and Cardiff, in Wales, and, at least at Edinburgh, broke all attendance records.

K BEGAN HER FIRST THREE-month season at Jerusalem in mid-May, 1961, with a staff of thirty and a labor force that would rise to 450 over the course of the dig. She found running the Jerusalem dig more demanding than Jericho had been, as it was a larger enterprise, with sites spread out all over the city, which meant Kathleen was constantly on the move. Although Roland de Vaux was officially co-director for the first three years, and from 1962 Doug Tushingham directed the excavations in the Armenian Garden inside the city, K tried to visit all the sites—perhaps a half dozen at any one time—each day. It was exhausting. To keep up with everything—visiting all the sites, hiking up and down the steep hill at the main site of Ophel where she spent most of her time, checking in on the Conservation Department, giving her staff weekly talks and tours of the sites, dealing with all the problems that arose in the excavation of a living city—would have been beyond most people. Doug Tushingham later described:

> K's indomitable determination to see and oversee all aspects of the work, day after day, involved climbing up and down the steep streets and slopes of Jerusalem in summer's heat, descending treacherous stairs into deep excavations, and struggling up again, working over and annotating great piles of pottery, drawing sections, and, in addition, carrying on diplomatic negotiations with officials of all kinds, civilian, and military, and ecclesiastical, on an endless variety of subjects, from supplies of drinking water to permission to dig an additional two meters here or there, from importunate tourists to labour disputes.[44]

Moreover, because of her post-Jericho fame, K was swamped with more applicants than she could take. As at Jericho, the dig was an international affair. In addition to British, American, Canadian, French, Jordanian, and Australian participants, Belgium, Holland, Sweden, New Zealand, Argentina, and Trinidad were also represented. Some of the young field supervisors were second-generation friends. Sebastian Payne, the son of her friend Joan Crowfoot Payne and grandson of John Crowfoot, dug with her at Jerusalem, as did Tim Strickland, son of Mike Strickland, a British army officer she had met while digging at Jericho. Chris Young's aunt Joan Clarke had dug with K both at Sabratha and Jericho. K interviewed applicants personally whenever she could, but people who knew her agreed that K was not always the best judge of character, and occasionally there were complaints about some of the people she took on.[45] Later she would be criticized for not recruiting more seasoned excavators. But training students was one of her goals, and she was happy to take on young people with little experience, although she might advise them to do some reading—such as Wheeler's *Archaeology from the Earth*—or to get experience on a British dig first.[46] K told at least one inexperienced young woman that she would first be put where she could not do any damage. Later, when Kathleen was convinced that an individual knew what he or she was doing, the person would be moved to a more complicated site. In addition, K also had the benefit of archaeologists who had been trained at Jericho—people such as Crystal Bennett, Peter Parr, Sven Holm-Neilson, Ahmed Shistawi, Doug Tushingham, and Basil Hennessy—who could provide more immediate supervision of the less experienced while she made her daily rounds.

The British School was not big enough to accommodate everybody. For the first two seasons, most of the staff was housed in Watson House, the former St. John's Eye Hospital—a lovely old Arab building in the middle of the Old City which has a garden with a view of the Mount of Olives—and an adjacent building, Strathearn House. In later seasons the British School rented additional space from the owner of the Husseini building, in which the BSAJ was housed, and so everyone could be put up either in the British School itself, in additional space in the Husseini building, or in an annex behind it. K thought these positively luxurious accommodations compared with conditions at Jericho;[47] water shortages, however, were sometimes a problem, and some seasons the staff were allowed only one shower a week.[48]

Jerusalem, like any large excavation, depended on the support of a staff of non-excavators. For most of the time, Theodora Newbould served as the expedition's housekeeper, a position Vivienne Catleugh had filled for several seasons at Jericho but never did at Jerusalem. Known to everyone as Theo, Newbould had presumably met K through Rik Wheeler, for whom she had worked as a field administrator for some years. A combination secretary/domestic bursar/advisor to the young, Newbould dealt with most of the day-to-day practical matters and was described by people who worked with her at Jerusalem as a wonderfully eccentric woman with a highly developed sense of honor (Figure 7.2).

In addition to Theo Newbould and the experienced field supervisors, K had the advantage of other staff members who had been at Jericho: Maggie Tushingham, Dorothy Marshall, Peter Dorrell, Terry Ball, Cecil Western, and Nancy Lord. Perhaps because the Jerusalem dig was larger and less intimate than Jericho had been, perhaps also because K was busier, perhaps because she

FIGURE 7.2: K and Theodora Newbould on payday.
Courtesy of Agnès Spycket.

was older and so the age difference between her and the younger site supervisors was that much greater, some participants thought that K was less social than she had been at Jericho. They perceived a sort of K "gang": an assortment of K's intimates, made up, to a large degree (although not entirely), of people who had been at Jericho, including the Tushinghams, Kim Wheeler, Terry Ball, Basil Hennessy, Peter Dorrell, Cecil Western, and Nancy Lord. It is in Jerusalem that more and more people remark on her shyness. People who knew her earlier are less likely to describe her in such terms.[49]

K herself provided a description of the typical workday in her popular account *Digging Up Jerusalem*. Since work began at 5 am (to avoid the heat later in the day), everyone was up and having a light snack by 4:30. The diggers were then driven in various vehicles to the half-dozen or so sites scattered around the city. About 9:30 a more substantial breakfast was served. The majority of the site supervisors, who were working on Ophel, would meet for breakfast at the "little dig house" on the top of the hill, while the others would be fed at their sites. (For those working on Ophel, the nearest toilet facilities were located at the top of the hill, a five-minute walk up the steep hill from some of the trenches. One former site supervisor recalls that rushing up the hill when suffering from "gippy tummy" was not a pleasant experience.)

Work was resumed until lunch at 2 pm. During the first year an unusually hot spell led to a tradition of another break at midday. Although the winter at Jericho could range from warm to quite chilly, Jerusalem in the summer was always hot. Early in the 1961 season, the Khamsin, the hot east wind blowing off the desert, caused the temperature to shoot up to over 100 degrees. None of the trenches was yet deep enough to provide any shade, and some of the site supervisors, especially those from more temperate climates, were feeling the heat. One day, much to everyone's relief, Madeline Parr, wife of Peter Parr, the permanent Secretary/Librarian of the BSAJ, suddenly appeared on site with some welcome iced lemonade. K later recalled, "I don't think any of us concerned will forget the blessed gulps of this liquid."[50] Although this was the worst heat wave of the entire dig, it established a tradition of a lemonade break from 12 to 12:10. As the trenches deepened, they provided some shade from the heat, but nothing could make them completely comfortable. At midday, with the sun shining directly overhead, there was no place to hide. Worse, with the heat reflected off the sides of the trench, it could become like an oven.

After a late lunch at the British School, there was a siesta until 4 pm. For K this was a very welcome and much-needed break, while some of the more youthful and energetic might head into the Old City. Pottery sorting took place after tea at 4 pm. Late afternoon was also the time when sections were drawn, and K might well return to one of the trenches with a site supervisor, working until dark.

Dinner was at 7 pm. For some of the site supervisors, drinks and singing on the roof afterward became a ritual, while K would often retire to her room for several more hours of work. Even though the Jerusalem expedition was not as isolated as Jericho had been, nevertheless, as at Jericho, the archaeologists occasionally organized their own celebrations, a party or special dinner. On a particularly memorable occasion, an impromptu game of cricket broke out after dinner when K decided that the Americans should have the game explained to them.

Local labor included several hundred men and boys, mostly from the local Arab village of Silwan. As at Jericho, these consisted of pickmen, shovel men, and basketboys. Some of the workmen were the prized "Jerichoans"—those Kathleen had trained at Jericho who had become highly skilled, professional diggers. K's foreman was Abul Jewas Abassi, known as Abu Mohammed, a local from Silwan who was generally charged with making things go smoothly. One of the great challenges of the site supervisors was to keep the baskets moving at a rapid clip along the lines of basketboys, sometimes as many as fifty working in a chain, passing along the baskets of earth. Terry Ball has a vivid memory of K standing on the slope of Ophel, hands on hips, "like some great emperor," shouting "Shugul!"—"Work!"— to keep things moving along. Certainly, the boys could sometimes be something of a trial. Mostly teenagers, some as young as twelve or thirteen, they often found the work dull; one lot amused themselves by asking English-speaking tourists the meaning of all the dirty words in English they could think of.

K BEGAN EXCAVATIONS IN 1961 to answer specific questions. First, was the "City of David," in fact, on the ridge of Ophel? Second, when did the city first spread to the western ridge, the so-called Mount Zion? And, finally, how authentic was the traditional site of the crucifixion and garden tomb on which the Church of the Holy Sepulchre was founded? Those questions were determined in part by where she was permitted to dig, which in turn depended on the availability of suitable spots in the crowded city and the willingness of owners to grant the necessary permissions. Kathleen very much wanted to excavate in the Jewish Quarter, in the southeastern part of the Old City, because that area encompassed all the periods that interested her, from the Iron Age to the Crusader period. This quarter of the city was still in ruins as a result of the fighting in 1948. K believed the authorities were interested in rebuilding the area, and hoped that they might be willing to move the refugees squatting there in order to permit excavations before work began.

That hope was disappointed, and Kathleen was not allowed to excavate in the Jewish Quarter in 1961. But the Moslem religious authorities, the Awqaf, gave the permission necessary for her to begin looking for the site of the original city on Ophel.[51] Here was another puzzle related to the City of David's location. The entrance to the water shaft of what had been identified as the earliest city by an earlier expedition appeared to be located outside the city walls, making it vulnerable in case of attack. Why put the entrance there?

The Jewish historian Josephus, writing in the first century A.D., believed that the original Jebusite and Davidic city had been on the western ridge. On the face of it, this made sense. The higher western slope seemed more suitable for the building of a fortified city, being broader and flatter than the narrow Ophel. In the early twentieth century, however, Père Vincent (a Dominican working at the École Biblique who K remembered quite vividly from her days at Samaria) had argued that the earliest city must have been on Ophel. Only then, he reasoned, would the city have had access to the permanent water supply of the Gihon spring (or Virgin's Fountain) at the bottom of the hill. Furthermore, he had suggested that the shaft and tunnel system discovered by Charles Warren had given access to the spring. This might explain the biblical story in which David conquered the strongly fortified city by penetrating the city through its water system. However, during his 1923–1925 excavations, R.A.S. Macalister had identified a wall at the top of the ridge as that of the original Jebusite city. If Macalister was right, then the shaft that led from the spring came to the surface 27 meters (80 feet) outside of the city wall, which would have been no help in case of attack.

Kathleen set out to solve this problem with Trench 1, an 11-meter-wide trench from Macalister's so-called Tower of David at the top of Ophel down the steep eastern side of the hill (Figure 7.3). This was a grueling and, at first, unrewarding trench to excavate. Digging on a steep 45-degree slope—so steep it was difficult to stand on and even more difficult to walk up—the excavators encountered massive amounts of stone debris four and five meters thick. Most of the first season was spent removing what K called this "ghastly stone tumble."[52] In width, the 11-meter-wide trench consisted of two squares of five

FIGURE 7.3: The eastern slope of Ophel, with K's squares down the side.
Courtesy of Jeremy Ritchie.

meters, supervised by a single site supervisor. The length of the trench that first season was determined arbitrarily by the number of field assistants available. K admitted that she initially laid out the trench at thirty-five meters because that was the point at which she ran out of site supervisors. Luckily, they were just barely enough. The expedition discovered a wall at the very end of the trench down the hill—in the final foot of the final square—which dated to the Middle Bronze Age, ca. 1800 B.C. (Figure 7.4). K later conceded that it was imprudent of her to declare at the time that they had uncovered the east wall of the first city, but subsequent excavation confirmed her claim. By the end of the 1962 season, K felt confident that this was, in fact, the wall of the city captured by David, and that it remained in use until the seventh century B.C. She had effectively stretched the earliest Jebusite-Davidic city down the eastern slope of Ophel some 160 feet farther than previously thought. The entrance to the shaft leading to Gihon came well within K's wall, and the problem of access to the spring was neatly solved[53] (Figure 7.5).

174

Figure 7.4: The original wall of Jerusalem. *Courtesy of Jeremy Ritchie.*

Other results were also apparent that first year. Fairly early on K became sure that Macalister's "Tower of David" was no such thing. It had been built

175

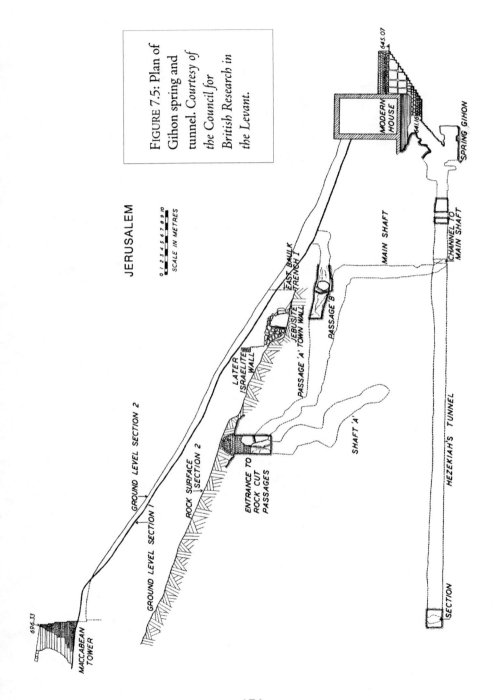

FIGURE 7.5: Plan of Gihon spring and tunnel. Courtesy of the Council for British Research in the Levant.

on the remains of buildings from the seventh century B.C., and dated only to the second century B.C., long after David. But Trench 1 had other surprises. On the upper part of the slope at the top of Trench 1, once they got past the layers of stone debris, the excavators uncovered artificial terraces erected on platforms supported by retaining walls. K believed that, built in the Late Bronze Age (ca. fourteenth–thirteenth century B.C.), these structures had been a way of extending the area at the top of the narrow ridge. She determined that they had originally been constructed by the Jebusites but were extended, and sometimes repaired, by the Israelites in later centuries.[54] In fact, she argued that they explained an ambiguous term found in the Hebrew Bible: II Samuel, I Chronicle, and I Kings contain references to David, Solomon, and Hezekiah building, rebuilding, or in some way being concerned with "millo." Since the root meaning of the Hebrew word is "filling," K argued, convincingly for some,[55] that the term refers to these artificial terraces (Figure 7.6), concluding that

> [t]he great quantity of debris overlying the houses dates from the Babylonian destruction of Jerusalem in 586 B.C. when the inhabitants of Judah were led into captivity. It has always been clear from the Biblical account how disastrous this was for Judah and the Jews; the extent of the physical disaster for Jerusalem has only become apparent as a result of these excavations.[56]

Whatever effort it must have taken on the part of the Israelites to repair and extend these terraces in the Iron Age, transporting the huge rocks up the slope and maneuvering them into place, great effort was also required to excavate their remains. The only way to remove the stones was to pound them into fragments small enough to be carted away, a procedure that took a heavy toll on the expedition's sledgehammers. Finally, Abu Mohammed, K's foreman, came up with a solution: "a tough looking individual" with the singular ability to look at a gigantic stone, sing a little song, and then expertly shatter it with a single blow.[57]

In addition to proving that the earliest Jerusalem had been located on the eastern ridge, K also wanted to determine when the city first spread to the western ridge, Mount Zion. Writing in the first century A.D., the historian Josephus described Jerusalem as being built on two ridges, the lower city on the smaller eastern ridge and an upper city on the western ridge. Both cities, he said, were surrounded by a wall built by David and Solomon. In addition, biblical references to the Mishneh, or "Second Quarter," suggested an addition to the original city of David. When had the city spread west onto Mount Zion?

FIGURE 7.6: The Jebusite terraces. *Courtesy of Jeremy Ritchie.*

To find this out involved investigating the wall that Bliss and Dickie had discovered, running south from the southwest corner of the Old City and eventually turning east to connect the eastern and western ridges. Kathleen's investigation was restricted by the fact that the demilitarized zone adjacent to the Israeli sector, the ominously named No-Man's Land, lay immediately to the west. In fact, the top of the ridge was in this off-limits zone. K did the best she could under the circumstances, beginning excavations at the very edge of No-Man's Land. To everyone's surprise, including K's, all the evidence for the origin of this wall pointed to a much later date than expected, leading her to contradict Josephus; the western ridge, at least at its southern end, had not been included in the city until the mid-first century A.D. (Later excavations in the Old City would lead her to the conclusion that Jerusalem had not spread to the western hill at all during the period of the Judean Monarchy.) She deduced that it was likely Herod Agrippa who had built Bliss and Dickie's wall. According to Josephus, Herod Agrippa had extended Jerusalem to the north. K argued that he had apparently done the same to the south.

Finally, K was able to excavate on one site within the Old City walls that first year, a place called the Muristan, just south of the Church of the Holy Sepulchre.[58] On property owned by the Order of St. John of Jerusalem, this site led to one of the more surprising, even unexpected, successes of the Jerusalem dig. The Church of the Holy Sepulchre had been established by Helena, mother of the emperor Constantine, in the early fourth century A.D. on the traditional site of Christ's crucifixion and tomb. According to the account in the Gospels, and the requirements of Jewish law, the site was outside the city's walls. Many people, K included, were perplexed upon first visiting the church to find it in the midst of the cramped Old City. The answer, of course, was that Calvary and the Holy Sepulchre must have been outside Jerusalem's walls not as they exist now, or even as they existed in A.D. 320, but as they existed ca. A.D. 30. Josephus, writing later in the first century, described the three north walls that existed at the time of Titus's conquest of Jerusalem in A.D. 70. The second wall mentioned by Josephus is the wall that must have been the outermost wall at the time of Christ's death; the crucifixion and burial must have taken place outside this wall. Since the Muristan was south of the Church of the Holy Sepulchre, if this area had been outside the north city wall ca. A.D. 30, the site of the Church of the Holy Sepulchre must have been as well (Figure 7.7). To K's surprise, she was able to confirm this reconstruction archaeologically.

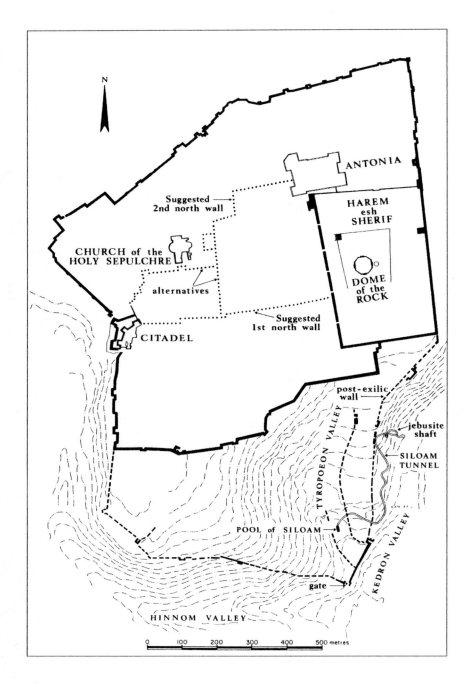

Labels within the figure:

N

ANTONIA

HAREM esh SHERIF

Suggested 2nd north wall

CHURCH of the HOLY SEPULCHRE

DOME of the ROCK

alternatives

Suggested 1st north wall

CITADEL

post-exilic wall

jebusite shaft

SILOAM TUNNEL

TYROPOEON VALLEY

KEDRON VALLEY

POOL of SILOAM

gate

HINNOM VALLEY

0   100   200   300   400   500 metres

FIGURE 7.7: Plan of alternatives for the second north wall of Jerusalem. *Courtesy of the Council for British Research in the Levant.*

In the middle of the crowded Old City, with no direct access to roads, the Muristan was not an easy place to dig. The vacant area available for excavation was only thirty by fifteen meters to begin with, and as the excavators dug downward, and debris began to pile up around them, the excavated area gradually contracted. When bedrock was finally reached in the 1963 season, the area excavated was only four by four meters. At one point K had to spend what was for the expedition a considerable amount of money to hire donkeys to haul the dirt away so that the excavators would have room to continue work. K herself admitted that she had despaired of success. But success came. Underneath the Byzantine layers, they found fill dated to the reconstruction of Jerusalem in the second century A.D. Directly underneath that was evidence of seventh-century B.C. quarrying. By the end of the 1963 season, K had come to the conclusion that between the seventh century B.C. and the second century A.D. the site had remained outside of the city walls. So, while she readily conceded that the archaeological evidence did not prove that the tradition upon which Helena relied was authentic, it did show that it *could* have been.

Initially, then, the excavations were quite successful, allowing K to claim that she had found the city of David. In November 1962 Kathleen gave a public talk in London to a packed house on the first two seasons at Jerusalem, at which her "exposition and explanation of those ghastly stones was quite brilliant."[59] At a party afterward K had a terrific time—until she fell asleep on a chair. She was exhausted.

AFTER TWENTY-SEVEN YEARS at the Institute of Archaeology, Kathleen left to become Principal of St. Hugh's College, Oxford, in August 1961. She had maintained her ties with Oxford and in 1960 had been delighted to be made an Honorary Fellow of Somerville. She had held the position of Lecturer in Palestinian Archaeology since 1948 despite recommendations that she be promoted to Reader or even Professor.[60] The headship of an Oxford college was a tremendous leap in prestige.

Kathleen might also have been ready for a change. In 1958 the Institute, having lost its lease on St. John's Lodge, abandoned the lovely building overlooking Regent's Park and moved into new quarters on Gordon Square in Bloomsbury. Although closer to the University of London and the British Museum, the new building didn't have the charm of the eighteenth-century mansion. Max Mallowan's reaction may have reflected that of his colleagues: "I regret to say that the external appearance of the building strikes me as hideous."[61] Despite concerns about having enough space for all of the archaeological collections, K made the best of things, telling Peter Parr that it wasn't too bad.[62] The new building was opened by the Queen Mother, Chancellor of the University of London, on April 29, 1958, twenty-one years to the day after the Institute had originally been opened at St. John's Lodge.

She was less sanguine about other developments. V. Gordon Childe had resigned as Director of the Institute in 1956, and W. F. "Peter" Grimes had become the new Director. Grimes got off to a dreadful start with K when he banned dogs in the new building and car-park. The fact that her dogs were old, frequently sick all over the place, and badly behaved did nothing to mitigate K's fury. She immediately resigned her post at the Institute. An emergency meeting of the Management Committee had to be called. The minutes do not record the details of the arrangement worked out, but somehow a crisis was averted.[63] Rachel Maxwell-Hyslop recalled that a compromise was reached whereby K's dogs were permitted in the car-park.[64]

One day while K was away in Jerusalem, a letter arrived from St. Hugh's College asking if she would allow her name to be considered as the next principal. Vivienne Catleugh forwarded the letter on to K, urging her to think seriously about it. The Principal of St. Hugh's, Emily Proctor, was retiring. Proctor, while an excellent scholar, was an austere, private woman, who had been uninterested in socializing with undergraduates. The College's Governing Body (made up of all the College Fellows) decided that the College needed a different kind of head, someone more outgoing who would take more interest in entertaining the undergraduates. Kathleen's name was suggested.[65]

After a round of weekend interviews, the Governing Body was considering three candidates, including K. None of the women was obviously the clear choice. In K's case, the College Fellows were a little put off by her Third Class degree in History. In order to help make up their minds, two of the College Fellows, Rachel Trickett and Mary Warnock, went to High Wycombe to see K at home. There they met "the real Kathleen": dressed in faded old clothes, chain smoking, with the ubiquitous dog trailing along at her heels. While they had come to discuss St. Hugh's and her views on its future, they found themselves talking about the dig in Jerusalem, gardening, and dogs. While K made no secret of her interest in the job at St. Hugh's, at the same time she made it clear that archaeology would remain her first priority. Even if they remained unconvinced that she was a real "intellectual," they were taken with her warmth, enthusiasm, and charm, and became convinced she was the woman for the job.[66] And, so, in August 1962 K became the new Principal of St. Hugh's.

K and Vivienne Catleugh had been living together in Hammersmith since the war, K working at the Institute and Catleugh for the Red Cross. Catleugh decided that she needed to go with her to Oxford. Before K made the move to St. Hugh's, she consulted Dame Janet Vaughn, the distinguished principal of Somerville College. According to Catleugh, Dame Janet told K that her three duties as Principal would consist of running the College, her own research, and entertaining, and she advised her that doing all three well on her own would be very demanding. So, K asked Catleugh to come to Oxford with her to run the domestic side of things, as she had been doing in Hammersmith for the last twenty years. Catleugh, who was ready to retire from the Red Cross, was convinced K needed her. So, she moved to Oxford with K, where she was known to all the Fellows of St. Hugh's as "My Friend from the Red Cross" because that was how K always referred to her.[67]

K MADE NO SECRET OF the fact that she didn't enjoy working at Jerusalem as much as she had Jericho. The stone rubble, for one thing, on the side of Ophel made digging difficult, even unpleasant, and often impossible to have the neat five by five meter squares and clean vertical sides so important to the Wheeler-Kenyon method. In *Digging Up Jerusalem* K expressed her frustration quite straightforwardly: "I have had my fill of this."[68] Moreover, she certainly found the dig more exhausting. She was older—and stouter—and needed her afternoon rest in a way she appears not to have done before.

Furthermore, she had numerous frustrations she had not faced at Jericho. Pilfering of artifacts was more of a problem. She was constrained by houses, local footpaths, and ongoing construction. Refugee squatters sometimes got in the way; one winter locals used one of the sites as a toilet.

Digging in Jerusalem was a particular headache because of the necessity of obtaining the combined consent of the city authorities, private landowners, and religious authorities. The need to get permissions and rent land made organization tricky because K did not want to publicize the dig and ask for money before she had a permit from the authorities, but she couldn't begin to negotiate with landowners until she had money.[69] K found her foreman Abu Mohammed particularly valuable when it came to bargaining with landowners: "If I felt the rent demanded was exorbitant, I would sweep out indignantly, and leave him to persuade the owner to reduce his terms, which he always did."[70]

Getting the necessary authorizations posed a real challenge. At one point K was getting no response from the various authorities, so she went to Jerusalem with the expressed intention of devoting herself to pestering the requisite individuals until she got the needed authorization.[71] Her government contacts proved useful in moving things along; the Governor of Jerusalem, Anwar Nuseibah, whom Kathleen quite liked, helped persuade the Awqaf to give permission to dig on their land.[72] In another instance the intervention of the Greek consul convinced the Greek Patriarchate to allow excavations on its property.[73]

And once permissions were obtained, they might be revoked. At one time it looked as though the Armenian Patriarchate would allow a hotel to begin construction in the Armenian Garden, where Doug Tushingham was digging.[74] In 1964 the excavations on the main site at Ophel were delayed three weeks because of problems getting permission from the army and the Awqaf.[75] At one point Crystal Bennett felt justified in threatening that K might just give up excavating in Jordan altogether if the Awqaf didn't give the necessary permission.[76] Permission to dig in the Jewish Quarter was eventually given in 1962, but these excavations came to a premature end when K could not get permission to continue in 1964. Although she must have been terribly disappointed, Kathleen restrained herself in print, writing only that this "is most unfortunate, as this is the area which holds out the best hope of securing dating evidence concerning the earliest stages of the walls of the present Old City."[77]

And still there was the difficulty, despite her fame, of raising the substantial sums of money Jerusalem required. She kept busy churning out articles to draw attention to the dig, such as those in the *Daily Telegraph*, *The Illustrated London News*, and the *Jewish Chronicle*, among others, and sometimes ended them with a plea: "[W]e . . . need the support of everyone interested in the history of this unique city."[78] Unlike Jericho, whose tombs had produced so many intact objects that could be given to museums and universities in exchange for financial support, Jerusalem was slow to produce these kinds of artifacts. The Emory University Museum Committee, for instance, at one time considered dropping its support of the excavations because of the lack of finds.[79] That was one reason why K was so pleased when, for instance, a cache of intact pots was found in 1962. Nevertheless, finances remained so strained that in 1965 she had to turn to the Russell Trust for a mid-season bailout, and the financial situation remained critical.[80] By the end of the final season, the dig was bankrupt.

THE FIRST TWO SEASONS AT Jerusalem were perhaps the most exciting and productive; the rest was almost an anticlimax. In the summer of 1963, K began on several new sites. While she was confident that she had located the eastern wall of the first Jerusalem, she wanted to continue to trace the outline of the earliest city. Although she did not have quite the success she had had with that first wall, in the end she was reasonably confident that she had been able to sketch—more or less—the outline of Jebusite-Davidic Jerusalem. While the Hinnon and Kedron valleys provided natural boundaries for ancient Jerusalem to the west, east, and south, there was no natural geographic boundary to the north. She assumed that the southern boundary of the city was determined by the southern tip of the Ophel ridge. But absent an obvious natural boundary on the north side, Kathleen began looking for the north wall of the earliest city. This search was greatly restricted because of the presence of human habitation—houses, gardens, paths, and the like—but also complicated by the destruction wrought by previous excavators who had obliterated the all-important stratigraphical evidence. In the end, K believed that she had bracketed the position of the northern wall, even if she could not claim to have definitely found it. The Moslem holy site, the Haram esh-Sherif, is located at the southeast corner of the Old City. It was built on the site of Herod's Temple, which itself had been built on the traditional site of the Temple of Solomon. The Haram esh-Sherif, therefore, is located on the site of Solomon's Temple. And according to the biblical account, Solomon built the temple on a threshing floor which K, not unreasonably, assumed had been outside the early city. So, K concluded, the site of the northern wall must be somewhere between her Trench 1, which had uncovered the eastern wall, and the Haram to the north.

And, indeed, she uncovered a complicated succession of walls in that area, crossing the crest of Ophel at a narrow section of the ridge. While the destruction of previous excavators and limited access made it impossible to date the walls stratigraphically, by excavating small areas to the north and south, she was able to bracket where she believed the original north wall must have been. No evidence of any occupation north of the complex of walls prior to the ninth or tenth century B.C. was found (too late to be within the earliest city), but much earlier occupation south of it was, leading K to conclude that the boundary of the earliest city was to be found in that tangle of walls. Grasping that she claimed to have located where the northern wall must have been rather than that she actually found it was apparently not as easy as it sounds, for in

September 1964 *The Times* erroneously reported that the northern wall itself had been uncovered. Quite probably to her great annoyance, she had to clarify the fact that while the location of the wall was known with reasonable certainty, the wall itself had not been located.[81]

Likewise, K would claim to have determined what must have been the location of the earliest city's western wall, without actually locating it. When she became convinced that the city had not spread to Mount Zion (the western ridge) until the first century A.D., Kathleen wanted to locate the western wall of the Jebusite and Davidic city on Ophel. Again, she made her argument using negative evidence. Excavation on several small sites just below the western crest of Ophel showed no Bronze or Iron Age deposits, so K concluded that the wall must have been built on what would have been a natural defensive position: the western edge of the eastern ridge. Extensive quarrying on Ophel during the Roman and Byzantine periods, however, made such occupation impossible to prove; if there had been a wall, earlier generations had removed it. K was nevertheless confident of her position. She was, however, good-natured enough to repeat, even while defending her interpretation, her friend Père de Vaux's remark that her plans of Jerusalem "consisted of a hypothetical line which happened to fit in with a few fixed points."[82] Her sketch of the outline of Jebusite and Davidic Jerusalem showed the city to have occupied about eleven square acres (Figure 7.8).

The admittedly limited archaeological evidence suggested that the original Jebusite city was not much altered after its conquest by the Israelites, ca. 1000 B.C. The terraces on the eastern slope of Ophel remained in use; the original Middle Bronze Age wall on the eastern slope also continued in use until about the seventh or eighth century B.C. Around that time it was replaced by another wall slightly uphill to the west. K believed that this wall had been rebuilt a number of times, but that some of the rebuilds had so completely disappeared due to the steepness of the slope that she could only infer their existence. (Later archaeologists disagreed that the wall had been repeatedly rebuilt.) K speculated that some of these repairs belonged to the time of King Hezekiah, ca. 700 B.C., when he was trying to defend against the Assyrians.[83]

But the most dramatic change in the outline of the early city occurred as a result of the Babylonian Exile, when the city was conquered and its inhabitants deported to Babylon. Early on, K's excavations indicated that on the eastern slope of Ophel, no remains were dated later than the destruction of the city by Nebuchadnezzar ca. 587 B.C. Further excavation revealed that when

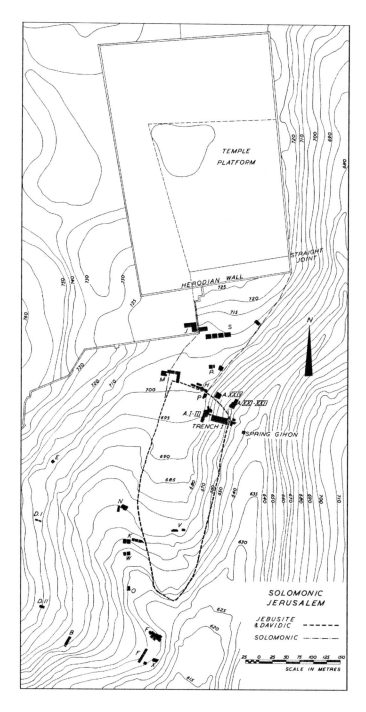

FIGURE 7.8: Plan of Jebusite, Davidic, and Solomonic Jerusalem.
Courtesy of the Council for British Research in the Levant.

187

Nehemiah rebuilt the walls about 440 B.C., they were built not down the slope, but on the crest of the ridge, probably because the population of the city was so small at the time. Since the Siloam Tunnel had in all probability been built by Hezekiah some 250 years earlier (ca. 700 B.C.), water could be channeled from the Gihon spring in the Kidron Valley at the base of the eastern slope of Ophel into a reservoir in the central valley, the Tyropoeon. Thus, it was no longer necessary to have walls far enough down the eastern slope to protect the entrance to the spring.

Kathleen also had hopes that excavations on one of her sites within the Old City might turn up the walls of post-Exilic or Maccabean Jerusalem. The excavations of C. N. Johns near the Citadel on the western edge of the Old City had uncovered evidence of the Maccabean walls, and K wanted to dig south of the Citadel at a site known as the Armenian Garden, located in the extreme southwest of the Old City. K was happy that she could turn over the excavation of this site to her friend Doug Tushingham who, with his wife Maggie, was able to join the expedition in 1962, representing the Royal Ontario Museum. The site was a large one, a pleasant change from the cramped conditions of most of the other excavation areas in Jerusalem. She was confident that the site would illuminate the development of the city on the western ridge, and was reasonably optimistic about finding remains of Hadrian's Aelia Capitolina, and the legionary camp established by Titus during the first Jewish revolt; possibly even part of Herod the Great's palace might be uncovered. Excavation in the Armenian Garden would continue through the end of the dig but, despite K's high hopes, proved disappointing. Some Roman remains and seventh-century B.C. material were found, but Doug Tushingham (and K) argued that the area wasn't occupied until the fifth century A.D. And although some significant Byzantine and Islamic remains were identified, this wasn't really what interested K. Tushingham did uncover a fragment of a lovely mosaic which K thought politic to have restored and sent to the Armenian Patriarch as a way of thanking him for letting them dig on the site.[84]

Kathleen was also interested in New Testament Jerusalem. Ancient Jerusalem reached its greatest extent—310 acres—under the grandson of Herod the Great, Herod Agrippa (A.D. 40–44). K had already argued that in the first season she had shown how Herod Agrippa had expanded the city to the south. According to the historian Josephus, he had also expanded the city to the north by adding another—or third—north wall. When K's excavations began, scholars believed that this wall was either on the same line as that of the present north wall of the Old City, or was another wall that ran about 400 meters to the north which had been discovered in the 1920s by Eleazar Sukenik and L. A. Mayer. Kathleen claimed to settle the question. She uncovered a foundation trench for the northernmost wall that included coins dated to the late A.D. 50s, making it too late to have been built by Herod Agrippa. Arguing that this wall faced south rather than north, and that its shoddy masonry indicated it had been built in a hurry, K began by thinking it was the south wall of Titus's camp, but came to believe it had been built by Titus to encircle the population during his siege of the city.[85]

This left the other possibility, which was that the third north wall, the wall of Herod Agrippa, ran along the line of the north wall of the sixteenth-century Old City. While K could not claim to have provided any evidence of this herself, she did think some of her students had. In 1964 the British School of Archaeology in Jerusalem, in cooperation with the Jordanian Department of Antiquities, began excavating along the north wall of the Old City at the Damascus Gate, first under Crystal Bennett and then Basil Hennessy. These excavations found the foundation trench of the original wall and showed that the wall under the Damascus Gate was no earlier than the first half of the first century A.D. and so probably attributable to Herod Agrippa.[86]

COMING UP WITH SOLUTIONS to old problems and continuing to outline the history of the evolution of the city was no doubt satisfying, but it didn't solve the problem of K's need for objects. Unlike Jericho with its artifact-filled tombs, Jerusalem was not providing the kind of complete objects that were so desirable. However, while digging on the eastern slope of Ophel, K located some of the most interesting finds of the Jerusalem excavations. North of Trench 1 the excavators came upon a shallow cave in the rock face, around which had been built a small enclosure plastered with mud. Within the walls of the enclosure was a large cache of intact pots which made Kathleen remember wistfully the hundreds of wonderfully preserved vessels found at Jericho. Adjacent was what appeared to be a cult center—a small room with two oblong monolithic pillars which K interpreted as cult stones or *mazzeboth*, like those condemned by the prophets of Israel because of their association with Canaanite deities. Nearby were the remains of what looked like an altar. This allowed K to interpret the pottery cache as a *favissa*, a repository for sacred vessels offered to a god and so no longer suitable for ordinary purposes[87] (Figure 7.9). The evidence of an unorthodox cult just outside the city walls

FIGURE 7.9: Cache of pottery K interpreted as a *favissa* near a sanctuary.
Courtesy of Jeremy Ritchie.

was archaeological testimony of the chasing after strange gods that the Hebrew prophets constantly railed against.

This wasn't even the most dramatic find in this area. In the 1966 season Andrew Moore, an Oxford undergraduate, was excavating in a square north of Trench 1 when he came upon a small niche in the side of a stone wall which had a large green object jammed into it. Immediately he suspected it was some sort of metal object. And right away he realized how important it would be to find a metal object in an Iron Age level at Jerusalem.

Kathleen, as bad luck would have it, was nowhere around. She had gone to lunch with General Odd Bull, head of the United Nations Truce Supervisory Commission at the old Government House of the Mandate, to which she had last been when she attended a dance there in 1935. Although security at Government House was extremely tight (located as it was between the Jordanian and Israeli sectors), K was let in the gate without proper authorization. A policeman whose young sons worked for her waved her through saying, "I know Miss Kenyon."[88]

While K was still away at lunch, Moore had his workmen clear carefully around the unknown object, without disturbing it. When everyone went back to the British School at 2 pm for lunch, he stayed put, sending a message to K to come when she could. She arrived back at the British School around 3 pm, looking forward to her afternoon siesta. But upon receiving this message, she quickly changed into dig clothes and hurried out to Ophel to see what was up.

By the time K arrived, a small crowd had gathered. Trying to hide her excitement at what would turn out to be the best find in Jerusalem so far, K squeezed herself into the small open space and with some effort, carefully and slowly extracted the object herself. It turned out to be several objects—a nest of buckets, a small bronze bucket with an iron handle, inside of which was another bronze bucket and inside of that a bronze jug. Alongside the buckets were several small, decayed iron objects.

Although they were simply ordinary household objects, these buckets were extraordinary, even unique finds, for they were the first bronze vessels found at a Palestinian town site rather than in a tomb. The outer bucket was in such good shape that it still held water from the previous winter's rains. The inner vessels were in much worse condition, and Cecil Western decided they needed more conservation than could be done in Jerusalem. They would have to go to the British Museum, and as soon as possible. This set in motion the somewhat melodramatically named "Operation Buckets of Blood": Kathleen phoned the British Embassy in Amman. The Embassy cabled the Foreign Office in London which contacted the airline BOAC. BOAC flew the buckets to London via diplomatic pouch, where they passed through customs as "used domestic utensils" before being whisked straightaway to the British Museum (Figure 7.10).

The excavations in Jerusalem would end on an even more dramatic note.

FIGURE 7.10: The smaller of the bronze buckets. *Courtesy of Jeremy Ritchie.*

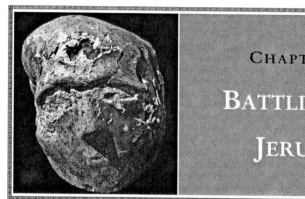

CHAPTER EIGHT

BATTLING OVER JERUSALEM

IN 1966 KATHLEEN'S ARCHAEOLOGICAL efforts were disrupted by her responsibilities as a Trustee of the Palestine Archaeological Museum for, in November of that year, the Museum was nationalized. Awni Dajani, the Director of Antiquities, had wanted to do this for years. When Jerusalem got a new governor, Dajani approached him on the matter, candidly admitting to K that the move had nakedly political and nationalistic motives.

Through Dajani, the new governor, Anwar Khatib, called an emergency meeting of the Trustees of the PAM to discuss the takeover of the museum by the government of Jordan.[1] K was not really surprised. She had long seen this as a real possibility. And she had no objection in principle to Jordan eventually assuming responsibility for the museum. But she was convinced that at present, the Jordanians were simply not prepared to run it properly, having no one in the Jordanian Department of Antiquities with any museum training. Yosef Saad, the present curator, was competent enough to work under the direction of the trustees, but K feared what would happen if the Department of Antiquities were to take over the administration of the museum. Her opinion was influenced in large part by the museum in Amman which she thought thoroughly disorganized.[2]

At the meeting of the trustees with Khatib on August 6, K was blunt about the lack of trained personnel and the disarray of the Amman Museum. The trustees managed to persuade him to agree that the PAM would not change hands until December 1. Before then, an Advisory Council (made up of representatives of the same international bodies the trustees represented) would be established that would advise on the appointment of a director to run the museum.[3] K insisted that this director must have museum training, and she fully expected that one would be brought in from abroad.[4]

Nevertheless, the Department of Antiquities gave signs of its determination to take over the PAM as soon as possible, and the trustees called another emergency meeting with the governor, hoping to prevent a premature takeover. He promised that nothing except an inventory of museum contents would take place until the appointment of a director and the new advisory body.[5] Yet, the next morning the *Jerusalem Times* proclaimed, "Government Takes Over Museum Here," and Department of Antiquities officials showed up at the museum, taking over Yosef Saad's office and demanding official documents.

K was furious. She was particularly angry that according to a *Jerusalem Times* article, the Department of Antiquities had appointed a committee to inventory the PAM's contents, charging that official records of the museum were incomplete and implying that valuable objects were missing.[6] Incensed that the trustees and Saad, whom she considered quite capable, should be accused of incompetence at best and dishonesty at worst, she shot off another letter of protest to Anwar Khatib, ending, "I realize that you must feel that I am always the person to make trouble. I can assure you that this is only because I am so deeply interested in the Museum and its future, and am so very interested in Jordan's good name."[7]

K's letter to the governor and another one from Père Pierre Benoit (President of PAM's Board of Trustees) to the Jordanian Prime Minister must have done some good because the Department of Antiquities began to back off a bit. Nevertheless, despite some indications that Gerald Harding, former Director of Antiquities, might be made director of the museum, at least temporarily,[8] in October Aref el Aref was suddenly appointed Director-General, without consultation with the trustees. Although K knew that Aref, a historian and former civil servant, was a well-respected individual, she did not believe him qualified to run the museum, and still hoped that Harding might be brought in as an advisor.[9] He was, but only for a short three months. In addition, Saad left in January, refusing to work at the PAM any longer.[10] In the months after the nationalization became official in December of 1966, the museum began to deteriorate.[11] K, as a member of the new Advisory Council, did all that she could from Oxford, having her contacts in Jordan keep an eye on the situation and writing nagging letters to the new Director-General. Finally, Aref summoned the Advisory Council to a meeting on July 3, 1967. But the Council was never to meet—for by July, the Museum was no longer in Jordanian hands.

SINCE 1948 JERUSALEM HAD been a divided city. A demilitarized No-Man's Land running roughly north to south, along the western wall of the Old City, divided the two sides. The reality of the military situation affected Kathleen's excavation. She couldn't, for example, look for evidence of Jerusalem's spread to the top of the western ridge because this was No Man's Land. The Armenian Garden was in the extreme southwest corner of the Old City where the army had dug trenches along the inside of the wall, and permission from the military authorities was needed to dig here.

The members of the Jerusalem excavations were always well aware that they were living in disputed territory. They knew that if they went through the Mandelbaum Gate into the Israeli sector, they wouldn't be allowed back into Arab Jerusalem. The occasional careless student stumbled into the zones that were off limits. One of the site supervisors who accidentally wandered into No-Man's Land was arrested by the Jordanian authorities and K had to retrieve him. On another occasion, two young men who had been out for an evening of drinking found themselves in what they suddenly realized were the minefields surrounding Hadassah Hospital. The discovery sobered them up considerably. Sometimes shots rang out over the border. One evening the group having drinks on the roof of the British School had to scramble down when firing began. The next morning spent bullets were found on the roof.

Tensions had remained high in the Middle East after the disturbances of 1956. Using Syria as a base, terrorists continued to launch attacks on Israel through Lebanon or Jordan, and by June of 1967 these tensions had reached a breaking point. In May the Soviet Union—wrongly as it turned out—informed the Egyptian government that Israel was planning to invade Syria. Egypt began rather ostentatiously preparing for war, to the great approval of the Arab world, sending troops into the Sinai. On May 17 President Nasser asked the UN to withdraw its troops from between Egypt and Israel. He also declared his decision to close the Straits of Tiran to Israeli shipping, an act Israel was bound to regard as an act of war. Despite recent tensions between Egypt and Jordan, the situation drew the countries closer together, and they agreed to a mutual defense pact. War was on the way.

By late May hostilities were clearly imminent, and the American and British consulates had advised their citizens to leave. Basil Hennessy, Director of the British School since November 1965, evacuated the residents of the School, including his wife and children, to Cyprus. On the morning of Monday, June 5, war broke out when the Israeli air force attacked and destroyed the Egyptian air command. Wednesday morning K phoned Rik Wheeler from the Principal's Lodging at St. Hugh's to tell him that Hennessy, who should have been in Jerusalem, was asleep in one of her spare rooms. The next morning Hennessy was in London, standing before Wheeler who as much as accused him of cowardice, dereliction of duty, and desertion in the face of the enemy. The interests of the School needed to be protected, and members of the BSAJ believed that having the director there during a time of crisis was critical. Hennessy's apparent desertion was a serious matter.

Hennessy's story was quite different. At the time, the BSAJ was in the process of moving to a new building in the Sheikh Jarrah quarter of the city, and he had found someone to take over the lease of the Husseini building, the current site of the British School. By late May, the prospective tenant, however, seemed to be backing out. Hennessy was afraid he was going to get stuck paying rent on two buildings and became convinced he needed go to London to see the Council of the BSAJ and explain his predicament. Consulting several knowledgeable people—including General Bull of the UN—he was told he probably had time to fly to London and back before war broke out. Accordingly, he left on June 4. By the time he arrived in Cyprus, where he had stopped en route to see his family, the fighting had started. He telephoned Kathleen to explain his situation, and she told him to continue on to England.

Basil Hennessy's and Rik Wheeler's recollections of subsequent events also differed. Wheeler claimed he told Hennessy he *would* go back to Jerusalem, which by this time had been taken by the Israelis. According to Hennessy, when Wheeler asked him if he wanted to return, he replied, "Of course." In all this K supported Hennessy, who was, after all, her student and a skilled archaeologist who had done a good job running the British School. She particularly objected to the high-handed way Wheeler had treated Hennessy, a fact that would later cause some friction between them.

Pulling the necessary strings, Wheeler got himself and Hennessy on a flight to Tel Aviv, where they caught a taxi to Jerusalem. The next evening they attended, as the guests of Carmella Yadin, wife of Yigael Yadin, a victory concert given by the Israeli Philharmonic Orchestra to celebrate the capture of East Jerusalem. Through the intervention of the Israeli Director of Antiquities Avraham Biran, Hennessy and Wheeler were driven into East Jerusalem on June 11, the day after the war ended, past dead bodies and the detritus of war, to the British School, which had already been looted. Wheeler dropped Hennessy off there with instructions to hold the fort.

The Six Day War ended with Israel occupying East Jerusalem and what would become known as the West Bank. Kathleen's feelings about this were not ambivalent, as she made clear in a letter to *The Times* on June 19. Given the attention that it would generate, Kathleen's letter is worth quoting in full:

> From the beginning of the conflagration in the Near East, the United Kingdom has declared that it is neutral. But it was also made very clear that this neutrality would not allow Israel to be annihilated. This was in accord with the feeling of the western world. Israel as a state existed, even though it had been formed at the expense of the Arab occupants of Palestine. Its achievements had been remarkable and the bravery and determination of its inhabitants deserved our fullest admiration.
>
> At a time when it seemed very probable that Israel would be overwhelmed by the united strength of her Arab neighbours, it was made very clear that the west would not allow this to happen. Then the incredible happened, and it was not Israel but Jordan that was overwhelmed, the smallest and most vulnerable of the Arab powers and for long a very loyal ally of Britain.
>
> Surely just as a week or so ago we were saying that the Arabs must not be allowed to get away with the fruits of successful war, so we must now say that the Israelis must not be able to keep the fruits of their invasion. Israel should be made to return to her pre-existing frontiers. Only by insisting on this, and doing our best to enforce it, can our neutrality be said to mean anything.
>
> Admittedly, some adjustments of the frontier would be reasonable. The Gaza strip is irrelevant to Egypt, and has a future only as a part of Israel. Some guarantee must be given about Sharm esh Sheikh, though it must be remarked that this controls access to Jordan's only port, as well as to a subsidiary Israeli port. The Israelis understandably feel that the Old City of Jerusalem must not be lost to them. But it must be remembered that it is equally important to the Arabs, and is inhabited by them. It must also be pointed out that there was a Jewish Temple in Jerusalem from the

time of Solomon, c. 960 B.C. to A.D. 70, when it was destroyed by Titus, a period of 1,030 years. Only 40 years has to be added to that to the time David first captured Jerusalem.

After a period of Roman and Christian control, Jerusalem was conquered by the Arabs in A.D. 636. Since then it has been the third most holy city of the Islamic world, a period to the present date of 1,331 years, interrupted by a bare century of Christian control in the Crusader period. The Jews have no prescriptive right to Jerusalem.

It must be accepted that the Israelis cannot in the future be denied access to the Old City. Their interests and those of the Muslim and the Christians must be safeguarded, and this is surely a function of the United Nations. Jerusalem should become an open city, with an area perhaps stretching from the Mount of Olives to the east, and from Government House to the south, but to the north only from the walls of the Old City itself, for outside it is the Arab new city which is just as much an Arab achievement as is the other new city a Jewish achievement.

Sympathy in the west with the Israelis is natural, for we have many of their co-religionists among us, and because we have a guilt-complex over the terrible fate of the Jews in Europe. But what most people do not remember today is that there was not a convenient empty space in the eastern Mediterranean to which the Jews could return after a diaspora of nearly 1,900 years. The creation of the state of Israel meant the expulsion or flight of about a million Arabs. This is the injustice the Arabs cannot stomach.

From 1952 to 1958 I carried out, as Director of the British School of Archaeology in Jerusalem, annual campaigns of excavations at Jericho. Our nearest neighbours were the 30,000 refugees in the Ain es Sultan camp. They were kept alive and healthy by the U.N.W.R.A., supported by Britain and America. The women were kept busy with household chores, but the men had no worthwhile occupation. Their thoughts were with, and their conversation about, their own houses, fields, shops and olive groves which they had inherited from their fathers.

This bitter sense of injustice remains. It will only be multiplied many times if a yet further area is seized by Israel. This is not the way to peace. It is a contribution to the build-up of greater antagonism.

Every effort must be made by the great powers to prevent it, if necessary by sanctions. If we were prepared to intervene if the war went one way, we should be prepared to intervene now that it has gone the other.[12]

Hoping to complete the final season despite the recent changed political situation, K went out to Jerusalem in early July to assess conditions on the ground. Things were less grim than feared: she found that the expedition's tools had been safely stored in the home of one of her foremen, and more damage had been done to her trenches by the winter rains than by the fighting. For the first time K had to deal with the Israeli authorities, but all went smoothly and she had no complaints about the Israeli Department of Antiquities. Despite her letter to *The Times*, she had a cordial meeting with Avraham Biran, who quickly agreed to give her the necessary Israeli permit to continue her excavations. Political reality made it necessary for K to get Israeli permission, but given her long history of association with the Jordanians and her belief that the Israeli occupation was illegal, she felt obligated to get Jordanian permission as well. So she set out for Amman, not being able to go the short distance across the Allenby bridge but having to fly to Cyprus and Beirut first. Her mission successful, she returned to Jerusalem at the end of July to begin excavations on August 4.[13]

Because of the delay and uncertainty, many people had made other plans in the meantime and could not—or would not—come. K was so shorthanded that she had to contact people she had initially rejected. But she managed to scrape together a relatively small crew of nineteen for the final season. Although she had been worried that she wouldn't be able to get her Jericho men, in the end she was able to report back to London that she was equipped "with a number of skilled old hands from Jericho."[14]

Many, including Kathleen, did not find it pleasant excavating in what had recently been a war zone and what was, in their view, occupied territory. They had the inconveniences of curfews, roadblocks, and the swarms of Israeli tourists who, so long barred from sites integral to the Jewish tradition, were eager to visit the site of the city of David. In some ways administration of the dig was made more complicated. Despite Israeli labor regulations, K was permitted to pay her workers at Jordanian rather than Israeli rates, but high inflation still meant that the money she had raised for three months barely lasted two. Numerous Israeli archaeologists—to K it seemed "every archaeologist in Israel"[15]—visited the excavations, many more than once. While the interest was flattering, it meant that she spent more time than she really wanted giving tours of the sites. K found the Israeli Department of Antiquities "excellent to deal with and most cooperative. There is the snag that they are so interested that they keep visiting one and having to be shown round," although she conceded that "perhaps this is better than the opposite extreme that we have been used to!"[16] .

Some annoyances were more serious. Many disapproved of the Israeli occupation and found it difficult to see their Arab friends under enemy occupation. Some of the members of the crew were offended—and deeply disturbed—by what they saw as the malicious and unnecessary harassment of, even gratuitous cruelty to, the Arab population. Tom Holland had a particularly nerve-wracking experience. He was still living in the old British School, in the Husseini building, while many of the others were in the new British School in Sheikh Jarrah, where meals were served. One evening after dinner the archaeologists heard an enormous explosion coming from the direction of the Husseini building. Rushing to the site they discovered that the Israelis had blown up the building next door. When Holland went up to his room, he discovered that all the windows had been blown out and broken glass covered his bed.

Despite such unpleasantness, it was a successful season, if only two months' long rather than the usual three. Kathleen was able to finish most of the work that she had planned to do, even if she wasn't able to excavate to bedrock everywhere. The most sensational find was made late in the season. Within the last two weeks of the dig, near the cache of pottery found in an earlier season, excavators located another cave and what was at the time the largest cache of pottery ever found in the Holy Land—some 1300 intact objects including jugs, bowls, lamps, and the largest cooking pot ever discovered. Among the artifacts were a number of human and animal figurines. Most of the human figures were female, interpreted as typical fertility symbols, associated with a fertility cult.

Some of the animal figures were horses with a disk on their forehead, which K guessed was associated with the worship of the sun. K provisionally interpreted the cache as another *favissa*, or divine offering, dating it to ca. 700 B.C.

This was a tremendous piece of luck. But coming so close to the end of the season, the excavators had to scramble to excavate, plan, and clear the cave. Moreover, all of the finds had to be conserved, drawn, and photographed properly. The cost of hiring the necessary people to do this used up the remaining funds of the dig. The Jerusalem expedition was completely broke.

SO, WITH THIS DISCOVERY, the Jerusalem excavations ended on at least a minor note of triumph. Still, it must have been a bitter way for Kathleen to end her career in the Middle East. She was certainly unhappy to see the West Bank and East Jerusalem in Israeli hands; she never considered the Israeli occupation legitimate, continuing to refer to these areas as "Israeli-occupied Jordan."[17] Her letter to *The Times* no doubt played a role in persistent rumors that she was anti-Semitic and refused to excavate under the Israelis. While she certainly did not relish the changes she saw taking place in East Jerusalem,[18] this was not the reason she ceased excavation after 1967. The Jerusalem excavations had originally only been expected to last five years or so. The seventh season, in 1967, was already intended to be the final one. At the age of 61, despite her passion for digging, K had many good reasons to retire from fieldwork, the completion of the Jericho and Jerusalem publications not least among them. If anything, the changed circumstances provided a temptation to go on; she seems to have contemplated additional seasons since some areas, such as the crest of Mount Zion, the western ridge, were now accessible. But as this would have delayed publication even further and as a considerable amount of money had been raised on the basis of concluding the excavations in 1967, she decided to make that year the final season as planned.[19]

But some have interpreted Kathleen's retirement from fieldwork as evidence of her political attitudes. To be sure, she did not attempt to hide where her sympathies lay, and this unquestionably affected her reputation. Eight years later an article by Hershel Shanks appeared in his new publication, *Biblical Archaeology Review*, asking "Kathleen Kenyon's Anti-Zionist Politics—Does It Affect Her Work?" Although the term he used was "anti-Zionist," more than one archaeologist interpreted Shanks as accusing her of anti-Semitism.

Was K an anti-Semite? Kathleen Kenyon was certainly not anti-Semitic if by that is meant dislike of Jews. Everyone who knew her well agrees. She was undoubtedly anti-Zionist. Convinced that Israel had been established at the expense of an innocent Palestinian population, she thought the Israeli occupation of the West Bank and annexation of Arab Jerusalem were wrong and illegal, and she never recognized Israel's claim over land acquired in 1967. She became involved with the Council for Arab- British Understanding, an organization formed after the Six Day War to promote understanding of the Arab point of view. On the other hand, she was willing to recognize Israel's existence as a fact, as her letter to *The Times* makes clear, and she clearly felt great sympathy for the suffering of the Jews under the Nazis.[20]

Undeniably, she had the prejudices of her upbringing. She was a product of the British Empire, and more than a little (what might now be termed) ethnocentric. A story is told about Kathleen being shown around Jerusalem after 1967 and having the Wolfson Towers, named after a British businessman and philanthropist, pointed out to her as a building named for one of her countrymen. "He's not my countryman," K retorted. "He's from Glasgow. And he speaks like a Glaswegian."[21] A Scot was not an Englishman.

It should not be surprising if, especially as a young woman, her habits of speech reflected the common prejudices of the age. When she was in her twenties, K wrote to Nora about being out to lunch, noticing the two women at the next table and "thinking what perfectly awful Jews they looked." Suddenly one of them turned and spoke to K, who was startled to realize that the ladies were acquaintances of hers.[22] K understood what a stereotypical Jewish appearance was supposed to be and that she didn't like it. In her time and place, it was not so terrible to say so. Kathleen's experience probably mirrored that of her contemporary Agatha Christie, of whom Henrietta McCall wrote, she "often made rather derogatory references to Jews in her books, as did many people of her age and class in conversation at the time. The horrors of the Second World War cured most of them of this unthinking prejudice."[23] The same could likely be said of Kathleen. No evidence in her personal or professional correspondence indicates race hatred or religious bigotry of any kind.

Other evidence, in fact, suggests the reverse. Her contact with the Israeli archeological establishment was limited before 1967 because the Jordanian authorities would have made it difficult for her to travel in Israel and still excavate in Jordan. Israelis were not permitted in Jordan at all,[24] but she trained Israeli students, such as Claire Epstein and B. S. J. Isserlin, in Britain and was on good professional terms with Israeli colleagues such as Trude Dothan, Magen Broshi , Yigael Yadin, and Nahman Avigad (with whom she had played tennis at Samaria in the 1930s).[25] After 1967, when she was no longer excavating in Jordan and so free to do so, she traveled in Israel regularly, visiting archaeological sites and debating with Israeli archaeologists (Figure 8.1). In the late summer of 1967, just after the war, she visited the American excavations at Gezer. After the war she also offered the Israeli Department of Antiquities assistance in obtaining a specialist from the British Museum to help with the preservation of the Dead Sea Scrolls (most of which were now in the possession of the Israelis), even if it meant resisting the British Foreign Office, which tended to be pro-Arab and anti-Israel.[26] Whatever her views of the legality and morality of the Israeli takeover, her principal concern continued to be archaeology.

In the immediate aftermath of the war, no one knew precisely what the long-term future of a British School of Archaeology in an Israeli Jerusalem would be. Kathleen believed that in the future it would be best to restrict the British School's excavations to eastern Jordan (that is, the non-occupied part) in order not to jeopardize the School's relations with the Arab world.[27] Shortly after the war ten members of the BSAJ (of whom Kathleen was *not* one) wrote a letter to Rik Wheeler as Chairman, requesting a special meeting to discuss whether or not to allow the School to remain in Jerusalem. Their aim was to transfer the School to Amman. Wheeler's position was that the BSAJ was a

FIGURE 8.1: Kathleen, Benjamin Mazar (*center*), and Avraham Biran (*far left*) at the Temple Mount excavations, ca. 1969/70. *Courtesy of Dr. Eilat Mazar.*

government-funded body specifically designated to support a school in Jerusalem, and Her Majesty's Government would not support such a relocation. K seems to have sided with Wheeler at this juncture, pointing out that because the School had been caught moving from one location to another, and was obligated to pay two rents at present, they did not have the resources to support an additional establishment in Amman. But she suggested that if independent funds could be obtained, a sort of outpost of the BSAJ could be set up in Amman. This was how matters were left for the time being. It was an issue that did not go away.[28]

The Six Day War also had unhappy consequences for K's friendship with Rik Wheeler. K was not only furious with Wheeler for the way he handled the Hennessy affair, but also because he took Hennessy with him to the victory concert given by the Israeli Philharmonic Orchestra. K (as well as many others) saw this as compromising the British School in the Arab world. The Basil Hennessy affair, according to Wheeler's biographer, did "lasting damage" to their long friendship and was "largely responsible for a clash between them that autumn."[29] In March of 1966 Wheeler had himself suggested that it was time for him to retire as Chairman of the School in Jerusalem and for K to take over. Subsequently, he had announced that he would wait until the Jerusalem excavations were over, since he had decided it would not be appropriate for Kathleen to become Chairman while still directing a major excavation for the BSAJ.[30] In the fall of 1967, however, several members of the Council were concerned that Wheeler's resignation so soon after the June war might be misconstrued.[31] Nevertheless, Wheeler wanted to resign but, according to Jacquetta Hawkes, he now considered Kathleen unsuitable after her open display of pro-Arab sympathy, refusing, however, to oppose her himself because of their long-standing friendship. K was duly elected Chairman of the BSAJ at the end of 1967. For her part (again, according to Hawkes), K was angry at Wheeler, maintaining that his opposition was actually rooted in her defense of Basil Hennessy. Furthermore, she even suspected that he might use his position in the British Academy to retaliate: "There is one real reason why I might not be considered suitable, and that is that there might be discrimination against the School in approaches to the Treasury through the British Academy. I am afraid things are as bad as that."[32] Despite this controversy, or perhaps because of it, Wheeler was quite gracious at the annual general meeting at which she was elected, reminding those present that had it not been for Kathleen, the British School would not have been reestablished after the

Second World War.[33] And despite whatever ill will the incident generated at the time, and whatever fears K may have had, Wheeler continued to support both K and the BSAJ.

MANY BELIEVED THAT JERUSALEM was not the grand finale that Kathleen's career deserved. This was in part because after 1967, Israeli archaeologists occupied what K must have thought an enviable position, much freer to excavate where they liked and for longer periods of time, sometimes year round, with extensive government support. In the next decade alone, more of Jerusalem would be excavated than had been done in the entire previous century. Consequently, K's accomplishments were to a large extent overshadowed and some of her conclusions modified.

The earliest findings of these Israeli excavations called into question some of K's results. In February 1968 Benjamin Mazar began excavations south and southwest of the Haram esh-Sherif, known to the Israelis as the Temple Mount. Without obtaining the consent of the Moslem authorities, the expedition began by using a bulldozer to open up a large area for exploration. Almost immediately Mazar uncovered an immense building complex, several walls of which had previously been located by K's expedition, which he identified as an Umayyad (early Arab) palace.[34] Roland de Vaux, K's assistant director who had supervised this area for her, had argued instead that these were Byzantine structures, hospices build by the Emperor Justinian in the sixth century. K accepted de Vaux's view that these were Byzantine buildings that had continued in use until the eleventh century, and were partially rebuilt in the Umayyad period.[35]

Israeli archaeologists contend that K's failure to recognize the large administrative complex was an example of the drawbacks of her emphasis on narrow trenches. Part of the problem, however, may well have been that K had been much more restricted in where and how much she was permitted to dig, so close to the Moslem holy site. In fact, she was never able to conclude her investigations here because the Awqaf withdrew permission after two seasons. Kathleen herself never accepted Mazar's conclusions, holding his excavation methods insufficiently rigorous.[36]

But she was forced to revise her opinion in light of the findings of her old colleague from Samaria, Nahman Avigad. On the basis of the sites she dug in the Old City and the trial trenches on the eastern slope of the western ridge, Mount Zion, Kathleen had concluded that Jerusalem was confined to the eastern hill, Ophel, during the First Temple Period, that is, between the tenth and sixth centuries B.C. But when Avigad began excavating on the northern end of the western hill, in the Jewish Quarter of the Old City in September 1969, he found an eighth-century B.C. wall that he attributed to Hezekiah. Avigad speculated that the wall continued down to the present-day Jaffa Gate in the west, and turned east to encompass both the western and eastern ridges, joining the Upper City to the original City of David. Such an outline seemed plausible because it would encompass the Siloam Pool, also built by Hezekiah to hold the water transported by tunnel from the Gihon spring in preparation for the Assyrian siege of 710 B.C.[37] Kathleen did acknowledge that the city expanded to the western ridge much earlier than she had believed, but would only concede that it had done so at its northern end, remaining adamant that her trial trenches had demonstrated "quite conclusively" that the southern part of the ridge was not enclosed by a wall until the first century A.D.[38]

One problem with her theory was that it gave the eighth-century city a decidedly odd shape (Figure 8.2). Another was that it left the Pool of Siloam outside of the eighth-century city walls. To account for this apparent oddity, K suggested that the pool was not an open reservoir but a rock-cut underground cistern which would have been hidden from view; however, she frankly admitted that she had no archaeological evidence to support this interpretation other than a channel that she believed had been cut into the rock in order to conceal the outflow of the pool. The question of the layout of Jerusalem in the First Temple Period is still a matter of debate, although most archaeologists now appear to accept Avigad's view.

Subsequent Israeli excavators also undermined K's conclusion that Josephus's Third Wall had followed the line of the north wall of the sixteenth-century Old City and that the northernmost wall—the wall 450 meters north of the Old City known as the Sukenik-Mayer wall—was a barrier built by Titus during his siege of Jerusalem. In the early 1970s Sara Ben-Arieh and Ehud Netzer excavated along this wall and found evidence that it faced north, which it would not have done had it been a wall of circumvallation.[39] They concluded that it must be the Third Wall, which most scholars today are inclined to accept, although this question also does not appear to be definitively resolved.[40]

Scholars, of course, argue over the interpretation of evidence on a regular basis, attacking one another's conclusions as a matter of course. But in K's case some of the attacks became very personal. In particular, the debate over the size of Jerusalem led to the suggestion that political bias might affect her archaeological interpretations. Hershel Shanks's 1975 article raised the ques-

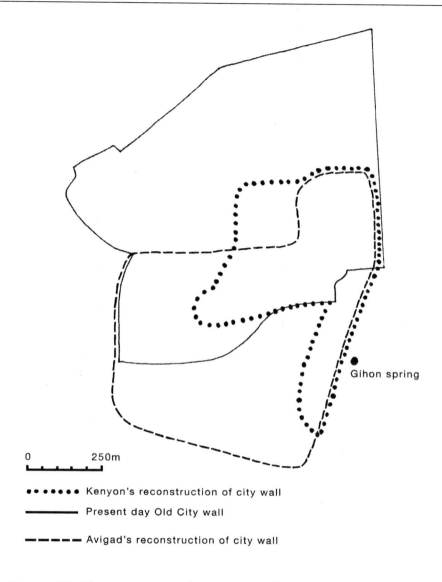

Gihon spring

●●●●●● Kenyon's reconstruction of city wall

———— Present day Old City wall

— — — — Avigad's reconstruction of city wall

FIGURE 8.2: Alternative views of ancient Jerusalem. *Drawing by Cindy Buob.*

tion explicitly. Although careful to point out that a number of her disagreements with Israeli archaeologists clearly had nothing to do with political differences, Shanks did raise the possibility that her minimalist views on the size of early Jerusalem—that is, her reluctance to acknowledge that the city had spread to the western ridge as early as the eighth century B.C.—was a result of her political predilections and a desire to minimize Jewish claims to the city. Not surprisingly, K was outraged by what she saw as an attack on her "professional integrity" and refused to respond to the question of her political views, tartly observing "that all real archaeologists would consider it quite unprofessional to enter into an argument with a critic, except on details of fact." She did, however, respond in print to specific questions Shanks had raised.[41]

No one who knew Kathleen Kenyon well believes that she would have deliberately skewed her archaeological conclusions to fit her political inclinations. Shanks himself did not claim to prove that she had. No doubt K disapproved of these Israeli excavations on principle; conducted in what she saw as occupied territory and so against UN conventions, she would have almost certainly thought them illegal. Admittedly, unconscious bias on her part, if it existed at all, would be almost impossible to prove. But if K's views reflected some sort of subconscious bias against Israeli archaeologists and their findings, is it likely that it had to do with something other than international politics. Among K and her peers, a sort of gentleman's agreement decreed that archaeologists did not start work on a site without consulting previous excavators.[42] The Mazar expedition, at least, did not observe this convention, and it is clear that some, perhaps including K, resented it.[43] But she was also always highly critical of Israeli methodology, believing that Israelis did not pay sufficient attention to stratigraphy. Finally, it must be said, whatever the merits of various arguments over the evidence, throughout her career Kathleen resisted changing her mind once she had made it up.

In fact, disagreement with K's conclusions about the size of early Jerusalem, as well as other of her conclusions, often reflects the most common critique of her excavations: she opened up areas that were too small and drew conclusions much broader than these small areas warranted. Archaeologist Amihai Mazar, for example, wrote that "[t]he results of the Israeli excavations in four areas of Jerusalem (south of the Temple Mount, in the Jewish Quarter, in the Armenian Garden and recently in the City of David) have proved many of Kenyon's conclusions wrong because these conclusions were based on sophisticated sections of debris layers in restricted areas."[44] Israeli archaeologists argued that they achieved more reliable results because they opened up wider areas. William Dever concurred, adding that Kathleen's "emphasis on sections may have been well suited to deep soundings on a typical tell like Jericho . . . but this approach did not prove satisfactory in dealing with monumental architecture, even residential areas, when expanses were so limited."[45] They had a point. Her results on the slope of Ophel, with its wider area of excavation, were more likely to be confirmed by subsequent excavation than results elsewhere. Yet, even here, excavations in later years made clear the advantages of opening up wide areas.[46] But as P.R.S. Moorey has pointed out, "her approach [in Jerusalem, as earlier at Samaria and Jericho] was as much a matter of tactics as of techniques. With the resources available to her, and the restricted areas accessible at the time, she believed that deep trenching and strict stratigraphical analysis were the most effective procedures."[47]

Although K worked on the publication of her excavations continually until her death, she never got around to even beginning the final report on Jerusalem. After she died, a subcommittee from the Council of the British School of Archaeology in Jerusalem took over responsibility for getting the final reports written, with Doug Tushingham serving as Honorary Editor-in-Chief. The volumes began appearing in due course: *Excavations in Jerusalem 1961–1967*, Volume I (1985) by Doug Tushingham was published first (he was, after all, writing up the results of his own work in the Armenian Garden); *Excavations in Jerusalem 1961–1967*, Volume II, *The Iron Age Extramural Quarter on the South-East Hill* (1990) was published by Henk Franken, who had dug at Jericho, and his student Margreet Steiner. Steiner also produced *Excavations by Kathleen M. Kenyon in Jerusalem 1961–1967*, Volume III, *The Settlement in the Bronze and Iron Ages* (2001); Kay Prag, one of K's Ph.D. students who had dug at Jerusalem (and took the title Director of the Ancient Jerusalem Project in 1993) produced, with Itzhak Eshel, *Excavations by K. M. Kenyon in Jerusalem 1961–1967*, Volume IV, *The Iron Age Cave Deposits on the South-east Hill and Isolated Burials and Cemeteries elsewhere* (1995). In 2005 Franken's *A History of Pottery and Potters in Ancient Jerusalem, Excavations by K. M. Kenyon in Jerusalem 1961–1967* appeared. And as of this writing, Kay Prag's *Excavations by K. M. Kenyon in Jerusalem 1961–1967: Discoveries in Hellenistic to Ottoman Jerusalem, Centenary Volume —Kathleen M. Kenyon 1906–1978*: Volume V (Levant Supplementary) is due to be published by Oxbow Books in February 2008.[48]

When a final report is written by someone other than the excavator, the resulting publication will probably not be what the original excavator would have produced. For example, Franken and Steiner rejected the pottery classification system K had used at Jerusalem, arguing that pottery shapes did not evolve as quickly as K had assumed, making "the accuracy that [she] had in mind impossible."[49] In addition, these reports reflected the interests of a discipline that had changed since the 1960s. Steiner, for instance, evaluated Jerusalem in its regional context, comparing it with other sites and considering its role in relation to those other sites,[50] questions that older generations of archaeologists had not attempted to address.

Some of K's preliminary conclusions published in her reports in the *Palestine Exploration Quarterly* and two popular books were revised. For example, the terraces on the side of Ophel that K had dated to the Bronze Age (fourteenth–thirteenth century B.C.), Steiner dated to ca. twelfth century B.C., the period of transition between the Late Bronze Age and the early Iron Age. (It should be noted, however, that many of K's dates for Jerusalem were tentative, and she said repeatedly that further precision would result from careful analysis of the pottery.) And while K had suspected that these terraces were built all down the eastern slope of Ophel, excavations by Yigael Shiloh had shown this not to be the case; Steiner suggested that the terraces were the foundation of some kind of fortification, rather than houses, as K had surmised.[51]

More ominously, however, Franken and Steiner's volumes revealed some serious problems with the records produced by the Jerusalem expedition, the authors reporting quite candidly that "the quality of the field documents is less than one would wish for."[52] Some of the plans and sections could not be found. They had either never been made or had vanished from the Jerusalem archive. In some cases the descriptions of stratigraphy could not be assigned to the sections to which they belonged, for lack of the necessary information. Some of the field notebooks kept by site supervisors lacked the locations of the layers they described; crucial information was sometimes missing from section drawings; some pottery phasing cards (used to keep track of how much of each type of pottery had been found in each structural phase) had not been updated when changes were made in the phasing of the layers (that is, when changes were made regarding which layers of stratigraphy would be grouped together to form a structural phase). This made the phasing and pottery cards essentially useless. Each archaeological deposit, identified on the basis of the texture and color of the soil, was supposed to receive its own number, but deposit numbers were never noted on the plans drawn by the surveyors at the end of each season.[53] All this was made worse by K's field notes, made in her own, often illegible handwriting.

How to explain these problems? Certainly, other scholars who used K's field records for other sites did not encounter such extensive difficulties. Ron Tappy found K's field notes from Samaria so thorough and meticulous that he was able to fruitfully reinterpret her results. Philip Kenrick was able to success-fully use the records from Sabratha to publish the excavation thirty years after its completion, noting that although some of the locations of the trenches were not noted in the archival material, her field notes were "basically pretty good."[54] Martin Biddle, a distinguished field archaeologist, the excavator of Winchester and now Professor of Archaeology at Hertford College, Oxford took issue with Hershel Shanks's claim that Steiner had documented "how incomplete, illegible, sloppy and just plain wrong [Kenyon's] excavation records are,"[55] writing that "[t]he 'slovenliness' of which Hershel Shanks accuses her is the antithesis of K as I saw her at work day after day for long hours drawing the main sections of Site H [at Jericho]."[56]

One explanation that accounts for certain difficulties with both the Sabratha and Jerusalem records is that K assumed she would be writing the final report: she knew where the trenches were located and which sections went with what trench. And, of course, she could read her own field notes. Known for her remarkable memory of the details of her sites, some of the information missing from the Jerusalem archives might well have been carried in K's head. She simply didn't anticipate the problems faced by someone else writing up her excavation notes. Kathleen was neither the first nor the last archaeologist to make this particular mistake.

Another possible explanation for the problems Franken and Steiner found is that Jerusalem was simply too much for Kathleen. The combined burdens of fundraising, administration, and excavation would have exhausted someone much younger. Conditions in Jerusalem were particularly trying: it was a com-plicated site to dig, and at any one time there might be half a dozen different excavation areas scattered throughout the city. Because K was committed to training students, she often took on relatively inexperienced field supervisors—who often changed from year to year—who may not always have been adequate-ly supervised. Certainly Steiner concluded that some were not. Franken himself had worked for K at Jericho and did not think that the quality of her work at Jerusalem matched it.[57] Even at Jericho there is evidence that Kathleen could be guilty of serious oversights. Willard Hamrick, for example, recalled that she neglected to give him proper instructions about keeping his site notebook.

So, in many respects Jerusalem indeed was not the farewell Kathleen should have had. Nevertheless, her very real accomplishments remain. She was the first to use modern stratigraphic techniques to prove that the City of David lay on the eastern ridge of Jerusalem and, in fact, the first to put the city's archaeology on a solid stratigraphic footing. And if many of the criticisms of her methods at Jerusalem and elsewhere have some merit, even the great archaeologists must be considered in the context of their times. As William Dever points out, advances in methodology wouldn't have been made without her: "Without Kenyon's bold efforts to grapple with the problems of three-dimensional recording of tells, the still newer methods would not have been possible."[58] And for that she should be remembered.

THE END OF THE 1967 SEASON was also the end of the useful life of the BSAJ's 1946 Pontiac, nicknamed "Ponty." The old wood-paneled station wagon had been on its last legs toward the end of the Jerusalem excavations, and someone suggested that a suitable end to the car—and the dig—would be to bury the vehicle in the massive trench in the Armenian Garden, which had to be filled in anyway. The interment ceremony was held with great fanfare (Figure 8.3): the lights were turned on (as for a funeral), and workmen pushed from behind as Doug Tushingham guided the car over the edge of the trench, jumping aside as the car rolled into its final resting place, the remainder of which was then filled in with a bulldozer. As she watched, K undoubtedly realized that this was the final moment of her final dig. And Kathleen Kenyon had tears in her eyes.

FIGURE 8.3: The end of the Jerusalem dig.
Courtesy of the Council for British Research in the Levant.

CHAPTER NINE

ST. HUGH'S AND ROSE HILL

B EING THE HEAD OF AN OXFORD college wasn't the same as directing an archaeological excavation. K couldn't simply give orders as she was accustomed to doing. The principal of St. Hugh's was no more than chairman of the Governing Body, which actually ran the college. To get anything done, she had to convince the Fellows of the College (who made up the Governing Body) by persuasion, using tact, negotiation, and compromise. The notoriously straightforward K excelled at none of these; she found this both frustrating and irritating. According to one of the college tutors Mary (later Baroness) Warnock, K "was inclined to lapse into talking to the Fellows as if we were native diggers,"[1] and to think them tiresome and recalcitrant when this did not work. Several members of the governing board later agreed that K could feel personally betrayed when Fellows she considered friends openly disagreed with her at meetings of the Governing Body. Although people who served with her on various archaeological committees believed that K respected people who stood up to her, she does seem to have expected the Fellows to follow her lead.

For their part, the Fellows seem to have had only a vague idea of K's professional accomplishments. Warnock, one of the most distinguished among them, thought that her contribution to archaeology consisted of "the discovery of new techniques for extracting fragile items unharmed from piles of rubble."[2] For the most part the Fellows thought Kathleen a bit out of place in an Oxford college, not truly an intellectual. On occasion, she unintentionally offered them amusement. For instance, when K and the College Fellows would meet for a drink before formally processing into the dining room for formal meals, K would knock back considerable quantities of gin. This meant that she had a tendency to garble the Latin grace recited before dinner, having particular difficulty with the phrase, *"quae ex liberalitate tua."* Nevertheless, the St. Hugh's Fellows were fond of Kathleen because she was hardworking, good-natured, and, above all, good for the college.

Even if the academic staff thought K inclined to be autocratic, the students did not; one student newspaper referred to her as "one of the least authoritarian" of the St. Hugh's staff.[3] Her young charges seem to have liked her or, at worst, considered her a distant, benign presence in their lives. The principal would not have seen much of them on an ordinary basis; day-to-day matters of discipline were taken care of by the dean. But K, with Vivienne Catleugh's help, did entertain undergraduates to sherry parties in the Principal's Lodgings. Never very good at small talk, K found making conversation with them trying and, as a result, few really enjoyed these parties. The clever ones quickly realized that she was considerably more interested in archaeology than she was in them and that the best way of drawing her into interesting conversation was to ask about her work. When one young woman asked about memorable finds from her excavations, she found the Principal "pleased by the question. She never gave the impression that her enthusiasm for her work had been touched by cynicism. She spoke first about a [gold] Roman ring, which she had found at [Leicester]. . . . It had come out of the ground as bright and fresh as the day it was buried. Then she described the skulls she had found at Jericho, with plaster faces moulded on them. She still spoke with wonder at their strangeness."[4]

If Kathleen was not particularly good at socializing with members of the Junior Common Room, she proved herself genuinely concerned with their best interests. Lacking the obsession of some of the dons with getting Firsts (not surprising, given her own undergraduate career), she wanted them to get the most out of their university experience. Cautioning that this would probably be their last chance for absolute freedom, she exhorted them to pursue their own interests, extracurricular as well as academic. She encouraged them to try acting, on one occasion directly contradicting a tutor who had earlier admonished the same group not even to think about it. Not all of her advice may have been equally welcome; she told one set of first-year students they shouldn't sleep so late in the mornings. But instances of her kindness and helpfulness abound: she let the Principal's Lodgings be used for a dance, gave an undergraduate whose housing arrangements fell through a place to live there, and suggested that St. Hugh's provide accommodations for overseas students during the vacations. Rachel Trickett, her successor at St. Hugh's, told this story:

On hearing at a dinner party that a young American who had just come up had been asked what he played (meaning rugger or soccer), and had replied 'the clarinet,' she laughed; but when her informant added that he had said, 'Not in my house, you don't,' she instantly put in, 'Well, he can play it in mine;' and he did.[5]

Perhaps remembering her own youthful impatience with rules and regulations, K was particularly sympathetic to student demands for greater autonomy, acknowledging that perhaps greater freedom was a good thing.[6] K's permission for the undergraduates to paint and redecorate their own rooms was thought sufficiently novel to merit a notice in *The Times*. Not only was St. Hugh's the first women's college to extend visiting hours for male visitors until 10 pm, but K's "late-night system," which allowed a single porter to let the students in however late they returned to the college (and thus not have to risk climbing over the wall), earned St. Hugh's the reputation of the most enlightened of the women's colleges. K was always willing to listen sympathetically to undergraduate desires and demands, and herself suggested the creation of a joint committee made up of both Fellows and undergraduates, which met regularly to discuss college matters. She did, however, expect them to go through proper channels: the occasion when the St. Hugh's girls staged a minor protest in the dining hall at dinner and presented her with a petition, upset her greatly. And although labeled a "progressive" by some,[7] the essentially conservative K was considerably less enthusiastic about the 1960s' greater sexual liberality, worrying that birth control advice being offered to unmarried women students would encourage promiscuity.[8]

One of the important achievements of K's tenure was the expansion of the college. Since the 1950s St. Hugh's had wanted to increase the numbers of undergraduates but in order to do, so needed the space to accommodate the additional bodies. Efforts had begun under her predecessor, but it was not until K's arrival that expansion got properly underway. The decision was made to begin building even before money had been raised. The new principal took an active part in the building projects, discussing plans, meeting with architects, and working hard to raise the necessary funds. The resulting construction meant that "St Hugh's for long periods during the [1960s] . . . resembled a construction camp,"[9] but student numbers (both undergraduates and postgraduates) went from 214 in 1960–1961 to 371 by the end of the decade.

By 1965 the New Building and the Buttery (a canteen that served light meals) had been completed, and with a grant given by the Wolfson Trust, work was begun on an additional building. Because this involved destruction of existing buildings, one of the college tutors organized a "demolition party." The records are circumspect, but plenty of gin seems to have been involved. As principal, K was invited and entered into the spirit of the thing, for she showed up with "her excavating tools . . . [and] knocked down a banister rail, chopped it into pieces, . . . [throwing] them through the skylight like darts."[10] The Wolfson Building was completed in 1967 and officially opened in May 1968 by Princess Alexandra (cousin to the Queen). K took the opportunity to introduce the royal visitor to her current badly behaved mongrel (he once bit a College Fellow), an airedale and collie mix named Angus, regaling the princess with the story of how the dog came to be named for her husband, Angus Ogilvy.[11]

Kathleen wasn't good at everything. She was generally agreed to be a clumsy and uninspiring speaker on college occasions such as the gaudies.[12] Although engaging on her own subject, she did not have a real grasp of what should be said in these circumstances; and just as she was hopeless at small talk, she never succeeded at being eloquent or witty at these affairs. Perhaps she realized this, for she made an effort to reduce the number of speeches she had to give on such occasions.

Characteristically, K was involved not merely with the college but with many aspects of Oxford life. She served on Hebdomadal Council, Oxford University's general policy-making board, where she earned a reputation for looking out for the interests of the colleges, particularly the women's colleges. Unfortunately it was in her efforts most closely associated with her field of archeology that Kathleen experienced her greatest failures. As a member of the Board of the Faculty of Anthropology and Geography (which also included prehistoric and European archaeology) she tried, unsuccessfully, to get archaeology accepted as an undergraduate degree course. A proposal for a joint honours school in Archaeology and Geography made some progress but in the end was rejected because of concerns that it would be difficult to arrange for the teaching of archaeology. Although there were a number of archaeologists in Oxford at the time, they were not organized into a single department and their efforts were not well coordinated. Much of the problem was the opposition of those like Christopher Hawkes, Kathleen's one-time dancing partner and now Professor of European Archaeology, who believed the subject should be taught only at the graduate level. By this time he and K were not on good terms, and his resistance may account in part for their unfriendly relations.

As Chairman of the Committee for the Pitt Rivers Museum, Kathleen was anxious to promote connections between archaeologists and anthropologists in the university as well as to raise funds for the development of the museum. But these plans were never realized, in large part because of circumstances over which K had no control. In addition, K failed in her efforts to reduce tensions between the anthropologists at the Institute of Social Anthropology and the ethnologists at the Pitt Rivers Museum. The relationships and rivalries involved were enormously complicated, and the academic politics involved were far too convoluted and Machiavellian for someone as straightforward as K to master; her best efforts achieved nothing. As with the Fellows of St. Hugh's, she may well have become frustrated with what she saw as the obstreperousness and recalcitrance of her university colleagues, for she told a reporter with a sigh, "It is hopeless at Oxford trying to get things through committee quickly. Everyone seems to want to have their say at great length."[13]

While archaeology at Oxford may have been K's greatest concern, the position of women in the university was also of genuine interest. She didn't actually think young women were as well off as they had been in her undergraduate days, in large part because they were getting married earlier; this, she was convinced, limited their academic prospects. Nevertheless, she wanted to increase the number and proportion of women at Oxford. The best way to do this, K believed, was through expansion of the existing women's colleges; hence her support of St. Hugh's building program. By the early 1970s, however, several of the men's colleges had proposed accepting women. According to one of her colleagues at St. Hugh's, K probably did not think that coeducational colleges would really be in the best interest of young women. Moreover, she was concerned about the impact of coeducation on the women's colleges. Yet, like the other principals of the women's colleges, she felt obliged to embrace any reform that would increase opportunities for women. In May 1972 a plan was debated in Congregation whereby five male colleges would admit women undergraduates for five years, at which time the experiment in coeducation would be reviewed. Kathleen spoke on behalf of the women's colleges:

> All five women's colleges have accepted this scheme. . . . We feel it would be wrong not to support what seems to be the easiest method of increasing the number of women at Oxford. . . . We also

would not feel it right to oppose a scheme whereby good academic women in the future would have the opportunity of fellowships at a man's college . . . with all the additional kudos and far greater financial reward. . . . But while we feel that we must accept the proposal, we are well aware that the immediate effect on the women's colleges may be very serious. . . . [T]here is a real risk that we shall drop back again into being second class citizens. . . . [G]irls may . . . put mixed colleges first, and we shall lose the best applicants. . . . [O]n one point we are clear — we are not going to drop our academic standards if the top of the list is creamed too much. Instead, the number of our entry must fall, and with it fee income. . . . I return to the fact that we have accepted the scheme put forward . . . [which is] a real and ordered experiment and not a rush into the unknown. We hope that the limitation in numbers will contain within acceptable limits any damaging results on the women's colleges. . . . If Congregation throws out or seriously modifies the Resolution . . . I believe the women's colleges will say that they cannot co-operate in a scheme to admit women to men's colleges that does not offer the proposed safeguards. The whole idea of Co-residence must surely then drop, for I hope that we can take it that no man's college will be sufficiently ungentlemanly to go forward ruthlessly over the collective dead bodies of the women's colleges.[14]

Yet, despite her position as the head of an Oxford college and her prominent role in the university itself, at a very basic level K remained a simple, relatively unsophisticated dirt archaeologist, an unpretentious woman who impressed "a terrified brand new undergraduate" with her naturalness and spontaneity by eating a prawn cocktail with her fingers. What this young woman, the same one to whom K waxed eloquent about the Leicester ring, took from her encounter with her college's principal was that, "in an age of smart restaurants, we could do with more people who eat with their fingers. In an age of cynical post-modernism . . . we could do with more people who never lose their wonder at the gleam of Roman gold in their own hand. We need more Kathleen Kenyons."[15]

THE NEW PRINCIPAL HAD made it clear when she took on St. Hugh's that her college responsibilities would not be allowed to interfere with the excavation of

Jerusalem. K agreed to remain in Oxford during the university term, condemning herself to digging during the hottest part of the year, a sacrifice that many of the Fellows at St. Hugh's probably did not fully appreciate. Not only was she away during the summer months, but she frequently had to make flying weekend visits to Jerusalem on Palestine Archaeological Museum and British School of Archaeology in Jerusalem business. One year, for example, she got a cable from Crystal Bennett, Assistant Director of the BSAJ, on the day after Christmas, announcing the discovery of a Crusader chapel at the Damascus Gate. K immediately dropped everything to fly out to Jerusalem.[16] Such travel was in addition to her normal load of college and university obligations, archaeological committee work, writing, and lectures all over the country. Her well-known stamina and energy stood her in good stead. Rachel Trickett recalled that Kathleen was known to "fly out to Jerusalem on a Friday morning; return on Monday evening; drive up to a prize-giving at some obscure school on the Tuesday; and conduct a Governing Body Meeting the following afternoon without showing any obvious signs of fatigue."[17] During the university term, K had time to pursue her own archaeological work only in the evenings. Still laboring diligently on the publication of both Sabratha and Jericho, she had packed the largest and most beautiful room in the Principal's Lodging with broken pottery. After a full day of college business, she would settle down to the writing up of her reports; passersby could see her light on late into the night.

Despite her objection to the Israeli takeover, K continued to visit Jerusalem regularly after 1967. Since losing her Jordanian excavation permit was no longer a risk, she was free to tour pre-1967 Israel as well. And she did. Whatever her views on Zionism or the occupation of the West Bank, Kathleen was considerably more interested in archaeology than international politics, telling Joe Callaway in 1968 that she planned to inspect Yigael Yadin's work at Hazor and Megiddo.[18] Sometimes in the 1970s she was escorted to Israeli archaeological sites by William Dever, head of the Albright Institute (formerly the American School of Oriental Research), or Graeme Auld, Assistant Director of the British School, or Crystal Bennett. She was coolly polite to those archaeologists of whom she disapproved, while getting into animated discussions with those she thought worth talking to. Dever recalled her visit to his excavation at Gezer in the late 1960s as one of the greatest days of his life in the field. For the Gezer crew, who were employing the Wheeler-Kenyon method, it was like a visit by royalty; everyone turned out to escort her around the site. After a while on this formal tour, however, K became restless, jumped into a trench, pulled a worn trowel out of her purse, and began scratching at the sections, explicating the stratigraphy to her surprised but eventually enthralled hosts. Her polite visit turned into an exhilarating four-hour seminar for the field director and crew. [19]

Kathleen remained critical of much Israeli archaeology, and in particular, Israeli archaeology in Jerusalem. Benjamin Mazar's excavations around the southwest corner of the Temple Mount (or Haram esh-Sherif) had come under fire both for being in violation of UN conventions against excavating in occupied territory and because of accusations that the excavations were done badly, in some cases actually endangering historic Islamic buildings. In 1974 condemnation of the Israeli excavations had resulted in sanctions being imposed against Israel by UNESCO as well as the exclusion of Israel from UNESCO's European region. K sided with the critics, protesting that tunneling along the western wall of the Haram esh-Sherif caused cracks in the Ribat Kurd, a thirteenth-century pilgrims' hospice built next to the Haram, and endangered other medieval buildings in the vicinity. Unsurprisingly, she also condemned the tunneling as very bad archaeology, as it destroyed stratigraphical evidence.[20]

Excavation in what was becoming known as the Occupied Territories continued to be a problem for the British School of Archaeology in Jerusalem. Members of the BSAJ, including K, wished to respect the UN's position that it was illegal, especially since Arab governments made it known that such excavation would be considered an "unfriendly act," which, it was feared, would have unfortunate repercussions for British archaeologists elsewhere.[21] Attempts were made to get around this prohibition. K had been able to complete the Jerusalem excavations because she had received the permission of the Jordanian, as well as Israeli, authorities. A subsequent BSAJ attempt to do the same did not meet with success: the Jordanians refused to give Basil Hennessy permission to continue his excavations at Samaria. By the summer of 1969, it was clear that the British School would be unable to conduct excavations in either Jerusalem or the West Bank for the foreseeable future.[22] So, excavation in the areas occupied by Israel, which included East Jerusalem, was out of the question, and the best that K could do was suggest that the BSAJ follow a policy of "lying low" for the time being.[23]

On the other hand, the Jordanian government did not want the British School moved from Jerusalem to Amman, because so doing would tacitly accept the Israeli occupation.[24] So Jordan, with which K sympathized, trapped the BSAJ: the School could not relocate to Amman in order to more easily supervise excavations east of the Jordan River, and it could not excavate at all in the West Bank or East Jerusalem. K despaired that "[p]rospects for continuing work in Palestine seem to get more and more gloomy."[25] The BSAJ dealt with this basically untenable situation in two ways. First, early in 1968 K suggested that while the BSAJ could not excavate in Jerusalem, it could begin an architectural survey of the Old City. Beginning modestly, this enterprise became the Jerusalem Architectural Survey, a ten-year project that resulted in the survey and recording of the Islamic buildings of medieval Jerusalem, many of which were later destroyed to permit redevelopment.[26]

In addition, even though the decision had been made not to relocate the BSAJ, a base of operations was clearly needed in Amman for British excavations in Jordan.[27] After 1967 the time-consuming and irksome border-crossing between Israeli-occupied Jerusalem and Jordan made overseeing archaeological projects in Jordan from Jerusalem awkward and inconvenient. Thus, early in 1968 two truckloads of excavation equipment were transported from Jerusalem to Amman.[28] What began as an effort to set up an Amman office of the BSAJ ended with the establishment of an autonomous institution. Crystal Bennett was primarily responsible for the creation of what became the Amman Institute and spent much of the 1970s running both the British School in Jerusalem and the office in Amman. Kathleen, however, fully supported her efforts, working to raise money from private sources and to secure a grant from the British Academy to support the Amman institution. Shortly before K's death in 1978, a grant was finally approved, and in 1980 Crystal Bennett became the first Director of the British Institute at Amman for Archaeology and History.

DOMESTICALLY, NOT MUCH CHANGED in these years. Vivienne Catleugh was still a fixture, running the house and, in many ways, K's life. The two women—K and Catleugh—were clearly dependent on each other but perhaps had lived together for too long; they frequently bickered, often to the embarrassment of their friends. Weekends were spent at the cottage in High Wycombe, where K gardened or worked on the Jericho pottery in the shed behind the house.

One cause for concern by the early 1970s was K's health. In her fifties and sixties she had put on a good deal of weight; her habits of eating and drinking were not conducive to slimness. A visitor dining at St. Hugh's noticed that K helped herself to two servings of the rich dessert.[29] She regularly consumed impressive quantities of alcohol, which, if rarely impairing her, certainly contributed to weight gain. Suffering from high blood pressure and shortness of breath, K made sporadic efforts at reform, going to a health spa on one occasion and, at one point, giving up smoking. But she didn't really take proper care of herself, much to Catleugh's aggravation, continuing to drink too much, eat too much, and work too hard. Andrew Moore, one of K's Ph.D. students, became convinced that she had had a heart attack in the early 1970s that she and Vivienne Catleugh were at pains to cover up.[30]

In the meantime, honors continued to accumulate. In 1964 Oxford had awarded her a doctorate on the basis of her many publications. In 1965 she had become a Trustee of the British Museum. She received the University of Glasgow Dalrymple Lectureship in Archaeology for 1968–1969 and gave the Haskell Lectures at Oberlin College in 1976. In 1969 the University of Exeter bestowed an honorary D. Litt. One of the awards of which she was most proud was conferred by King Hussein of Jordan when she was made Grand Officer, Order of Istiqlal. It was in 1973, however, that Kathleen's career received its crowning achievement, when she was named a Dame Commander of the Order of the British Empire, becoming Dame Kathleen, for "services to archaeology"[31] (Figure 9.1). Although Kathleen was extremely gratified by the honor, she reacted with her usual modesty: "It adds a lot to one's pleasure to know that one's friends are pleased, and they certainly have been embarrassingly kind. It is most satisfactory that archaeology has been recognized in this way."[32]

IN HER FINAL TERM AT St. Hugh's, Kathleen had the distinction of being asked by the undergraduates to give a talk on her own work, the first principal ever to be requested to give a lecture to the entire college. As she spoke on Jericho, K pointed to a slide of her Arab workmen. "They," she bluntly told the assembled young women, "were far less trouble to me than you are."[33] As gruff as she might have been, they clearly recognized her affection and concern for them, for this was not the final honor K received from the Junior Common Room. The undergraduates also asked that the New Building, which she had worked so hard to build, be rechristened the Kenyon Building.

The affection she had generated among staff, colleagues, and undergraduates was evident at her retirement in 1973. Celebrations ranged from a party hosted by the Junior Common Room to a dinner in London given by the Association of Senior Members, and gifts ranged from the album of pictures of St. Hugh's given to her by the staff of the college to the gift of luggage pre-

FIGURE 9.1: The new Dame Kathleen (*center*), with Vivienne Catleugh (*left*), and Nora Kenyon Ritchie (*right*). *Courtesy of Janet Heath.*

sented by the Fellows. K was particularly flattered by the number of former undergraduates at the London dinner who had not been at St. Hugh's while she was principal. As part of the festivities, a portrait of K was unveiled at a party in the college to join those of the college's other principals in Morden Hall. Painted by Carel Weight, professor at the Royal College of Art, it was disliked by many who found it unflattering, emphasizing as it did her ungainly figure; others liked it better, believing that the portrait caught K's peculiar vulnerability.

In the summer of 1973, K packed up and retired with Vivienne Catleugh, the dogs, and five moving vans full of potsherds to Rose Hill, the estate she had inherited from her father in northeast Wales. Kathleen had no trouble settling into this neighborhood with which she had had connections all of her life. Pradoe, where Sir Frederic had been born, was only half an hour away, and K became friendly with its current owner, her second cousin Colonel John Kenyon. She and Catleugh were active in the local community, attending the parish church of St. Hilary, Erbistock, where Kathleen was a member of the Parochial Church Council. And while they socialized with distinguished neighbors such as Sir William and Lady Lowther and Brigadier and Mrs. Gwydyr Jones, they also opened up Rose Hill to the entire village on several occasions. K's status as "the dame" was both assured and respected. When her visiting niece was injured in a car accident, the constable sent to interview her found himself being interviewed instead by Kathleen. All he managed to get in was an occasional, "Yes, Dame Kathleen," "No, Dame Kathleen."

K loved life in the county. Since her childhood days when her family lived at the British Museum during the week and in Surrey on the weekend, she had always had a country residence. Rose Hill was an estate of about 100 acres, the house itself on a slight hill with a lovely view of the Dee Valley. Although she had a gardener, K herself worked energetically on the estate, planting trees, picking fruit, and pruning hedges. She and Catleugh worked in the garden in the afternoons, K frequently riding around on a tractor.

K had told Joe Callaway that in her retirement she planned to "get on with archaeology,"[34] and so she did. Several rooms in the large house were given over to pottery, and mornings and evenings spent in them (afternoons were for the garden). Rik Wheeler's third wife Kim had left him some years before and had lived for a time with K at St. Hugh's, working on the Jericho reports. Lady Wheeler accompanied K to Rose Hill to continue working on the publication of Jericho. As K worked steadily through the Jericho pottery, she managed to combine her archaeological work with her estate renovation; when the potsherds could be discarded, she tossed them into the duck pond to make an island.

If working almost full time on Jericho was not enough, other projects included *The Bible and Recent Archaeology*, based on the Haskell Lectures, as well as a fourth edition of *Archaeology in the Holy Land*. Professional correspondence, book reviews, trips to London for committee meetings, and, naturally, the local Shropshire archaeological society,[35] also occupied her. But she wasn't too busy to track down the answer to a query from a complete stranger. When a schoolgirl wrote to ask a local archaeological question, K told a friend, "Wasn't it lucky, I had an idea about it and I found some details so I could write and tell her what she wanted to know."[36]

In the last year or two of her life, K had opportunities to reunite with friends, students, and colleagues in a celebration of archaeological achievements. Her seventieth birthday was celebrated in high style in Oxford in January 1976. Although essays for her festschrift had been commissioned well ahead of time, problems with publishers meant that at the party in Oxford she could only be offered a list of the essays contributed in her honor. The actual volume did not appear for another two years.[37] November 1977 saw one more reunion of sorts when, as part of the 100th anniversary of the Deutscher Verein zur Erforschung Palästinas (German Society for the Exploration of Palestine), K was awarded an honorary Doctorate of Theology from Evangelisch-theologische Facultät der Eberhard-Karls-Universität in Tübingen, Germany; many of her archaeological contemporaries were present to witness the event. She gave a lecture on her excavations in Jerusalem, which did not satisfy all in attendance because the lecture was on *her* excavations; she did not discuss subsequent Israeli findings.[38] Doug Tushingham, however, happily reported, "I cannot say that I ever saw her in higher spirits, more proud of her accomplishments and more confident of her ability to finish her writing commitments."[39]

But Rik Wheeler's death in 1976 must have reminded K of the passage of time. And she recognized that she herself was slowing down. In July 1978, just a month after delivering her last lecture to the Palestine Exploration Fund on "Archaeological Problems and Biblical History," she retired as Chairman of the British School of Archaeology in Jerusalem, pleading increasing hearing loss as an excuse. After serving as either director or chairman for twenty-seven years, Kathleen felt it was time to turn things over to someone else.[40] Then she went home to Rose Hill.

Just five weeks later, on the evening of August 18, K was alone in the main house. Vivienne Catleugh was in Norfolk visiting relatives, while Kim Wheeler was living in the nearby coach house. As far as anyone knows, K worked in her study as usual that night, the dogs following her into the bedroom when she retired. Unusually, however, the side door to the house was left unlocked, so perhaps she felt unwell that evening. Early the next morning Kim Wheeler received a phone call from K saying that she was very ill. The doctor arrived to find K unconscious from a massive stroke. She was admitted to Wrexham Hospital where she lingered for five days before dying on August 24, just five days after Max Mallowan. She was seventy-two years old.

Students, friends, and colleagues grieved for K in Britain, America, Australia, Canada, and Jordan. Obituaries appeared all over the world, from *The Times* of London to the *Jordan Times* and *Washington Post*. Memorial services were held on October 25 at St. James, Piccadilly, where the blessing was given by the Archbishop of Canterbury, and on November 10 at The University Church of St. Mary the Virgin, Oxford, where the address was given by Rachel Trickett, Principal of St. Hugh's College. But in the small, packed church of St. Hilary on August 29, the funeral service was conducted by the local rector. After "Jerusalem the Golden" was sung and Psalm 122 ("O Pray for the peace of Jerusalem") recited, the Reverend Peter Jones reminded the congregation that "one so erudite and distinguished lived amongst us so humbly and simply in Christian fellowship."[41] Dame Kathleen was then laid to rest in the small churchyard overlooking the River Dee, under a tombstone that read, "Blessed are the pure in heart for they shall see God."

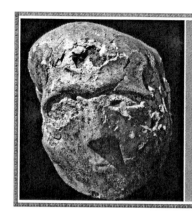

"Ancient Jerusalem Was Built on a Platform." *Daily Telegraph* (3 September 1962).

"Ancient Jerusalem." *Discovery* (April 1962): 18–23.

"Ancient Jerusalem." *Scientific American* 213, No. 1 (July 1965): 84–91.

Archaeology in the Holy Land. New York: Frederick A. Praeger, 1960.

Beginning in Archaeology. 2d ed. London: J. M. Dent & Sons Ltd, 1953.

"Biblical Jerusalem." *Expedition* V, No. 1 (Fall 1962): 32–35.

"The British School of Archaeology in Jerusalem. The New School Building." *Palestine Exploration Quarterly* 99 (1957): 97-100.

"The Bronze Age Tombs of Jericho." *Illustrated London News* (3 October 1953): 520–523.

"Conference on the Future of Archaeology." *Nature* 152 (18 September 1943): 320–321.

"The Council for British Archaeology." *The Museums Journal* 44 (1944): 91–92.

Digging Up Jericho. New York: Frederick A. Praeger, Inc., 1957.

Digging Up Jerusalem. New York: Frederick A. Praeger, Inc., 1974.

"Earliest Jericho." *Antiquity* 33 (1959): 5–9.

"Early Jericho." *Antiquity* 26 (1952): 116–122.

"An Essay on Archaeological Technique: The Publication of Results from the Excavation of a Tell." *Harvard Theological Review* 64 (1971): 271–279.

"Excavation Methods in Palestine." *Quarterly Statement* (1939): 29–40.

"Excavations at Breedon-on-the Hill, 1946." *Transactions of the Leicestershire Archaeological Society* XXVI (1950): 17–68.

"Excavations at Jericho, 1952. Interim Report." *Palestine Exploration Quarterly* 84 (1952): 4–6.

"Excavations at Jericho, 1952." *Palestine Exploration Quarterly* 84 (1952): 62–82.

"Excavations at Jericho, 1953." *Palestine Exploration Quarterly* (1953): 81–96.

"Excavations at Jericho, 1954." *Palestine Exploration Quarterly* (1954): 45–63.

"Excavations at Jericho, 1955." *Palestine Exploration Quarterly* 87 (1955): 108–117.

"Excavations at Jericho, 1956." *Palestine Exploration Quarterly* 88 (1956): 67–83.

"Excavations at Jericho, 1957." *Palestine Exploration Quarterly* (1957): 101–107.

"Excavations at Jericho, 1957–58." *Palestine Exploration Quarterly* (1960): 88–113.

Excavations at Jericho. Vol. 2. *The Tombs Excavated in 1955–8*. Jerusalem: The British School of Archaeology in Jerusalem, 1965.

(and T. A. Holland). *Excavations at Jericho*. Vol. 3. *The Architecture and Stratigraphy of the Tell*. London: The British School of Archaeology in Jerusalem, 1981.

"Excavations at Jerusalem, 1961." *Antiquity* XXXVI (1962): 93–96.

Excavations at Jewry Wall Site, Leicester. Oxford: Report of the Research Committee of the Society of Antiquaries No. XV, 1948.

"Excavations at Sutton Walls Camp, Herefordshire, 1948–1950." *Transactions of the Woolhope Naturalists' Field Club*, XXXIII, Part II (1950):148–154.

"Excavations at Sutton Walls, Herefordshire, 1948–1951." *The Archaeological Journal* 110 (1953): 1–87.

"Excavations at Viroconium in Insula 9, 1952–3." *Transactions of the Shropshire Archaeological Society* LX (1980): 5–74.

"Excavations at Viroconium, 1936–37." *Archaeologia* 88 (1940): 175–227.

Excavations at Wroxeter 1936. Shrewsbury: Brown & Brinnand, Ltd., 1937.

"Excavations in Jerusalem, 1961." *Palestine Exploration Quarterly* 94 (1962): 72–89.

"Excavations in Jerusalem, 1961–1963." *Biblical Archaeologist* 27 (1964): 34–52.

"Excavations in Jerusalem, 1962." *Palestine Exploration Quarterly* 95 (1963): 7–21.

"Excavations in Jerusalem, 1963." *Palestine Exploration Quarterly* 96 (1964): 7–18.

"Excavations in Jerusalem, 1964." *Palestine Exploration Quarterly* 97 (1965): 9–20.

"Excavations in Jerusalem, 1965." *Palestine Exploration Quarterly* 98 (1966): 73–88.

"Excavations in Jerusalem, 1966." *Palestine Exploration Quarterly* 99 (1967): 67–73.

"Excavations in Jerusalem, 1967." *Palestine Exploration Quarterly* 100 (1968): 97–111.

Excavations in Southwark, 1945–47. Research Papers of the Surrey Archaeological Society No. 5, 1959.

"Excavations on the Wrekin, Shropshire, 1939." *The Archaeological Journal* 99 (1942): 99–109.

"Father Roland De Vaux, O. P." *Levant* 4 (1972): v–x.

"Grace Mary Crowfoot." *Palestine Exploration Quarterly* (1957): 154.

"The Holy City from Today to 1800 B.C." *Illustrated London News* (21 April 1962): 619–621.

"In Search of Ancient Jerusalem." *Illustrated London News* (14 April 1962): 578–580.

"Israelite Jerusalem." In *Near Eastern Archaeology in the Twentieth Century: Essays in Honor of Nelson Glueck*, edited by James A. Sanders. New York: Doubleday & Company, 1970.

"Jericho." In *The New Encyclopedia of Archaeological Excavations in the Holy Land*, Vol. 2, edited by Ephraim Stern. Jerusalem: Israel Exploration Society, 1993

"Jericho." *Archaeology* 20 (1967): 268–275.

"Jericho." In *Archaeology and Old Testament Study*, edited by D. Winton Thomas. Oxford: Clarendon Press, 1967.

"Jericho and Its Setting in Near Eastern History." *Antiquity* 30 (1956): 184–195.

"Jericho and the Origins of Agriculture." *The Advancement of Science* (July 1960): 118–120.

"Jericho Before Joshua." *The Listener* (4 June 1953): 929.

(and A. D. Tushingham) "Jericho Gives Up Its Secrets." *National Geographic* (December 1953): 853–870.

"The Jericho of Abraham's Time." *Illustrated London News* (19 May 1956): 352–355.

"Jericho—The World's Oldest Town." *Illustrated London News* (13 October 1956): 611–613.

Jerusalem: Excavating 3000 Years of History. London: Thames and Hudson, 1967.

"The Jerusalem Excavations." *The Jewish Chronicle* (2 February 1962): 2.

"The Jewry Wall." *The Archaeological Journal* (1955): 160.

"John Winter Crowfoot." *Palestine Exploration Quarterly* 92 (1960): 161–163.

"Mankind's Earliest Walled Town." *Illustrated London News* (17 October 1953): 603–604.

"Megiddo, Hazor, Samaria and Chronology." *Bulletin of the Institute of Archaeology* 4 (1964): 143–156.

"New Excavations at Samaria." *Discovery* (December 1932): 377–380.

"New Finds in Jerusalem." *The Jewish Chronicle* (26 January 1962): 15–18.

"The Oldest Town in the World," *The Sunday Times*, May 1, 1955.

"Phoenician, Roman, Byzantine: The Three Cities of Tripolitanian Sabratha." *Illustrated London News* (March 29, 1952): 538–539.

"Progress at Jericho," *The Listener* (17 April 1952): 621.

"Reply to Professor Braidwood." *Antiquity* 31 (1957): 82–84.

"A Roman Forum Found in the Heart of Leicester." *Illustrated London News* 13. (February 1937): 256–259.

The Roman Theatre of Verulamium. Reprinted from the *St. Albans and Hertfordshire Architectural and Archaeological Society's Transactions*, 1934.

"The Roman Theatre of Verulamium, St. Albans." *Archaeologia* LXXXV (1935): 213–261.

(and Sheppard S. Frere). *The Roman Theatre of Verulamium (St. Albans)*. Official guide to site. Reprinted from the *St. Albans and Hertfordshire Architectural and Archaeological Society's Transactions*, 1934.

"Search for North Wall of David's City." *The Daily Telegraph* (September 4, 1962).

"A Secret of Southern Africa." *The Kodak Magazine* 8, No. 5. (May 1930): 78–79.

"Sir Mortimer Wheeler." *Levant* 9 (1977): i–ii.

"Some Notes on the History of Jericho in the Second Millennium B.C." *Palestine Exploration Quarterly* 83 (1951): 101–138.

"The Victoria Falls, Rhodesia." *The Kodak Magazine* 8, No. 9 (September 1930): 166–167.

"Women in Academic Life." *Journal of Biosocial Science*, Supplement 2 (1970): 107–118.

"The World's Oldest Known Township." *Illustrated London News* (12 May 1956).

ABBREVIATIONS
AND NOTES

ABBREVIATIONS

AK: Amy Kenyon

BBC: British Broadcasting Corporation Written Archives Centre

Bodl Library: Bodleian Library

BRC: British Red Cross Museum and Archives

BSAJ: British School of Archaeology in Jerusalem

CBA: Council for British Archaeology

CBRL: Council for British Research in the Levant

DUJo: Digging Up Jericho

DUJm: Digging Up Jerusalem

FK: Frederic Kenyon

GCT: Gertrude Caton-Thompson

IAMC: Institute of Archaeology Management Committee

JM: Sir John Myres

JWM: The Jewry Wall Museum & Site Archives

KK: Kathleen Kenyon

KMKC: Kathleen M. Kenyon Collection, Baylor University.

NK/NKR: Nora Kenyon/ Nora Kenyon Ritchie

PAM: Palestine Archaeological Museum

PEF: Palestine Exploration Fund

PEQ: *Palestine Exploration Quarterly*

PP: Peter Parr

QS: PEF *Quarterly Statement*

REMW: Robert Eric Mortimer Wheeler

SBTS: Southern Baptist Theological Seminary

SHC: St. Hugh's College Archives

VC: Vivienne Catleugh

Unless otherwise noted, all correspondence of KK, FK, AK, and NKR is to be found in the possession of Janet Ritchie Heath.

NOTES

Prologue

[1] The skulls were originally dated to ca. 5000 B.C., but this was later revised in light of C-14 dating. The skulls are now believed to date to 6000 BC or even earlier.

Chapter 1

General recollections of Kathleen Kenyon's childhood are based on Nora Kenyon Ritchie's Memoirs #1 and #2 (Heath collection), as well as interviews with Janet Ritchie Heath, Vivienne Catleugh, and Jeremy Ritchie. Some information about KK's education is from Kathleen Kenyon, "Digging for History—From Zimbabwe to Jericho via Southwark," Kathleen M. Kenyon Collection, Baylor University [KMKC].

General information about Sir Frederic Kenyon comes from Wilkins, *Kenyon Family Histories*; Frederic Kenyon, "Autobiographica" (Heath collection); and Bell, *Sir Frederic George Kenyon*, 269–294.

General background on St. Paul's Girls' School is from the SPGS archives, as well as from Avery, *Best Type of Girl*; Bailes, *Once a Paulina*; Gray, *Gladly Wolde He Lerne*; Hirschfield, *St. Paul's Girls' School*; and Hopkinson, *Incense Tree*. General background on Somerville and Oxford is based on accounts in Harrison, *History of the University of Oxford*; Adams, *Somerville for Women*; Withers, *Lifespan*; Brittain, *The Women at Oxford*; Jones, *Margery Fry*; and KK, "Women in Academic Life."

[1] Letter from Frederic Kenyon to G. F. Barwick, February 3, 1914, quoted in Miller, *That Noble Cabinet*, 292.

[2] Rose, *King George V*, 263.

[3] Bell, 270.

[4] Prag, "Kathleen Kenyon and the Holy Land," 121–122.

[5] AK to FK, 19 April 1906.

6 AK to FK, 5 August 1913.
7 AK to FK, 9 April 1906.
8 AK to FK, 10 August 1908.
9 AK to FK, 22 March 1907.
10 AK to FK, 5 August 1908.
11 AK to FK, probably 31 July 1914.
12 KK to FK, undated but apparently from Rose Hill, fall 1914.
13 AK to FK, 24 August 1914.
14 KK to AK, 2 September (1923?).
15 Winifred Pye, *Eothen School (1892–1942)*. Printed for the Eothen Jubilee Fund. Surrey History Centre.
16 Hopkinson, 39.
17 Beatrice de Cardi, interview.
18 FK to NK, 26 February 1917.
19 FK to AK, 5 August 1917.
20 See, for example, FK to NK, 26 February 1917.
21 KK, "Digging for History."
22 KK to AK, 3 December 1924.
23 Frances Gray to FK, 18 July 1925.
24 KK to AK, 19 January 1926.
25 KK to NK, 29 October 1925.
26 K to NK, 7 February 1926.
27 KK to AK, 22 February 1926.
28 KK to AK, 13 March 1926.
29 KK to NK, 26 January 1926.
30 NK to AK, 11 March 1928.
31 KK to AK, 19 January 1926.
32 Butcher, Sarnia. Diary, 15 January 1954.
33 KK to AK, 13 January 1926; KK to AK, 29 April 1926.
34 E.g., KK to AK, 5 November 1925; KK to AK, 12 February 1926; KK to AK, 20 October 1927.
35 KK to AK, 22 February 1926; KK to NK, 2 March 1926.
36 KK to AK, 5 November 1925.
37 KK to AK, 30 October 1927.
38 KK to NK, 19 May 1929.
39 KK to NK, 14 March 1929.
40 E.g., KK to NK, 19 May 1926; KK to NK, 14 March 1927.
41 Quoted by Tushingham in "Kathleen Mary Kenyon," 557.
42 KK to NK, 2 March 1926.
43 KK to AK, 13 March 1926; KK to NK, 12 March 1926.
44 KK to AK, 21 March 1926.
45 FK to NK, 12 February 1928.
46 *Isis Magazine*, 2 November 1927.

[47]NK to FK, 7 November 1927.
[48]FK to JM, 12 November 1928. Bodl. Library, Myres MS 71, fols. 106–107.
[49]Memorial address given by John Ward Perkins, October 25, 1978, St. James, Piccadilly, London.
[50]FK, "Autobiographica."
[51]KK to AK, 31 January 1926.
[52]KK to NK, 30 January 1927.
[53]Withers, 33.
[54]NK to FK, 27 July 1930.

Chapter 2

This account of Gertrude Caton-Thompson [GCT] and her expedition to Zimbabwe is based on Clark, "Gertrude Caton-Thompson"; KK, "A Secret of Southern Africa," and "Digging for History" (KMKC, Baylor University); Caton-Thompson, *Mixed Memoirs*; "The Southern Rhodesian Ruins"; and *The Zimbabwe Culture*; and the local South African newspapers: *Bulawayo Chronicle*, 18 May, 27 July, 3 August 1929; *The Cape Times*, 18 March 1928; 28 September 1929; *Johannesburg Star*, 23 January 1930.

[1] Frederic Kenyon [FK] to John Myres [JM], 12 November 1928, Bodl. Library, Myres MS 71, fols. 106–107.
[2] GCT to JM, 13 November 1928, Bodl. Library, Myres MS 71, fol. 109.
[3] The British Association for the Advancement of Science to JM, 19 November 1928, Bodl. Library, Myres MS 71, fol. 113.
[4] KK, "Digging for History."
[5] KK to AK, 24 March 1929.
[6] KK to NK, 31 March 1929.
[7] KK to NK, 19 May 1929.
[8] KK to AK, 13 April 1929, St. Hugh's College, Letters of KK [SHC].
[9] KK to NK, 19 May 1929; KK to AK, 13 April 1929, SHC.
[10]KK to NK, 21 April 1929, SHC.
[11]KK to AK, 13 April 1929, SHC.
[12]*Cape Times*, 18 March 1929.
[13]Drower, "Gertrude Caton-Thompson," 351–379.
[14]KK to NK, 21 April 1929. In *Mixed Memoirs* GCT tells a slightly different version of this story, one that stresses her own authority. She says that *she* kept the workers until after dark. A version of the story that appeared in *The Bulawayo Chronicle* on 27 July 1929 tends to agree with K's account.
[15]KK to NK, 21 April 1929, SHC.
[16]GCT, "The Southern Rhodesian Ruins," 621. In her publication of this site, *Zimbabwe Culture*, GCT concedes that "the term Bantu used in a generic sense invites reproach, but until anthropologists provide a substitute it seems inevitable" (p. 10).
[17]KK, "Digging for History."

[18] KK to AK, 13 April 1929; KK to NK, 21 April 1929; both in SHC.

[19] NKR, Memoir #1; FK to JM, 12 November 1928, Bodl. Library, Myres MS 71, fols. 106–107.

[20] KK to FK, 12 May 1929; KK to NK, 19 May 1929.

[21] KK to NK, 21 April 1929, SHC; KK to NK, 19 May 1929.

[22] KK to AK, 9 June 1929.

[23] KK to NK, 19 May 1929.

[24] Vivienne Catleugh [VC], interview.

[25] KK to FK, 12 May 1929.

[26] KK to AK, 7 July 1929.

[27] FK to NK, 5 November 1929; FK to NK, 22 October 1929.

[28] KK to FK, 12 May 1929.

[29] KK to AK, 26 May 1929, SHC. GCT, *Zimbabwe Culture*, 67; GCT to FK, 15 July 1929. In *Mixed Memoirs*, GCT gives a date for the Sung china as thirteenth–fourteenth century A.D. (p. 122).

[30] GCT, *Zimbabwe Culture*, 76; KK to AK, 9 June 1929.

[31] KK to AK, 9 June 1929.

[32] GCT to FK, 15 July 1929.

[33] GCT, *Mixed Memoirs*, 136.

[34] Or Chibvumani. GCT, *Zimbabwe Culture*, 151.

[35] KK to FK, 31 August 1929.

[36] KK to NK, 8 September 1929, SHC.

[37] KK, "Victoria Falls, Rhodesia," 166.

[38] KK to FK, 24 September 1929.

[39] KK to FK, 15 October 1929; KK to AK, 22 October 1929.

Chapter 3

For the excavations at St. Albans, Roman Verulamium, I have relied on Hawkes's biography of Sir Mortimer Wheeler; Mortimer Wheeler, *Archaeology from the Earth* and *Still Digging*; and R. E. M. Wheeler and T. V. Wheeler, *Verulamium: A Belgic and Two Roman Cities*.

John Crowfoot's reports in the *Palestine Exploration Quarterly* [PEQ] and The Palestine Exploration Fund's *Quarterly Statement* describe the Samaria excavations, as do KK, "New Excavations at Samaria"; Avigad, "Samaria," in *The New Encyclopedia of Archaeological Excavations in the Holy Land*; Tappy, "Samaria," in *The Oxford Encyclopedia of Archaeology in the Near East*; Moorey, "Kathleen Kenyon and Palestinian Archaeology"; and Tappy, *The Archaeology of Israelite Samaria*, Vols. 1 and 2.

[1] FK to JM, 23 May 1930, Bodl. Library, Myres MS 72, fol. 93.

[2] FK to NK, 5 November 1929.

[3] GCT to FK, 15 July 1929.

[4] KK to NK, 29 January 1930.

[5] KK, "Digging for History"; KK to NK, 19 February 1930.

[6] FK to NK, 19 February 1930; KK to NK, 2 February 1930; FK to NK, 23 January 1930.

[7] KK to FK, 8 November 1929; Vivienne Catleugh [VC], interview; FK to NK, 9 February 1930.

[8] FK to NK, 27 January 1930.

[9] KK to NK 28 November 1933.

[10] E.g., KK to NK, 23 April 1932; KK to AK, 2 March 1933.

[11] Jeremy Ritchie, interview; NK to John Ritchie, 2 September 1935.

[12] KK to NK, 20 October 1933.

[13] KK to NK, 5 May 1930.

[14] Rachel Maxwell-Hyslop, interview. It was part of Kenyon family lore that Wheeler learned his archaeology from his wife.

[15] KK to NK, 31 July 1930; KK to FK, 10 August 1930.

[16] KK, "Sir Mortimer Wheeler," i–ii.

[17] KK to FK, 10 August 1930.

[18] VC, interview.

[19] KK to NK, 8 November 1933.

[20] KK to NK, 31 July 1930; KK to AK, 16 September 1932.

[21] KK to NK, 31 July 1930.

[22] KK to AK, 28 October 1933.

[23] R.E.M. and T.V. Wheeler, 23.

[24] KK, "Digging for History."

[25] KK to NK, 31 July 1930; KK to NK, 10 August 1930.

[26] KK to NK, 11 September 1933; KK to AK, 3, 16 September 1933.

[27] KK to NK, 1 October 1933.

[28] KK to NK, 8 November 1933.

[29] KK, "The Roman Theatre of Verulamium, St. Albans," 213–261; *The Roman Theatre of Verulamium*; KK and Sheppard S. Frere, *The Roman Theatre of Verulamium (St. Albans)*. Further excavation of the site in 1959 suggested that originally the theater had been part of the sacred area of the temple, implying a ritual or cultic purpose. See S. S. Frere, "Excavations at Verulamium 1959," 12–13, and *Verulamium Excavations*, Vol. II, 73–74.

[30] Myres, "Verulamium," 16–25. See also Wilkes, "Kathleen Kenyon in Roman Britain," 105.

[31] Hawkes, 159. Reproduced from *Adventurer in Archaeology: The Biography of Sir Mortimer Wheeler* by Jacquetta Hawkes (Copyright © Estate of Jacquetta Hawkes 1982) by permission of PFD(www.pfd.co.uk) on behalf of the Estate of Jacquetta Hawkes.

[32] Wilkes, 104. Subsequent excavations in the late 1950s and early 1960s did demonstrate that some of Wheeler's conclusions were premature. For example, they showed that the Belgic *oppidum* extended beyond Prae Wood, and that some of the Roman structures had been misdated because of mistakes Wheeler made with the pottery. The Fosse, which Wheeler believed represented "the first Roman Verulamium," was shown to date from the second century A.D., and so was not part of the early Roman city. The excavator Sheppard

Frere also argued that the city was not affected by the third-century crisis. Only in the fourth century did Verulamium begin a gradual decline. Since much of the evidence for the city's decline came from the use of the theater as a trash dump, once Frere had suggested that the theater had a religious purpose, it was easier to argue that its disuse was the result of conversion to Christianity in the fourth century rather than economic decline. Frere, *Verulamium Excavations*, Vol. II, 21.

[33] Quoted in Moorey, *A Century of Biblical Archaeology*, 19.

[34] First Annual Report, 1920: Ordinances, 1921, BSAJ General File, Palestine Exploration Fund [PEF].

[35] FK, "Britain's Task and British Opportunity in the Near East: A School of Archaeology in Jerusalem," Bodl. Library Myres MS 55, fol. 13.

[36] FK to JM, 22 November 1926, Bodl. Library, Myres MS 54, fol. 120; *Quarterly Statement [QS] of the Palestine Exploration Fund* (1930), 24.

[37] PEF Minute Book 8, 15 January 1930; BSAJ minutes, 15 January 1930; PEF. This was not the last time the possibility of merging the two organizations was brought up. See BSAJ Minutes, 14 June 1935, and PEF Minute Book 9, 12 May 1955, PEF.

[38] PEF Minute Book 8, 12 November 1930, PEF.

[39] Also spelled Sebaste or Sabastiya.

[40] It was not uncommon for Jews living in Palestine in this period to take Hebrew names.

[41] Elisabeth Crowfoot, "Grace Mary Crowfoot, 1877–1957," http://www.brown.edu/Research/Breaking_Ground/.

[42] KK to AK, 6 April 1931.

[43] KK, "Grace Mary Crowfoot," 154.

[44] Crowfoot, Kenyon, and Sukenik, *Buildings at Samaria*, xvi.

[45] KK to AK, 3 May 1933.

[46] Elisabeth Crowfoot, interview.

[47] KK to AK, 6 April 1931; KK to NK, 4 April 1933.

[48] Elizabeth Murray to her mother, 28 April 1933, Elizabeth Murray correspondence, PEF.

[49] Elizabeth Murray to her mother, 14, 17, April 1933, Elizabeth Murray correspondence, PEF.

[50] KK to NK, 4 April 1933.

[51] KK to NK, 15 May 1933

[52] Elizabeth Murray to her mother, 17 April 1933, Elizabeth Murray correspondence, PEF; KK to NK, 15 June 1933.

[53] Roger Moorey noted the similarities in technique that K used at both St. Albans and Samaria: Moorey, *A Century of Biblical Archaeology*, 63.

[54] Diana Crowfoot Rowley, interview.

[55] KK to FK, 12 June 1932.

[56] Moorey, *A Century of Biblical Archaeology*, 35.

[57] The work of William F. Albright at Tell Beit Mirsim in the late 1920s and early 1930s was crucial to this, as were the excavations at Megiddo. While much of the work from these sites was still unpublished when K was working at Samaria, the findings were

being circulated by word of mouth. As a result of visits back and forth between the various excavations, K would have had a good idea of what was going on at these sites. I am grateful to Rupert Chapman for pointing this out to me. See also Moorey, *A Century of Biblical Archaeology*, 69–71.

[58] Elizabeth Murray to her mother, 3 March 1933, Elizabeth Murray correspondence, PEF.

[59] KK to AK, 30 May 1935.

[60] Albright, "Recent Progress in Palestinian Archaeology," 21.

[61] G. E. Wright, "Israelite Samaria," 17.

[62] Aharoni and Amiran, "New Scheme," 180; G. E. Wright, "Israelite Samaria," 20–21.

[63] Tappy, "Samaria," 464. Of course, strictly speaking, the *terminus post quem* is not the construction date itself, but the date after which construction must have taken place.

[64] As Peter Parr pointed out to me, when these archaeologists argued that the pottery KK ascribed to her Period 1 must have existed prior to the building of Omri's palace, they are correct. But this does not tell us by how long the pottery preceded the palace. They date some of the Samarian pottery, based on comparisons with material from other sites, to the tenth or eleventh century B.C., long before Omri. But this method of dating depends on the reliability of these other excavations, which can often result in merely circular arguments.

[65] KK, "Megiddo, Hazor, Samaria and Chronology," 145–148.

[66] Tushingham, "Kathleen Mary Kenyon," 560–561.

[67] KK, "The summit buildings and constructions," in Crowfoot, Kenyon, and Sukenik, *Buildings at Samaria*, 93.

[68] Charles Burney, interview.

[69] Tappy, *The Archaeology of Israelite Samaria*, Vol. I, 7.

[70] Ron Tappy, interview.

[71] KK to NK, 28 April 1935; Diana Crowfoot Rowley, interview.

[72] KK to AK, 7 June 1935.

[73] KK to NK, 16 July 1935.

[74] KK to NK, 28 April 1935.

[75] KK to NK, 28 April 1935.

[76] KK to AK, 30 May 1935

[77] KK to NK, 20, 28 April 1935.

[78] KK to NK, 28 April 28, 1935; KK to FK, 29 June 1933. Kathleen was to note in her obituary of John Crowfoot that "he frankly disliked" dealing with stratification. KK, "John Winter Crowfoot," 161.

[79] KK to AK, 7 June 1935.

[80] KK to FK, 29 June 1933.

[81] KK to NK, 21 January 1934.

[82] KK to AK, 28 June 1935.

[83] KK to NK, 23 May 1935.

[84] Joan Crowfoot Payne, interview; NK to John Ritchie, 31 August 1935.

[85] KK to NK, 16 July 1935.

[86] KK to AK, 16 July 1935.

[87] KK to NK, 16 July 1935. According to Diana Crowfoot Rowley, the Crowfoot girls were a bit worried that K might want to take too much charge of things herself.

[88] KK, "Roadtrip." This is the nickname I have given the untitled, handwritten manuscript describing the journey in the KMKC, Baylor University. Probably written with the intention of publication, it appears never to have been completed.

[89] KK to NK, 16 July 1935; KK to AK, 21 July 1935; KK, "Roadtrip."

[90] KK, "Roadtrip"; KK to AK, 21 July 1935.

[91] Joan Crowfoot Payne, personal communication; Diana Crowfoot Rowley, interview; KK, "Roadtrip."

[92] KK, "Roadtrip."

[93] KK, "Roadtrip"; Diana Crowfoot Rowley, interview. Mrs. Rowley's recollection of this trip differs slightly from K's, but in general I have relied on K's account on the grounds that it was probably written soon after the event.

[94] Diana Crowfoot Rowley, interview.

[95] Joan Crowfoot Payne, personal communication; Diana Crowfoot Rowley, interview; NK to John Ritchie, 23 August 1935; NK to John Ritchie, 27 August 1935; NK to John Ritchie, 31 August 1935; NK to John Ritchie, 1 September 1935.

Chapter 4

[1] Hawkes, *Adventurer in Archaeology*, 132. Reproduced from Adventurer in Archaeology: the Biography of Sir Mortimer Wheeler by Jacquetta Hawkes (Copyright © Estate of Jacquetta Hawkes 1982) by permission of PFD (www.pfd.co.uk) on behalf of the Estate of Jacquetta Hawkes.

[2] NK to John Ritchie, 1 September 1935.

[3] NKR to John Ritchie, 20 August 1940

[4] Beatrice de Cardi, interview.

[5] E.g., KK to NK, 13 March 1933; 4 April 1933.

[6] Diana Crowfoot Rowley, interview.

[7] Elisabeth Crowfoot, interview.

[8] KK to NK, 8 November 1933.

[9] KK to NK, 15 June 1933.

[10] KK to NK, 15 December 1933.

[11] KK to NK, 8 November 1933

[12] KK to FK, 1 May 1931.

[13] E.g., FK to NK, 23 January 1930.

[14] "Under the Ground," *The Times* (London), 11 July 1960.

[15] Steele, "The College Head," 15.

[16] KK to NK, 4 April 1933; KK to NK, 15 May 1933; KK to AK, 22 May 1933; KK to AK, 8 June 1933; KK to NK, 9 March 1934.

[17] Cecil Weston, interview; KK to NK, 20 May 1930; 21 January 1934; 28 March 1934; FK to NK, 21 March 1934; 11 April 1934.

[18] REM Wheeler [REMW] to KK, 8 July 1935, Institute of Archaeology Management Committee [IAMC] Minutes.

[19] Hawkes, 130; Evans, "First Half-Century," 3–10.

[20] KK to NK, 16 July 1935.

[21] See the correspondence between Flinders Petrie and KK, Petrie Correspondence, A611/4 Box 1. See also Ucko, "Biography of a Collection," 359–361.

[22] FK to *The Times* (London), 18 April 1936.

[23] Wheeler, *Still Digging*, 90.

[24] KK to E. Perowne, 2 February 1939, Senate House Files, Institute of Archaeology, London.

[25] NK to JR, 5 September 1935.

[26] REMW to KK, 8 July 1935, IAMC Minutes.

[27] KK, *Excavations at Wroxeter 1936*, and "Excavations at Viroconium, 1936–37"; see also White and Barker, *Wroxeter*, 25–26.

[28] Wilkes, "Kathleen Kenyon in Roman Britain," 106–107.

[29] KK, "Excavations on the Wrekin, Shropshire, 1939," 99–109; "Wrekin's Old British City," *Wellington Journal & Shrewsbury News*, 19 August 1939.

[30] H. W. Hawkins, "Mystery of Roman Leicester," *Leicester Evening Mail*, 26 November 1937. In the 1930s, Roman Leicester was known as Ratae Coritanorum, but in the 1960s re-examination of the evidence led to a name change. Ratae Coritanorum became Ratae Corieltauvorum, and the Iron Age tribe the Coritani became the Corieltauvi.

[31] E. E. Lowe to Colin Ellis, 10 May 1937; Colin Ellis to E. E. Lowe, 30 November 1939; both in Jewry Wall Museum & Site Archives [JWM].

[32] KK, *Excavations at Jewry Wall*, 1.

[33] KK, "A Roman Forum Found in the Heart of Leicester."

[34] "Leicester's Roman Forum to be Preserved," *Leicester Evening Mail*, 24 February 1937.

[35] Jewry Wall Excavations Committee, Colin Ellis, "Chairman's Report" (March 24, 1937), JWM.

[36] KK to Colin Ellis, 24 February 1937, JWM.

[37] Murial Shaw to JWM, 1 December 1999, JWM.

[38] KK to Colin Ellis, 7 April 1937, JWM; KK to JM, 8 July 1936; both at the Bodl. Library, Myres MS 22, fol. 61.

[39] KK, *Excavations at Jewry Wall*, 3.

[40] Jennifer Peel Jones, interview; unpublished memoir of May Peel, in the possession of Jennifer Peel.

[41] KK to Colin Ellis, 31 March 1938, JWM.

[42] Memorandum to the Museum and Libraries Committee by Dr. E. E. Lowe (31 March 1938); KK to Colin Ellis, 31 March 1938; both at the JWM.

[43] KK, "Digging for History."

[44] "The Roman Midlands," *Archaeology is an Adventure*, 28 October 1934, British Broadcasting Corporation Written Archives Centre [BBC].

[45] KK, *Excavations at Jewry Wall*, 6.

[46] Taylor and Goodchild, "Review," 142–145.

47 KK, "Jewry Wall," 160.
48 "Jewry Wall Finds Most Important For Years," *The Leicester Mercury*, 6 July 1936.
49 Hebditch and Mellor, "Forum and Basilica," 1–80.
50 Taylor and Goodchild, 142.
51 Webster, *Archaeologist at Large*, 56.
52 Wilkes, 103.
53 Colin Ellis to REMW, 9 December 1938; 16 December 1948; both at JWM.
54 KK, "The Roman Forum at Leicester," KMKC, Baylor University.
55 FK to Colin Ellis, 25 December 1938, JWM.
56 Vivienne Catleugh [VC], interview.
57 NKR, Memoir #1, Heath collection.
58 KK to NKR, 19 February 1939.
59 KK to NKR, 17 July 1940.
60 VC, interview.
61 Visitor's book of Winifred Williamson, now in the possession of Ann Mitchell.
62 Beatrice de Cardi, interview.
63 Thomas Holland, interview.
64 Letter to author from Maggie Tushingham.
65 That was certainly the view of both VC (interview) and NKR ("When the Two Dames Met," *Wrexham Leader*, 8 September 1978).
66 Letter to author from Maggie Tushingham.
67 KK to AK, 7 April 1938.
68 Draft of circular on the projected "Conference of the Problems and Prospects of European Archaeology," Senate House Files, Institute of Archaeology, London.
69 Janet Heath, interview.
70 FK, letter to *The Times* (London), 14 April 1938.
71 NKR to John Ritchie, 20 August 1939.
72 NKR to John Ritchie, 19 June 1940.
73 FK, "Autobiographica," Heath collection.
74 Sandars, "Gordon Childe," 11.
75 KK to NKR, 20 May 1930, Heath collection; KK, War Service Record Card, British Red Cross Museum and Archives [BRC].
76 "Leading Field Archaeologist to Give Lecture in Glasgow," *The Glasgow Herald*, 18 February 1969.
77 Sharp, *British Red Cross Hammersmith*, 7.
78 VC, interview; Sharp, 8; BRCS County of London Branch Annual Reports, 1939–1945; KK, War Service Record Card; VC, War Service Record Card, BRC.
79 Now Shepherds Bush Road.
80 Sharp, 7–14. The statistics concerning membership in Sharp's book and the British Red Cross Archives Library do not agree, but it is nevertheless clear that in the early years of the war, membership grew significantly.
81 Talbot, "Memories," 27–28; NKR to John Ritchie, April 19, 1940.
82 IAMC Minutes, 30 September 1941.

83 Sharp, 8.
84 KK to NKR, 13 February 1941; KK to FK, 31 January, 9 February 1941.
85 FK to NRK, 30 August 1944.
86 VC, interview; FK to NKR, 22 January 1941; 14 September 1941, 2 November 1941; 29 December 1941; 7 May 1942; 26 May 1942.
87 KK to NKR, 8 November 1941.
88 KK to NKR, 9 December 1941; 26 December 1941; Sharp 12.
89 KK to NKR, 31 November 1941.
90 KK to NKR, 1 March 1942; FK to NKR, 28 February 1942.
91 Sharp, 8–9; KK to NKR, 1 March 1942.
92 FK to NKR, 27 March 1942; FK to NRK, 6 April 1942.
93 KK to NKR, 1 March 1941.
94 KK to NKR, 22 March 1942.
95 VC, interview; KK to NKR, 9 December 1941; 1 March 1942; FK to NKR, 28 February 1942.
96 Senate Minutes 2141, Report from the Institute of Archaeology, 21 June, 1944, University of London Library; Edward Perowne to KK, November 1940; Edward Perowne to E. S. M. Belloni, 19 November 1940, Senate House Files, Institute of Archaeology, London.
97 Senate Minutes 323, 11 December 1940; Senate Minutes 2083, 17 June 1942, University of London Library; IAMC Minutes, 20 January 1941, Institute of Archaeology, London.
98 Senate Minutes 1074, 25 February 1942; Senate Minutes 2083, 17 June 1942, University of London Library.
99 News Review, 4 May 1944, in Senate House files, Institute of Archaeology, London; KK to NKR, 9, 26 December 1941.
100 KK to NKR, 1 March 1942.
101 IAMC Minutes, 23 February 1942, 2 October 1942.
102 Evans, 14; The Times (London), 16 March 1943.
103 IAMC Minutes, 19 December 1942.
104 KK to John Crowfoot, 17 February 1943, Senate House Files, Institute of Archaeology, London.
105 KK to S. R. K. Glanville, 23 March 1943, Senate House Files, Institute of Archaeology, London.
106 Conference on the Future of Archaeology, 75–76.
107 KK to John Crowfoot, 17 February 1943, Senate House Files, Institute of Archaeology, London.
108 "Archaeology and Replanning," The Times, 9 August 1943; KK, "Conference on the Future of Archaeology," 320–321.
109 Conference on the Future of Archaeology, 70.
110 Conference on the Future of Archaeology, 40.
111 Conference on the Problems and Prospects of European Archaeology, 4.
112 VC, interview.

[113] KK to Molly Crowfoot, 20 October 1994, KMKC, Baylor University.

[114] "Notes and Notices," *The Museums Journal* 43, September, 1943, 89; KK, "The Council for British Archaeology," *The Museums Journal* 44, September 1944, 91–92; CBA Minute Books, 4 May 1943, Council for British Archaeology; 8 March 1944; A. W. Clapham, letter to *The Times* (London), 11 April 1944.

[115] CBA Minute Books, 4 May 1948.

[116] CBA Minute Books, 16 November, 16 December 1948.

[117] CBA Minute Books, 23 October 1945.

[118] CBA Minute Books, 2 June 1949; Beatrice de Cardi, interview. For further discussion of the early history of the CBA and Kathleen's role, see Morris, "Breathing the Future."

[119] Surrey Archaeological Society, Annual General Meeting (Report 1942), Annual General Meeting (Report 1943), Surrey Archaeological Society Archives.

[120] CBA Minute Books, 29 May 1945; Surrey Archaeological Society, Annual General Meeting (Report 1945); KK, *Excavations in Southwark, 1945–47*, 9.

[121] CBA Minute Books, 27 November 1945; 29 January 1946; 28 May 1946.

[122] KK, "Excavations at Breedon-on-the Hill," 67–68.

[123] CBA Minute Books, 29 October 1946; 26 November 1946.

[124] CBA Minute Books, 30 September 1947; 8 June 1948.

[125] Morgan, "Reports of Sectional Editors for 1949," 89; KK, "Excavations at Sutton Walls, 1948–1950;" "Excavations at Sutton Walls, 1948–1951," 1–32.

[126] IAMC Minutes, 30 April 1936.

[127] IAMC Minutes, "Institute of Archaeology Lectureship in Palestinian Archaeology," Annex A.

[128] IAMC Minutes, 9 October 1947.

[129] KK to Colin Ellis, 24 February 1937, JWM.

[130] Hawkes, 216–217.

[131] VC, interview.

[132] KK, "Essay on Archaeological Technique," 273; Quartermaster of First Battalion of Grenadier Guards to KK, 24 September 24, 1951, KMKC, Baylor University.

[133] Navy, Army, Air Force Institute, an organization that provided shops, clubs, and canteens for the military.

[134] VC, interview; Joan Kirk Clarke, interview.

[135] The broken pieces of the pots are pictured in a photograph of the burial, Plate 11b. The author writes, "One of the graves . . . contained three large pieces of a painted vessel which were noted in the site record as 'possibly intrusive': this seems to me unlikely in view of their suggestive positions in the grave and the substantial cover slabs which were *in situ* before the grave was opened. . . . SUBSEQUENT NOTE: One print of the photograph reproduced in pl. 11b has been annotated by JBWP - 'The pots are bogus.'" Kenrick, *Excavations at Sabratha 1948–1951*, p. 34, n. 2.

[136] Nicholas Thomas, interview; Philip Kenrick, interview.

[137] British School at Rome, 44th Annual Report to Subscribers (1948–49); British School at Rome, 45th Annual Report to Subscribers (1949–50); British School at Rome, 46th Annual Report to Subscribers (1950–51).

[138] KK, *Excavations at Southwark*, 10.
[139] Philip Kenrick, interview.
[140] Kenrick, "Excavations at Sabratha, 1948–1951," 51–52.
[141] Kenrick, *Excavations at Sabratha 1948–1951*, 3.

Chapter 5

For earlier work at Jericho, I have relied on Bartlett's *Jericho*; Holland, "Jericho" in *Oxford Encyclopedia of the Archaeology of the Ancient Near East*"; Kenyon, "Jericho," in *The New Encyclopedia of Archaeological Excavations in the Holy Land*; and Moorey, *Excavation in Palestine*.

John Garstang's PEF *Quarterly Statement* articles, listed in the bibliography, describe his excavations.

KK published her accounts of findings at Jericho in annual reports to the Palestine Exploration Fund as well as other works listed in the bibliography. I have also made use of the following unpublished sources: KK, "Digging Up Jericho," British Broadcasting Corporation Written Archives Centre [BBC]; and "Digging at Jericho," unpublished PEF lecture, KMKC, Baylor University.

The following also provided helpful information: Marshall, "Excavating Under Jericho"; Margaret Wheeler, *Walls of Jericho*; Tushingham, "Kathleen Mary Kenyon"; Ruby, *Jericho: Dreams, Ruins, Phantoms*; and Johnstone, *Buried Treasure*. I have also made use of David Spurgeon's series of articles in the Toronto *Globe and Mail* from January to April 1956.

For discussions of KK's methodology at Jericho, see KK, *Digging Up Jericho* (*DUJo*), 34–35; *Digging Up Jerusalem* (*DUJm*), 68; Margaret Wheeler, *Walls of Jericho*, 23–24; Moorey, *Excavation in Palestine*, 28–30, 61–63; and Huckaby " Analysis of the Methodology of Kathleen M. Kenyon."

For camp life on the Jericho dig, see Margaret Wheeler, "The Lighter Side of Dig Life"; Callaway, "Dame Kathleen Kenyon"; A. D. and Maggie Tushingham, "Dame Kathleen Kenyon," ix. In addition, I had access to the following unpublished sources: diary notes of Sarnia Butcher; Martin Biddle, unpublished typescript sent to author (see Chapter 8, n. 56), "Kathleen Kenyon," letters to the author from Henk Franken, Svend Holm-Nielson, and Maggie Tushingham.

I have also used personal recollections of the Jericho excavations: interviews with Terry Ball, Martin Biddle, Charles Burney, Sarnia Butcher, Vivienne Catleugh, Joan Kirk Clarke, Robert Dyson, John Evans, Basil Hennessy, Philip Hammond, Willard Hamrick, Robert North, Peter Parr, Ahmed Shistawi, David Spurgeon, Peter Pedrette, Lawrence Toombs, Doug and Maggie Tushingham, Gus van Beek, and Cecil Western.

I made use of an interview with Dahoud Jibrin conducted by Minna Lönnqvist, December 10, 1996. I am grateful to Dr. Lönnqvist for allowing me access to her notes.

[1] Moorey, *A Century of Biblical Archaeology*, 64.
[2] F. Kenyon, *Bible and Modern Scholarship*, 14, n. 1. I am grateful to Gary C. Huckaby's Ph.D. dissertation for calling my attention to this point.

3 KK, "Some Notes on the History of Jericho," 122.

4 Minute Book 8, 18 February, 21 March 1944, Palestine Exploration Fund [PEF]. She eventually published such a book, *Archaeology in the Holy Land*, in 1960.

5 BSAJ Minutes, 22 May 1947; Minute Book 9, 15 February 1949; both at PEF.

6 BSAJ Minutes, 5 December 1950, PEF.

7 BSAJ Minutes, 9 February, 1 March 1951; Minute Book 9, 27 February 1951; both at PEF.

8 BSAJ Minutes, 9 February, 21 June 1951, PEF.

9 Tushingham, "Kathleen Mary Kenyon," 576–568; Doug and Maggie Tushingham, interview.

10 R. E. M. Wheeler, *Archaeology from the Earth* (1954), 30. By permission of Oxford University Press.

11 Dever, "Two Approaches to Archaeological Method," 1.

12 Wright, "Archaeological Method in Palestine," 125–126, especially n. 22.

13 See discussion of method in Dever, "Two Approaches to Archaeological Method" and "Archaeological Method in Israel," as well as Moorey, 24–32.

14 KK, "Excavation Methods in Palestine," 35.

15 KK, *DUJo*, 26.

16 KK to NKR, 27 January 1952.

17 KK to NKR, 27 January 1952.

18 A. Shistawi, interview.

19 Letter to author from Maggie Tushingham; Doug and Maggie Tushingham, interview.

20 KK, *DUJm*, 75.

21 KK to NKR, 5 February 1953.

22 Margaret Wheeler, *Walls of Jericho*, 73–74.

23 Balter, *The Goddess and the Bull*, 17–18.

24 Interview with Dahoud Jibrin conducted by Minna Lönnqvist, 10 December 1996.

25 Tushingham, "Kathleen Mary Kenyon," 54.

26 Eventually, K would dig three main trenches in the mound: Trench I in the west side, Trench II on the northern end, and Trench III on the southern end. In addition, she would open up various smaller squares in the northern half of the mound.

27 See, for example, F. Kenyon, *Bible and Modern Scholarship*, 15. For Kathleen's view of the Old Testament, see KK, "Palestine in the Time of the Old Testament," BBC broadcast, Tuesday, May 31, 1955, KMKC, Baylor University; KK, "Archaeology and History," KMKC, Baylor University.

28 *Conference on the Future of Archaeology*, 35.

29 KK to NKR, 27 January 1952.

30 See, for example, KK, *DUJo*, 261–263, or "Jericho and Its Setting in Near Eastern History," 195.

31 Tushingham, "Excavations at Old Testament Jericho," 52; KK, "Early Jericho," 118.

32 E.g., KK to NKR, February 5, 1953; 13 February 1955.

33 KK to NKR, 7 March 1952.

34 KK to NKR, 7 March 1952.

[35] Zeuner, "Notes on the Bronze Age Tombs," 126–127.

[36] KK to Antony Derville, 29 October 1956, BBC; letter to author from Mary Alexander.

[37] KK to NKR, 27 January 1952.

[38] KK to NKR, 13 February 1955.

[39] K herself confirmed this story to Iain Davidson some years later.

[40] KK to NKR, 13 February 1955; KK, *DUJo*, 50; Margaret Wheeler, *Walls of Jericho*, 144–145.

[41] BSAJ Minutes, 9 May 1952; 26 June 1952; Minute Book 9, 26 June 1952; both at PEF.

Chapter 6

For KK's life at the Institute of Archaeology, I have relied on interviews with John Evans, Sarnia Butcher, Ros Henry, Vivienne Catleugh and Lawrence Toombs, as well as Callaway, "Dame Kathleen Kenyon."

[1] KK to NKR, 27 January 1952.

[2] Dever, "Kathleen Kenyon," 526.

[3] BSAJ Minutes, 14 October 1952. I am grateful to the The Council for British Research in the Levant [CBRL] for permission to reproduce BSAJ Minutes.

[4] KK to NKR, 5 February 1953.

[5] A. D. Tushingham, *ASOR Jerusalem and Baghdad Archaeological Newsletter #8*, 2 April 1953.

[6] This account of the "lowest boat race in history" is based on A. D. Tushingham's account in the *ASOR Jerusalem and Baghdad Archaeological Newsletter #8* (2 April 1953), as well as interviews with Doug and Maggie Tushingham, Cecil Western, and Peter Parr.

[7] Robert North, interview.

[8] For descriptions of the discovery of the portrait skulls, see KK, *DUJo*, 60–62; "Jericho Before Joshua," 930; "Father Roland De Vaux, O. P., viii–vix; KK and Tushingham, "Jericho Gives Up Its Secrets,"853; Ruby, *Jericho: Dreams, Ruins, Phantoms*, 126–128. In addition, I have had the benefit of interviews with Doug and Maggie Tushingham, Vivienne Catleugh, Cecil Western, and Peter Parr.

[9] KK, *Archaeology in the Holy Land*, 52.

[10] KK, *DUJo*, 63.

[11] At least the lecture notes preserved in the KMKC at Baylor University are minimal.

[12] Mallowan, *Mallowan's Memoirs*, 239.

[13] See, for example, Mallowan, *Mallowan's Memoirs*, 239, and "Department of Western Asiatic Archaeology 1947–62," 160.

[14] Vivienne Catleugh [VC], interview.

[15] VC, interview; "When the Two Dames Met", *Wrexham Leader*, 8 September 1978.

[16] KK to NKR, 27 December (1955?)

[17] KK to NKR, 13 September 1952.

[18] According to John Wilkes, "Although Kenyon had completed her report on the digging by 1956, the complete publication did not appear until 1980. Students had apparently

been allowed to take away the pottery for study and drawing and recovery of the material was both protracted and incomplete." Wilkes, "Kathleen Kenyon in Roman Britain," 104. See also KK, "Excavations at Viroconium in Insula 9, 1952–3," 5–74.

19 Mallowan, "Department of Western Asiatic Archaeology 1947–62,"160.

20 Information on these various broadcasts can be found in the BBC Written Archives Centre [BBC].

21 KK to the BBC, 16 August 1956; KK to "Women's Hour", 7 November 7, 1956, BBC.

22 See, for example, BSAJ Minutes, 6 October 1953, PEF.

23 R. E. M. Wheeler, The British Academy 1949–1968, 21.

24 KK, "Excavation Methods." Institute of Archaeology Proposed Occasional Paper, KMKC, Baylor University.

25 Robert H. Dyson, Jr, "Digging Up Jericho by Kathleen Kenyon," The Middle East Journal 12 (1958), 336.

26 Donald Redford, interview.

27 Butcher, diary, March 3, 1954.

28 Moorey, "Kathleen Kenyon and Palestinian Archaeology," 9.

29 See, for example, Parr, "Proto-Urban Jericho," 396.

30 Roland de Vaux to KK, 4 July 1960, KMKC, Baylor University.

31 KK to Peter Parr, 29 November 1959, BSAJ Paper Archives #2, PEF.

32 KK to NKR, 7 February 1954.

33 KK to NKR, 7 February 1954.

34 KK to Lorna Moore, 8 January 1954, BBC.

35 KK to NKR, 7 February 1954.

36 KK, Archaeology in the Holy Land, 54.

37 KK, "Excavations at Jericho 1954," 51.

38 KK to NKR, 15 February 1954.

39 But now dated to ca. 8500 B.C.

40 KK, "Excavations at Jericho 1954," 61.

41 KK, "The Oldest Town in the World."

42 For the story of Zeuner's investigations, see Margaret Wheeler, Walls of Jericho, 110–114; and KK, Digging Up Jericho (DUJo), 249–250. For the results of these investigations, see Zeuner, "Notes on the Bronze Age Tombs of Jericho," 118–128; and Sheila Dorrell, "The Preservation of Organic Material in the Tombs at Jericho," in KK, Excavations at Jericho, Vol. 2, 704–707.

43 Jonathan Tubb, interview.

44 KK, DUJo, 251.

45 KK to NKR, 7 February 1954; KK to NKR, 13 February 1955.

46 KK to NKR, 15 February 1954.

47 KK to NKR, 13 February 1955.

48 KK to NKR, 24 December 1957.

49 PEF Minutes, 19 May 1954; 15 December 1954; 12 May 1955, PEF.

50 Butcher, diary, February 1, 1954.

51 Starlings were a local delicacy, and sometimes their feathers were plucked so the birds could not fly.

[52] KK to NKR, 16 February 1955.

[53] KK to NKR, 13 February 1955.

[54] KK to NKR, 10 January 1956.

[55] KK to NKR, 10 January 1956; KK to NKR, 16 February 1956.

[56] KK to Paul Johnstone, 6 February 1956, BBC.

[57] For views of the local Arab population I have relied on interviews with Vivienne Catleugh and Monique Brinkman; Margaret Wheeler, *Walls of Jericho*, 87–88; and David Spurgeon's series of articles in the Toronto *Globe and Mail*.

[58] KK, "Jordan Today," handwritten manuscript, KMKC, Baylor University. At the time of the 1956 crisis, she also wrote a letter to *The Times* (London) (7 November 1956) stating that the British government's actions made her "feel that I shall be ashamed to return to Jordan even if it proves again possible."

[59] KK to Nora, 16 February 1956; Maggie Tushingham, interview.

[60] KK, "Sir Mortimer Wheeler."

[61] KK to BBC, 16 August 1956, BBC.

[62] KK to NKR, March (day uncertain) 1957.

[63] KK, "The British School of Archaeology in Jerusalem. The New School Building," PEQ (1957), 99; BSAJ Minutes, 24 July 1956; 7 May 1958, PEF; KK to NKR, March (day uncertain) 1957.

[64] KK to NKR, 24 December 1957.

[65] P. G. Dorrell, "Stone vessels, tools, and objects," in Kenyon and Holland, *Excavations at Jericho* 3, 485–575.

[66] KK, "Excavations at Jericho, 1957–58," 90.

[67] Most archaeologists preferred Early Bronze IV (ca. 2400–2100 B.C.)

[68] Braidwood, "Jericho and Its Setting in Near Eastern History," 73–81. See also R. E. M. Wheeler, "Anniversary Address," 166; KK, "Jericho and Its Setting in Near Eastern Archaeology," 184–195; and KK, "Reply to Professor Braidwood," 82–84.

[69] KK, "Reply to Professor Braidwood," 84.

[70] Parr, "Proto-Urban Jericho," 389–398. In this article Parr also mentions others who have reanalyzed the Jericho excavations.

[71] Laughlin, *Archaeology and the Bible*, 65–66.

[72] Bar-Yosef, "The Walls of Jericho," 157–162.

[73] Wood, "Did the Israelites Conquer Jericho?" 45–59.

[74] Amihai Mazar, 44.

[75] Laughlin, 49.

[76] Laughlin, 51.

[77] Tubb, "MB IIA Period in Palestine," 59.

[78] Laughlin, 59.

[79] Moorey, *Excavation in Palestine*, 63–64.

[80] Albright, "Reports on Excavation in the Near and Middle East," 31.

[81] See, for example, Dever, "Kathleen Kenyon," 534; Parr, "Proto-Urban Jericho," 396; French, "Review of *Excavations at Jericho*"; Oates, "Review of *Excavation at Jericho*"; Oates, "Review of *Excavations at Jericho*, Vol. 4 and Vol. 5"; and Watkins, "Review of *Excavations at Jericho*, Vol. 3."

[82] Watkins, "Review of Kenyon and Holland, *Excavations at Jericho.*"

[83] Moorey, "Kathleen Kenyon and Palestinian Archaeology," 6.

[84] Dever, "Two Approaches to Archaeological Method," 1.

[85] Letter to author, Henk Franken; Franken, "A. D. Tushingham and K. M. Kenyon: An Appreciation."

[86] KK to PP, 7 April 1959, BSAJ Paper archive #2, PEF.

[87] KK to NKR, 13 February 1955.

[88] Moorey, "Kathleen Kenyon and Palestinian Archaeology," 7.

[89] KK to PP, March (day uncertain) 1959, BSAJ Paper Archive #2, PEF; KK to NKR, March 14, 1959; Schedule of Lecture Tour of America, March/April 1959, Heath collection.

[90] KK to PP, March (day uncertain) 1959, BSAJ Paper Archive #2, PEF; KK to NKR, 14 March 1959; Schedule of Lecture Tour of American, March/April 1959, Heath collection..

[91] Willard Hamrick, interview. In the 1950s, British buildings had two water tanks, a cold tank and a hot tank. Usually only one of these was suitable for drinking without boiling.

[92] KK to PP, March (day uncertain) 1959, BSAJ Paper archive #2, PEF; KK to NKR, 14 March 1959, 7 April 1959.

[93] "A member of the family," *The Kenyon Clipsheet*, May 1959, Kenyon College, Greenslade Special Collection & Archives.

Chapter 7

For KK's description and interpretation of the Jerusalem excavations, I have relied on her annual reports to the PEF ("Excavations in Jerusalem," 1961 through 1967); *Digging Up Jerusalem* (*DUJm*); *Jerusalem: Excavating 3000 Years of History*; and various articles she published on the excavations, which are listed in the bibliography.

Interviews with the following provided very helpful accounts of the Jerusalem dig: Terry Ball, Ian Blake, Monique Brinkman, Stephanie Dalley, Iain Davidson, Gloria Fenner, Willard Hamrick, Basil Hennessy, Thomas Holland, Andrew Moore, Roger Moorey, Peter Parr, Sebastian Payne, Ann Seawright, Ahmed Shistawi, Agnès Spycket, Mary Swiney, John Strange, A. D. Tushingham, Maggie Tushingham, Jessica Rawson, Donald Redford, Cecil Western, and Christopher Young. Letters from Svend Holm-Nielson and Tim Strickland provided additional information. Numerous letters from Maggie Tushingham answered many of my questions. The following articles also provided useful information: Hadidi, "Kathleen Kenyon and her Place in Palestinian Archaeology"; Callaway, "Dame Kathleen Kenyon, 1906–1978"; Prag, "Moving Onward. Australians Uncovering Ancient Jordan"; and Tushingham, "Kathleen Mary Kenyon."

[1] Tushingham, "Kathleen Mary Kenyon," 571.

[2] KK, *DUJm*, 191, n. 1.

[3] M. Avi-Yonah, "Excavations in Jerusalem," 21.

[4] KK to PP, 20 May 1958. BSAJ Paper archives #2.

[5] KK, "Excavations in Jerusalem: Problems and Plans," KMKC, Baylor University.

[6] Ibid.

[7] Tushingham, "Kathleen Mary Kenyon," 572.

[8] Lawrence Toombs, interview.

[9] BSAJ Minutes, 2 February 1959, PEF.

[10] See, for example, NK to John Ritchie, 1 March1935; KK to NK, 28 March 1934; 8 March 1935; 30 December 1952.

[11] Prag, "Kathleen Kenyon and Archaeology in the Holy Land,"114; Lawrence Toombs, interview; see also KK to NKR, 27 January 1952.

[12] "Leading field archaeologist to give lecture in Glasgow," *The Glasgow Herald*, 18 February 1969.

[13] KK, "Excavations in Jerusalem: Problems and Plans,"handwritten speech in KMKC, Baylor University.

[14] The term "Ophel" seems to have been used to refer an acropolis, essentially a walled fort on a hilltop. See Eilat Mazar, "The Royal Quarter of Biblical Jerusalem," 64.

[15] KK, *DUJm*, 29–30.

[16] "Annual Report, 1956–57," *Proceedings of the British Academy* XLIII (1957): 5.

[17] Minutes of the PAM Board of Trustees, 28 November 1959; 7 May 1960, KMKC, Baylor University.

[18] Allegro, *The Dead Sea Scrolls*, 194.

[19] KK to Roland de Vaux, 28 January 1960; KK to Frank Francis, April 14, 1960; both in the KMKC, Baylor University. For a description of these excavations, see Stutchbury, "Excavations in the Kidron Valley."

[20] KK to John Allegro, 6 January 1960, KMKC, Baylor University.

[21] John Allegro to KK, 6 January 1960, KMKC, Baylor University.

[22] KK to PP, 4 February 1960, BSAJ Paper archive #2, PEF.

[23] KK to Roland de Vaux, 28 January 1960, KMKC, Baylor University. The Parker Expedition was the one in 1911 that had been rumored to have been looking for treasure beneath the Temple Mount and eventually had had to flee Jerusalem. But it managed to clear out the Siloam Tunnel, part of an elaborate tunnel system connected to the Gihon spring on the eastern slope of Ophel. Most importantly, Père Hugues Vincent was able to publish much of what had been found.

[24] John Allegro, "Dead Sea Scrolls Emergency," *Daily Telegraph*, 6 January 1960; KK to *Daily Telegraph*, 4 February 1960.

[25] For example, KK to REMW, 4 August 1961, KMKC, Baylor University.

[26] Memo, "The Dead Sea Scrolls"; REMW to A. A. F. Haigh, 15 February 1960; both in the KMKC, Baylor University.

[27] Copies of correspondence describing these negotiations are found in the KMKC, Baylor University.

[28] KK to REMW, 3 July, 12 July 1961; REMW to KK 29 July 1961; both in the KMKC, Baylor University.

[29] PP to KK, 27 April 1960, BSAJ Paper archive #2, PEF.

[30] John Allegro, "New Dead Sea Scrolls Search," *The Sunday Times*, 18 December 1960; *Sunday Times*, 1, 8, 22, January 1961.

[31] REMW to KK, 29 July 1961, KMKC, Baylor University.

[32] Peter Parr to KK, 2 October 1961. BSAJ Paper archive #2, PEF.

[33] KK to Frank Francis, 14 April 1960; REMW to KK, 31 July 1961; KK to REMW, 4 August 1961; KK to John Henniker-Major, 4 August 1961; all in the KMKC, Baylor University.

[34] Correspondence concerning these negotiations is found in the KMKC, Baylor University.

[35] KK to REMW, 31 March 1962; memo, "Answers to the charges brought against the Museum by Dr. Allegro in his letter of April 2, 1962 to Mr. H. E. Macomber"; in the KMKC, Baylor University.

[36] John Allegro to W. B. Macomber, 2 April 1962; John Allegro to Willie Morris, 2 April 1962; KK to Frank Francis, 12 April 1962; all in the KMKC, Baylor University. "British Show of Scrolls Baulked," *Daily Telegraph*, 17 April 1962.

[37] KK to Frank Francis, 12 April 1962, KMKC, Baylor University.

[38] KK, "Dead Sea Scrolls. Report on New Material Brought to the Palestine Archaeological Museum," 30 April 1962; REMW to Brian Heddy, 17 August 1962; KK to REMW, 15 August 1962; all in the KMKC, Baylor University.

[39] G. R. Driver to REMW, 5 September 1962; "The Jericho Papyri. Informal meeting held at the British Academy, 9 October 1962"; both in the KMKC, Baylor University.

[40] Roland de Vaux to KK, 19 November 1962; KK to G. R. Driver, 27 November 1962; KK to R. de Vaux, 29 November 1962; all in the KMKC, Baylor University.

[41] KK to REMW, 27 November 1962; Roland de Vaux to KK, 19 November 1962; both in the KMKC, Baylor University. For the American version of the scrolls' purchase, see King, *American Archaeology in the Mideast*," 159–160.

[42] KK to Editor, *The Sunday Times* (London), 23 November 1965; KK to Roland de Vaux, 14 December 1965; Peter Hiley, correspondence editor, *The Sunday Times* to KK, 27 November 1965; all letters in KMKC, Baylor University.

[43] KK to S. Dearden, 24 November 1965, KMKC, Baylor University.

[44] Tushingham, "Kathleen Mary Kenyon," 575.

[45] For K as a bad judge of character, see, for example, Trickett, "Dame Kathleen Kenyon," 36.

[46] Western, "Dame Kathleen Kenyon, D.B.E.," iv; Sebastian Payne and Chris Young, interviews.

[47] KK, *DUJm*, 70–71.

[48] Memo to prospective staff, "Excavations in Jerusalem, 1964," in BSAJ General File, PEF.

[49] Not everyone in Jerusalem agrees with the observation that K was shy. Sebastian Payne, for example, does not. As he pointed out to me, her reaction to people depended on the context: she would have been less likely to seem shy to people she knew well or in situations in which she felt confident.

[50] KK, *DUJm*, 72.

[51] KK, "Excavations in Jerusalem"; KK, "Excavations in Jerusalem. Notes on scheme, on steps taken and results," both in BSAJ General File, PEF; KK, "Proposed excavations in Jerusalem," KMKC, Baylor University.

[52] KK to REMW, 3 July 1961, KMKC, Baylor University.

[53] Now two Israeli archaeologists argue that Warren's Shaft was never intended as a water shaft. See Reich and Shukron, "Light at the End of the Tunnel," 23–33, 72. Even their reinterpretation of the Warren Shaft System, however, still allows the spring to be accessed from within the city wall K located.

[54] In her publication of the Jerusalem excavations, M. L. Steiner dated the terraces to the twelfth–early thirteenth centuries B.C. See Steiner, *Excavations by Kathleen M. Kenyon in Jerusalem 1961–1967*, Vol. III, 24.

[55] See, for example, Bahat, "Jerusalem," 226; or James, "The Revelation of Jerusalem," 36.

[56] KK, "Ancient Jerusalem," *Scientific American*, 88.

[57] KK, *DUJm*, 102.

[58] During the 1961 season, excavation of another site within the Old City, a site just within and to the east of the Dung Gate, was begun by the Jordanian Department of Antiquities, with the Jerusalem Expedition acting in an advisory capacity. In 1962 and 1963, Roland de Vaux excavated in this area as an official part of Kathleen's Jerusalem excavations.

[59] Geraldine Talbot to Crystal Bennett, 21 November 1962, BSAJ Paper archives #2, PEF.

[60] Note from Director, 13 April 1960; Institute of Archaeology, Quinquennium 1957–1962, 592; Development Policy in the Quinquennium 1962–1967, 2; all from Senate House Files, Institute of Archaeology, London; IAMC Minutes, 1956–1961, 2 February 1960.

[61] Memo from Max Mallowan to Director, 7 January 1955, Senate House Files, Institute of Archaeology, London.

[62] KK to PP, 20 March 1958, BSAJ Paper archive #2, PEF.

[63] IAMC Minutes, 27 May 1957; W. F. Grimes to IAMC, 14 June 1957; IAMC Minutes, 4 June 1957.

[64] Rachel Maxwell-Hyslop, interview.

[65] Mary Warnock, interview; Susan Wood, interview.

[66] Trickett, "Dame Kathleen Kenyon," 35–36; Warnock, *Mary Warnock: A Memoir*, 125; Mary Warnock, interview.

[67] Warnock, *Mary Warnock: A Memoir*, 125.

[68] KK, *DUJm*, 5, 67, 130.

[69] KK to Peter Parr [PP], 15 July 1960. BSAJ Paper archive #2, PEF.

[70] KK, *DUJm*, 73.

[71] KK to Charles Johnstone, 31 August 1960, KMKC, Baylor University.

[72] PP to KK, 10 March 1962; Crystal Bennett to Doug Tushingham, 18 May 1964, BSAJ Paper archive #2; BSAJ minutes, 16 June 1964; all at PEF.

[73] KK to REMW, 3 July 1961, KMKC, Baylor University.

[74] Crystal Bennett to KK, 11 June 1963, BSAJ Paper archive #2, PEF.

[75] BSAJ Minutes, 16 June 1964, PEF; KK, "Excavations in Jerusalem, 1964," 9.

[76] Crystal Bennett to KK, 6 July 1964. BSAJ Paper archive #2, PEF.

[77] KK, "Excavations in Jerusalem, 1964," 9.

[78] KK, "Ancient Jerusalem," *Discovery*, 23.

[79] Emory University Museum Annual Report to the President, 1967–68. Special Collections, Woodruff Library, Emory University.

[80] KK to REMW, 3 September 1966, KMKC, Baylor University.

[81] "Ancient Jerusalem Wall Uncovered," *The Times* (London), 25 September 1964; "Jerusalem Wall: Search Continues," *The Times* (London), 28 September 1964.

[82] KK, *DUJm*, 94.

[83] M. L. Steiner argued that Kathleen probably thought that the wall had been rebuilt repeatedly because of "the recesses in the face of the wall. These recesses, however, are more likely to represent the ledges where once wooden beams had been incorporated into the masonry of the wall." Steiner also dates the wall earlier than K did, to the first half of the seventh century. Franken and Steiner, *Excavations in Jerusalem 1961–1967*, Vol. II, 56.

[84] KK to Armenian Patriarch, 22 September 1964, BSAJ General File, PEF.

[85] Willard Hamrick, who was one of K's site supervisors, came up with a different explanation for this wall. He argued that it was a barrier built by the inhabitants of Jerusalem during the First Revolt. See Hamrick, "New Excavations at Sukenik's 'Third Wall'" ; "The Third North Wall of Agrippa I" ; "The Fourth North Wall of Jerusalem."

[86] This point is still debated, but K's position is not generally accepted. See chapter 8.

[87] Kathleen's interpretations of a *masseboth* and *favissa* have been disputed by several authors. See M. L. Steiner and the authors she cites, in *Excavations in Jerusalem 1961–1967*, Vol. II, 24.

[88] KK, *DUJm*, 133.

Chapter 8

For general accounts of the effect of the Six Day War on the BSAJ, I have used William Dever, "Archaeology and the Six Day War," and information received from Terry Ball. For the Hennessy affair I have relied on interviews with Basil Hennessy, Joe D. Seger, and Terry Ball; Hawkes, *Adventurer in Archaeology*; and the BSAJ archives at the PEF.

For KK's own view of the effect of the war on the 1967 season, see her 1967 *PEQ* report, her memo, "Report to the Council of the BSAJ. Visit to Jerusalem and Amman," (14 July 1967), BSAJ General File, and her letter to Joe Callaway, 27 February 1968, Southern Baptist Theological Seminary [SBTS].

For Israeli views of KK's Jerusalem excavations I benefited from interviews with Avraham Biran, Magen Broshi, Meir Ben Dov, William Dever, Hillel Geva, Amihai Mazar, Eilat Mazar, Ronny Reich, David Ussishkin, and Seymour Gitin, as well as an e-mail from Dan Bahat. I have also made use of Avigad, *Discovering Jerusalem*; Amihai Mazar, "Israeli Archaeologists"; and Broshi, "'Digging Up Jerusalem'—A Critique."

[1] Memorandum of KK, 30 July 1966; KK to Frank Francis, 27 July 1966; both in KMKC, Baylor University.

[2] KK to Sayid Wasfi Tell, 4 August 1966; KK to REMW, 10 August 1966; both in KMKC, Baylor University.

[3] KK, "Extraordinary Meeting of the Trustees of the Palestine Archaeological Museum to Discuss the Proposal of the Jordanian Government to Take Over the Museum," 9 August 1966, KMKC, Baylor University.

[4] KK to REMW, 10 August 1966; KK to Frank Francis, 29 August 1966; both in KMKC, Baylor University.

[5] KK to Governor Anwar Khatib, 15 August, 18 August; KK, "Notes on Emergency Meeting of the Board of Trustees of 31 August, 1966," 2 September 1966; all in KMKC, Baylor University.

[6] *Jerusalem Times*, 1 September 1966.

[7] KK to Governor Anwar Khatib, 2 September 1966, KMKC, Baylor University.

[8] KK, "Progress Report up to 18.9.66"; KK to G. L. Harding, 8 September 1966; both in KMKC, Baylor University.

[9] KK, "Report on the Final Meeting of Trustees," 28 November 1966, KMKC, Baylor University.

[10] Eric Fletcher to KK, 8 May 1967; KK to Eric Fletcher, 16 May 1967; both in the KMKC, Baylor University.

[11] G. L. Harding to KK, 15 December 1966, 14 February 1967; J. P. Tripp to KK, 18 April 1967; all in the KMKC, Baylor University.

[12] KK, *The Times* (London), 19 June 1967.

[13] KK, "Report to the Council of the BSAJ. Visit to Jerusalem and Amman," 14 July 1967, BSAJ General File, PEF; Avraham Biran, interview.

[14] KK, "Excavations in Jerusalem, 1967," 98.

[15] KK, "Excavations in Jerusalem, 1967," 98.

[16] KK to Joe Callaway, 27 February 1968, SBTS.

[17] See, for example, her reply to *BAR's* inquiry about her use of the term "Palestine:" KK to *Biblical Archaeology Review [BAR]*, (November/December 1978), 45.

[18] KK to Joe Callaway, 27 February 1968, SBTS.

[19] "Permit Given for Jerusalem Dig," *The Times* (London), 16 March 1961; BSAJ Minutes, 3 July, 1967, PEF; KK, "Excavations in Jerusalem, 1967," 97.

[20] KK's review of General Odd Bull, *War and Peace in the Middle East. The Experiences and Views of an UN Observer* (1976), KMKC, Baylor University. Where, or whether, this was published is uncertain.

[21] Magen Broshi, interview.

[22] KK to NK, 15 December 1933.

[23] McCall, *Life of Max Mallowan*, 109.

[24] The Jordanians were so determined to prevent Jews from entering Jordan that students working on Kathleen's excavations in Jerusalem were required to present paperwork documenting their religion. See memo to students participating in 1964 Jerusalem excavations, "Excavations in Jerusalem, 1964," BSAJ General File, PEF.

[25] Trude Dothan said that when she studied at the Institute of Archaeology in London, K was quite helpful to her. Magen Broshi called her a "sport" because even after he wrote

253

a review critical of *Digging Up Jerusalem*, K was quite willing to remain on good terms with him, even conceding that some of his criticisms were warranted. Although Yigael Yadin's biographer implies that Yadin did not like K, there is no evidence that she did not like him. Her friends and colleagues recall that although she criticized his archaeology, she had a high opinion of him personally and they corresponded about professional matters in a friendly way.

[26] A. Biran to KK, 5 November 1967; KK to REMW, 14 November 1967; KK to T. C. Skeat, 14 November; all in the KMKC, Baylor University.

[27] BSAJ Minutes, 3 July 1967, PEF.

[28] Letter to Chair, BSAJ, undated; reply from REMW, 2 October 1967; Minutes of Special Meeting of BSAJ, 27 November 1967, all in BSAJ General File, PEF.

[29] Hawkes, 351. Reproduced from *Adventurer in Archaeology: the Biography of Sir Mortimer Wheeler by Jacquetta Hawkes* (Copyright © Estate of Jacquetta Hawkes 1982) by permission of PFD (www.pfd.co.uk) on behalf of the Estate of Jacquetta Hawkes.

[30] BSAJ Minutes, 4 March, 21 October 1966, PEF.

[31] BSAJ Minutes, 24 October 1966, PEF.

[32] Quoted in Hawkes, 351–352.

[33] BSAJ Minutes, 1 December 1967, PEF.

[34] For a description of these excavations, see B. Mazar, *The Mountain of the Lord*; Ben Dov, *In the Shadow of the Temple*.

[35] Kenyon, *Digging Up Jerusalem (DUJm)*, 275–278.

[36] Kenyon, *DUJm*, 277–278. Some other archaeologists seem to agree that Mazar was not the best excavator, nor was he using the most up-to-date methods. See, for example, Shanks, "Kathleen Kenyon's Anti-Zionist Politics,' 4; and Lapp, "Captive Treasures,"38–39.

[37] Avigad, *Discovering Jerusalem*, 28–30; Avigad, "The Upper City," 469–475.

[38] Kenyon, *DUJm*, 147–148, 158–160.

[39] Ben-Arieh and Netzer, "Excavations along the 'Third Wall' of Jerusalem, 1972–1974," 97–107.

[40] See Hershel Shanks's discussion of this question in "The Jerusalem Wall that Shouldn't be There." Although K did not respond in print to Ben-Arieh and Netzer's findings, Shanks says that she never changed her mind about the Third Wall. But Magen Broshi told me that she admitted to him he was right about some of his criticisms of *Digging Up Jerusalem*, although he could not remember which one. Possibly she meant the question of the Third Wall.

[41] "Kathleen Kenyon Replies to BAR," *Biblical Archaeology Review* 2, no. 1 (1976): 12–13.

[42] Lapp, 38. Other archaeologists agree that this sentiment existed.

[43] KK, *DUJm*, 278.

[44] A. Mazar, "Israeli Archaeologists," 120–121.

[45] Dever, "Kathleen Kenyon," 535.

[46] See, for example, Shiloh, *Excavations at the City of David*; Reich and Shukron, "Jerusalem City Dump in the Late Temple Period"; Franken, "Excavations of the British School of Archaeology in Jerusalem on the Southeast Hill in Light of Subsequent Research."

[47] Moorey, *A Century of Biblical Archaeology*, 124.

[48] Kay Prag expects the final volume of the Jerusalem excavations to be completed in the near future.

[49] Franken and Steiner, *Excavations in Jerusalem 1961–1967*, 5.

[50] Steiner, *Excavations by Kathleen M. Kenyon in Jerusalem 1961–1967*, Vol. III, 112.

[51] Steiner, Vol. III, 24, 38.

[52] Franken and Steiner, 1.

[53] Franken and Steiner, 1; Steiner, Vol. III, 2.

[54] Kenrick, *Excavations at Sabratha 1948–1951*, 4; Phillip Kenrick, interview.

[55] Shanks, "The Mistress of Stratigraphy Had Clay Feet," 53.

[56] Martin Biddle, "Kathleen Kenyon," unpublished typescript sent to author.

[57] Letter to author, Henk Franken, 15 October 2001.

[58] Dever, "Kathleen Kenyon," 542.

Chapter 9

For KK's life at St. Hugh's I have relied on interviews with Allison Brackenbury, Avril Bruten, Vivienne Catleugh, Peter Gathercole, Thomas Holland, Tony Lyford, E. M. Major, Janet Balfour, Joanna Trollope, Mary Warnock, and Susan Wood. Letters from Audrey Colson, Annette Blampied, and Allison Brackenbury were also helpful, as was an e-mail from Selina Hastings. I am grateful to St. Hugh's College for making available to me notes on KK's tenure by Margery Sweeting. In addition, I made use of the following published material: Cooper, "Dame Kathleen's Work as Principal of St. Hugh's and in the University of Oxford"; Trickett, "Dame Kathleen Kenyon"; Warnock, *Mary Warnock: A Memoir*; West, "Reminiscences of Seven Decades"; the Joint Common Room and Principal's reports found in the *St. Hugh's Chronicle*; and KK's own "Women in Academic Life."

K's life at Rose Hill is based on interviews with Colonel John Kenyon, Vivienne Catleugh, Thomas Holland, Janet Heath, Jeremy Ritchie; the Rev. Peter Jones, "Erbistock," *Parish Magazine*, October 1978; and a letter from Tim Strickland.

[1] Mary Warnock, interview.

[2] Warnock, *Mary Warnock: A Memoir*, 124.

[3] *Cherwell* (Oxford University), 15 October 1971.

[4] Alison Brackenbury, letter to author.

[5] Trickett, "Dame Kathleen Kenyon," 39.

[6] Steele, "The College Head ," 15.

[7] See, for example, *Cherwell*, 9 February 1964.

[8] *Cherwell*, 16 November 1966; Steele, 15.

[9] Priscilla West, "Reminiscences of Seven Decades", 186. Reproduced with permission of Palgrave Macmillian.

[10] West, 189. Reproduced with permission of Palgrave Macmillian.

[11] "Leading field archaeologist to give lecture in Glasgow," *The Glasgow Herald*, 18 February 1969.

[12] Reunions of former undergraduates, known in Oxford as the Senior Members of the University.

[13] Steele.

[14] KK, typescript in KMKC, Baylor University; printed in *Oxford University Gazette,* cii (1971/72).

[15] Alison Brakenbury, letter to author.

[16] Kenyon, *Digging Up Jerusalem,* 278–279.

[17] Trickett, 37–38.

[18] KK to Joseph Callaway, 26 November 1968, Southern Baptist Theological Seminary [SBTS].

[19] William Dever, interview.

[20] KK to *The Times* (London), 17 August 1972; L. Gress, "Leading Palestine archaeologist blasts Israeli methods of digging up Jerusalem," *Jordan Times,* 31 July 1977.

[21] BSAJ Minutes, 31 July 1969, PEF. The BSAJ had reason to be concerned that its continued presence in occupied Jerusalem threatened the position of British Schools in other Arab countries and was eager to have its position made clear to other Arab governments. One rumor reported to the BSAJ was that the British School in Baghdad was in trouble with the Iraqi government because of the BSAJ's "continued presence" in Jerusalem. (BSAJ Minutes, 31 July 1969). Max Mallowan wrote that an American expedition had been refused permission to excavate in Iraq because of American excavations in the West Bank (BSAJ Minutes, 24 September 1969). K's experience at the Third International Conference on Asian Archaeology held in Bahrain, March 1970, illustrates the difficulties she faced. At the conference K supported a resolution that essentially reaffirmed the UNESCO position, but she also proposed an amendment to the first draft of the resolution that left out parts of the original motion she felt improperly political. She was distressed because *The Sunday Telegraph* had inaccurately reported that she had opposed the original motion condemning the Israeli actions; K feared that that misrepresentation of her views could damage the BSAJ ("Arabs Ban Jerusalem Digs," *Sunday Telegraph,* 8 March 1970; KK to *The Sunday Telegraph,* 13 March 1970, KMKC; KK to *The Sunday Telegraph,* 23 March 1970, KMKC, Baylor University). I am grateful to Michael Rice for allowing me to read the account of this incident in his unpublished memoir.

[22] BSAJ Minutes, 17 February 1969; 31 July 1969; both at PEF.

[23] BSAJ Minutes, 31 July 1969, PEF.

[24] BSAJ Minutes, 2 February 1968; 13 March 1970; both at PEF.

[25] KK to Joe Callaway, 28 October 1969, SBTS. According to Andrew Moore, one of K's Ph.D. students, she wanted to have the BSAJ sponsor his dig in Syria in the early 1970s. Moore, who was concerned about the possible repercussions in Syria of BSAJ sponsorship, refused.

[26] BSAJ Minutes, 20 March 1968, 31 July 1969, PEF; Talbot, "Crystal Bennett," 2. See also Burgoyne, *Mameluke Jerusalem: An Architectural Survey.*

[27] And elsewhere. With much of what had been Jordanian territory now effectively off-limits to British archaeologists, K showed a growing interest in promoting archaeology in the surrounding region, in Syria and elsewhere.

[28] *Levant* 2 (1970): iii.

[29] Ann Mitchell, interview. Early in K's tenure Chef Tony Lyford had been hired by St. Hugh's. While the food at the college noticeably improved, probably this did not help K's waistline.

[30] Andrew Moore, interview.

[31] "The New Year's Honours List," *Daily Telegraph*, 1 January 1973.

[32] KK to Joseph Callaway, 3 February 1973, SBTS.

[33] Alison Brakenbury, letter to author, 17 October 2000.

[34] KK to Joseph Callaway, 3 February 1973, SBTS.

[35] "Kathleen Mary Kenyon," *Transactions of the Shropshire Archaeological Society*, 60 (1975–76), 131.

[36] Quoted, in Trickett, 39.

[37] Moorey and Parr, *Archaeology in the Levant*, vii; KK to Joseph Callaway, 23 June 1978, SBTS.

[38] William Dever, interview; Shanks, "An Archaeological Romance," 27.

[39] Tushingham," Kathleen Mary Kenyon," 580.

[40] BSAJ Minutes, 10 July 1978, PEF.

[41] Funeral address of Rev. Peter Jones, typescript provided to the author by Jeremy Ritchie.

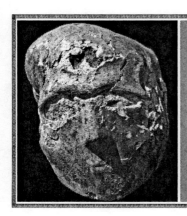

REFERENCES

MANUSCRIPT SOURCES

Heath, Janet Ritchie, collection of manuscripts. Handwritten, untitled memoirs of Nora Kenyon Ritchie [labeled here Memoirs #1 and #2]. Frederic Kenyon, "Autobiographica." Letters of Frederic Kenyon [FK], Amy Kenyon [AK], Kathleen Kenyon [KK], and Nora Kenyon Ritchie [NKR].

Baylor University. Kathleen M. Kenyon Collection [KMKC].

Bodleian Library, Oxford. Myres MSS.

British Broadcasting Corporation [BBC] Written Archives Centre. Correspondence.

British Red Cross Museum and Archives. County of London Branch Annual Reports. War Service Records.

Butcher, Sarnia. Diary.

Council for British Archaeology [CBA]. CBA Minute Books.

Emory University. Special Collections, Woodruff Library. Emory University Museum Annual Report to the President, 1967–68.

Institute of Archaeology, London. Petrie Correspondence. Senate House Files. Institute of Archaeology Management Committee Minutes [IAMC].

The Jewry Wall Museum & Site Archives. Correspondence.

Jones, Jennifer Peel. Unpublished memoir of May Peel.

Kenyon College. Greenslade Special Collections & Archives. *The Kenyon Clipsheet.*

Palestine Exploration Fund [PEF]. Minutes of the British School of Archaeology in Jerusalem. BSAJ Paper archives. BSAJ General File. Minutes of the Palestine Exploration Fund. Elizabeth Murray correspondence.

St. Hugh's College, Oxford [SHC]. *St. Hugh's Chronicle.* Letters of KK.

Surrey Archaeological Society Archives. Surrey Archaeological Society Annual General Meeting Reports.

University of London Library, Historic Collection. Senate Minutes.

Surrey History Centre. Pye, Winifred. *Eothen School (1892–1942).*

GENERAL WORKS

Adams, Pauline. *Somerville for Women.* Oxford: Oxford University Press, 1996.

Aharoni, Y., and Ruth Amiran. "A New Scheme for the Sub-Division of the Iron Age in Palestine." *Israel Exploration Journal* 8 (1958): 171–184.

Albright, W. F. "Recent Progress in Palestinian Archaeology: Samaria-Sebaste III and Hazor I." *Bulletin of the American Schools of Oriental Research* 150 (April, 1958): 21–24.

—. "Reports on Excavation in the Near and Middle East." *Bulletin of the American Schools of Oriental Research* 158 (April, 1960): 31, 37–39.

Allegro, John. *The Dead Sea Scrolls: A Reappraisal.* Harmondsworth, England: Penguin Books, 1956.

—. "Dead Sea Scrolls Emergency." *Daily Telegraph,* 6 January 1960.

—. "New Dead Sea Scrolls Search." *The Sunday Times,* 18 December 1960.

—. *Search in the Desert.* New York: Doubleday & Company, 1964.

"Ancient Jerusalem Wall Uncovered." *The Times* (London). 25 September 1964.

"Annual Report, 1956–57." *Proceedings of the British Academy* XLIII (1957): 5.

Avery, Gillian. *The Best Type of Girl: A History of the Girls' Independent Schools.* London: Andre Deutsch Ltd., 1991.

Avigad, Nahman. *Discovering Jerusalem.* Nashville: Thomas Nelson Publishers, 1983.

—. Samaria. In *The New Encyclopedia of Archaeological Excavations in the Holy Land,* edited by Ephraim Stern. Jerusalem: Israel Exploration Society, 1993.

—. "The Upper City." In "Revealing Biblical Jerusalem." In *Biblical Archaeology Today. Proceedings of the International Congress on Biblical Archaeology, Jerusalem, April 1984,* pp. 469–475. Jerusalem: Israel Exploration Society, 1985.

Avi-Yonah, M. "Excavations in Jerusalem—Review and Evaluation." In *Jerusalem Revealed: Archaeology in the Holy City 1968–1974,* edited by Yigael Yadin. New Haven and London: Yale University Press and the Israel Exploration Society, 1976.

Bahat, Dan. "Jerusalem." In *Oxford Encyclopedia of Archaeology in the Ancient Near East,* edited by Eric Meyers. American Schools of Oriental Research. Oxford: Oxford University Press, 1997.

Bailes, Howard. *Once a Paulina . . . A History of St. Paul's Girls' School.* London: James & James Ltd., 2000.

Balter, Michael. *The Goddess and the Bull.* New York: Free Press, 2005.

Bartlett, John R. *Jericho.* Grand Rapids, Michigan: William H. Eerdmans, 1982.

Bar-Yosef, O. "The Walls of Jericho: An Alternative Explanation." *Current Anthropology* 27, No. 2 (April 1986): 157–162.

Bell, H. I. "Sir Frederic George Kenyon, 1863–1952." *Proceedings of the British Academy* 38 (1952): 269–294.

Ben Dov, Meir. Translated by Ina Friedman. *In the Shadow of the Temple: The Discovery of Ancient Jerusalem.* New York: Harper & Row, 1985.

Ben-Arieh, Sara, and E. Netzer. "Excavations along the 'Third Wall' of Jerusalem, 1972–1974." *Israel Exploration Journal* 24, No. 2 (1974): 97–107.

Braidwood, Robert J. "Jericho and Its Setting in Near Eastern History." *Antiquity* 31 (1957): 73–81.

British School at Rome. 44th Annual Report to Subscribers (1948–49).

British School at Rome. 45th Annual Report to Subscribers (1949–50).

British School at Rome. 46th Annual Report to Subscribers (1950–51).

"British Show of Scrolls Baulked." *Daily Telegraph,* 17 April 1962.

Brittain, Vera. *The Women at Oxford: A Fragment of History.* London: George G. Harrap & Co., 1960.

Broshi, Magen. "'Digging Up Jerusalem' — A Critique." *British Archaeological Review* 1, No. 3 (1975): 1, 18–21.

Burgoyne, Michael. *Mameluke Jerusalem: An Architectural Survey.* Jerusalem: British School of Archaeology in Jerusalem, 1987.

Callaway, Joseph. "Dame Kathleen Kenyon." *Biblical Archaeologist* 42 (1979): 122–125.

Caton-Thompson. "The Southern Rhodesian Ruins: Recent Archaeological Investigations." *Nature* (19 October 1929): 619–621.

—. *The Zimbabwe Culture: Ruins and Reactions.* 2nd ed. London: Frank Cass and Co. Ltd., 1971.

—. *Mixed Memoirs.* Tyne & Wear: The Paradigm Press, 1983.

Clark, Graham. "Gertrude Caton-Thompson." *Proceedings of the British Academy* LXXI (1985): 523–531.

Conference on the Future of Archaeology. Held at the University of London, Institute of Archaeology, August 6th to 8th, 1943. Published as Occasional Paper No. 5 by the University of London Institute of Archaeology, 1944.

Conference on the Problems and Prospects of European Archaeology. Held at the University of London, September 16–17, 1044. Published as Occasional Paper No. 6 by the University of London Institute of Archaeology, 1945.

Cooper, T. C. "Dame Kathleen's Work as Principal of St. Hugh's and in the University of Oxford." *St. Hugh's Chronicle* 65 (1991–1992): 69–72.

Crowfoot, Elisabeth. "Grace Mary Crowfoot, 1877–1957." *http://www.brown.edu/ Research/Breaking_Ground/.*

Crowfoot, J. W. "Work of the Joint Expedition to Samaria-Sebastiya, April and May, 1931." *Quarterly Statement* (1931): 139–142.

—. "Excavations at Samaria, 1931." *Quarterly Statement* (1932): 8–34.

—. "Discoveries in Ahab's Capital." *Illustrated London News.* (24 January 1933): 84–85.

—. "Report for the Season, 1931–1932." *Quarterly Statement* (1933): 34–38.

—. "Report for the Season, 1932–1933." *Quarterly Statement* (1933): 175–183.

—. "Samaria: Interim Report on the Work in 1933." *Quarterly Statement* (1933): 129–136.

—. "Report for the Season, 1934–35." *Palestine Exploration Quarterly* (1936): 64.

—. "Report of the 1935 Samaria Excavations." *Palestine Exploration Quarterly* (1935): 182–194.

Crowfoot, J. W., and G. M. Crowfoot. "The Ivories from Samaria." *Quarterly Statement* (1933): 7–26.

Crowfoot, J. W., Kathleen M. Kenyon, and E. L. Sukenik. *The Buildings of Samaria. Samaria-Sebaste* I. London: PEF, 1942.

Crowfoot, J. W., and G. M. Crowfoot. *Early Ivories from Samaria, Samaria-Sebaste* II. London; PEF, 1938.

Crowfoot, J. W., G. M. Crowfoot, and Kathleen M. Kenyon. *The Objects from Samaria, Samaria-Sebaste* III. London: PEF, 1957.

Dever, William. "Archaeology and the Six Day War." *Biblical Archaeologist* XXX, No. 3 (1967): 73, 102–107.

—. "Two Approaches to Archaeological Method—The Architectural and the Stratigraphic." *Eretz-Israel* 11 (1973): 1–8.

—. "Archaeological Method in Israel: A Continuing Revolution." *Biblical Archaeologist* (Winter 1980): 41–48.

—. "Kathleen Kenyon." In *Breaking Ground: Pioneering Women Archaeologists*, edited by Getzel M. Cohen and Martha Sharp Joukowsky. Ann Arbor: University of Michigan Press, 2006.

Dorrell, P. G. "Stone Vessels, Tools, and Objects." In *Excavations at Jericho*, Vol. 3: *The Architecture and Stratigraphy of the Tell*, by Kathleen Kenyon and T. A. Holland, pp. 485–575. London: The British School of Archaeology in Jerusalem, 1981.

Dorrell, Sheila. "The Preservation of Organic Material in the Tombs at Jericho." In *Excavations at Jericho*, Vol. 2, *The Tombs Excavated in 1955–8*, by Kathleen Kenyon. Jerusalem: The British School of Archaeology in Jerusalem, 1965.

Drinkard, Joel, Gerald L. Mattingly, Jr., and Maxwell Miller, eds. *Benchmarks in Time and Culture: An Introduction to the History and Methodology of Syro-Palestinian Archaeology*. Atlanta: Scholars Press, 1988.

Drower, Margaret S. "Gertrude Caton-Thompson." In *Breaking Ground: Pioneering Women Archaeologists*, edited by Getzel M. Cohen and Martha Sharp Joukowsky. Ann Arbor: University of Michigan Press, 2006.

Dyson, Robert H. Jr. "*Digging Up Jericho* by Kathleen Kenyon." *The Middle East Journal* 12 (1958), 336.

Evans, John D. "The First Half-Century — and After." *Bulletin of the Institute of Archaeology* 24 (1987): 1–25.

Fanning, Michael. "Kathleen M. Kenyon's Interpretation of the History of Old Testament Times: An Analysis of its Genesis, Development, and Significance." Ph.D. dissertation, Baylor University, 1992.

Franken, H. J. "The Excavations of the British School of Archaeology in Jerusalem on the Southeast Hill in Light of Subsequent Research." *Levant* XIV (1987):129–135.

—. "A. D. Tushingham and K. M. Kenyon: An Appreciation." *Palestine Exploration Quarterly* 135, No. 1 (January–June 2003): 4.

Franken, H. J., and M. L. Steiner. *Excavations in Jerusalem 1961–1967*, Vol. II. *The Iron Age Extramural Quarter on the South-East Hill*. Oxford: Oxford University Press, 1990.

French, Elizabeth. "Review of *Excavations at Jericho*, Vol. 3." *Journal of Semitic Studies* XXVIII, No. 1 (Spring 1983): 151–152.

Frere, Sheppard S. "Excavations at Verulamium 1959." *The Antiquaries Journal* XL, Nos. 1–2 (January–April 1960): 1–24.

—. *Verulamium Excavations*, Vol. II. Reports of the Research Committee of the Society of Antiquaries of London, No. XLI, 1983.

Garstang, John. "Jericho. Sir Charles Marston's Expedition of 1930." *Quarterly Statement* (1930): 123–132.

—. "The Walls of Jericho. The Marston-Melchett Expedition of 1931. *Quarterly Statement* (1931): 186–196.

—. "The Walls of Jericho Excavated." *Illustrated London News* (17 January 1931): 94–99.

—. "A Third Season at Jericho." *Quarterly Statement* (1932): 149–153.

Geva, Hillel, ed. *Ancient Jerusalem Revealed*. Jerusalem: Israel Exploration Society; Washington, DC: Biblical Archaeology Society, 1994.

Gray, Frances. *And Gladly Wolde He Lerne and Gladly Teach: A Book about Learning and Teaching*. London: Sampson, Low, Marston and Co., 1931.

Gress, L. "Leading Palestine Archaeologist Blasts Israeli Methods of Digging Up Jerusalem. *Jordan Times*, 31 July 1977.

Griffin, Penny, ed. *St. Hugh's: One Hundred Years of Women's Education in Oxford*. London: Macmillan and Co., 1986.

Hadidi, Adnan. "Kathleen Kenyon and Her Place in Palestinian Archaeology." *Annual of the Department of Antiquities* 21 (1976): 7–17. Amman Department of Antiquities, Hashemite Kingdom of Jordan.

Hall, Richard. *Prehistoric Rhodesia*. Philadelphia: George W. Jacobs & Co., 1909.

Hamrick, E. W. "New Excavations at Sukenik's 'Third Wall.'" *Bulletin of the American Schools of Oriental Research* 183 (1966): 19–26.

—. "The Third North Wall of Agrippa I." *Biblical Archaeologist* 40 (1977):18–23.

—. "The Fourth North Wall of Jerusalem: 'A Barrier Wall' of the First Century, A.D." *Levant* XIII (1981): 262–266.

Harrison, Brian, ed. *A History of the University of Oxford*. Vol. 8, *The Twentieth Century*. Oxford: Oxford University Press, 1994.

Hawkes, Jacquetta. *Adventurer in Archaeology. The Biography of Sir Mortimer Wheeler*. New York: St. Martin's Press, 1982.

Hawkins, H.W. "Mystery of Roman Leicester." *Leicester Evening Mail*, 26 November 1937.

Hebditch, Max, and Jean Mellor. "The Forum and Basilica of Roman Leicester." *Britannia* 4 (1973): 1–80.

Hirschfield, M. G., ed. *St. Paul's Girls' School, 1904–1954*. London: The Favil Press Ltd., n.d.

Holland, Thomas. "Jericho." In *The Oxford Encyclopedia of Archaeology in the Near East*, Vol. 3, edited by Eric M. Meyers. American Schools of Oriental Research. Oxford and New York: Oxford University Press, 1997.

—. "Kathleen Mary Kenyon." In *Encyclopedia of Archaeology: The Great Archaeologists*, Vol. 2, edited by Tim Murray. Santa Barbara, CA: ABC-Clio, 1999.

Hopkinson, Diana. *The Incense Tree*. London: Routledge & Kagan Paul, 1968.

Huckaby, Gary C. "An Analysis of the Methodology of Kathleen M. Kenyon in Relation to Biblical Archaeology in Palestine with a Focus on Jericho." Ph.D. dissertation, Southwestern Baptist Theological Seminary, 1984.

James, Frances. "The Revelation of Jerusalem: A Review of Archaeological Research." *Expedition* 22 (Fall 1979): 33–43.

"Jerusalem Wall: Search Continues." *The Times* (London). 28 September 1964.

"Jewry Wall Finds Most Important for Years." *The Leicester Mercury*, 6 July 1936.

Johnstone, Paul. *Buried Treasure*. London: Phoenix House Ltd., 1957.

Jones, Enid Huws. *Margery Fry: The Essential Amateur*. Oxford: Oxford University Press, 1966.

Jones, Peter. "Erbistock." *Parish Magazine*, October, 1978.

"Kathleen Mary Kenyon." *Transactions of the Shropshire Archaeological Society* 60 (1975-76): 131.

Kehoe, Alice, with Mary Ann Levine. "Women's Work." In *The Cambridge Illustrated History of Archaeology*, edited by Lord Renfrew and Paul G. Bahn. Cambridge: Cambridge University Press, 1996.

Kenrick, Philip M. "Excavations at Sabratha, 1948–1951." *Libyan Studies* 13 (1982): 51–60.

—. *Excavations at Sabratha, 1948–1951*. Society for the Promotion of Roman Studies. Journal of Roman Studies Monograph No. 2, 1986.

Kenyon, Frederic. *The British Museum in War Time*. Glasgow: Jackson, Wylie and Co., 1934.

—. *The Bible and Modern Scholarship*. New York: Harper and Brothers Publishers, 1949.

King, Phillip J. *American Archaeology in the Mideast: A History of the American Schools of Oriental Research*. Winona Lake, IN: Eisenbrauns, 1983.

Lapp, Paul. "Captive Treasures." *Mid East* X, No. 1 (1970): 35–42.

Laughlin, John C. H. *Archaeology and the Bible*. London and New York: Routlege, 2000.

"Leicester's Roman Forum to be Preserved." *Leicester Evening Mail*, 24 February 1937.

Mallowan, M. E. L. "Department of Western Asiatic Archaeology 1947–62: Retrospect." *Bulletin of the Institute of Archaeology* 4 (1964): 157–163.

—. *Mallowan's Memoirs*. New York: Dodd, Mead & Company, 1977.

Mare, W. Harold. *The Archaeology of the Jerusalem Area*. Grand Rapids, Michigan: Baker Book House, 1987.

Marshall, Dorothy. "Excavating Under Jericho." *The Glasgow Herald* (28 March 1952).

Mazar, Amihai. "Israeli Archaeologists." In *Benchmarks in Time and Culture: An Introduction to Palestinian Archaeology*, edited by Joel Drinkard, Gerald L. Mattingly, and J. Maxwell Miller. Atlanta: Scholars Press, 1988.

—. *Archaeology in the Land of the Bible, 10,000–586 B.C.E.* New York: Doubleday, 1990.

Mazar, Benjamin. *The Mountain of the Lord: Excavating in Jerusalem*. New York: Doubleday & Company, 1975.

Mazar, Eilat. "The Royal Quarter of Biblical Jerusalem: The Ophel." In *Ancient Jerusalem Revealed*, edited by Hillel Geva. Jerusalem: Israel Exploration Society; Washington, D.C.: Biblical Archaeology Society, 1994.

McCall, Henrietta. *The Life of Max Mallowan: Archaeology and Agatha Christie*. London: The British Museum Press, 2001.

Meyers, Eric M., ed. *The Oxford Encyclopedia of Archaeology in the Near East*. 5 vols. American Schools of Oriental Research. Oxford: Oxford University Press, 1997.

Miller, Edward. *That Noble Cabinet: A History of the British Museum.* Athens, OH: Ohio University Press, 1974.

Moorey, P. R. S. "Kathleen Kenyon and Palestinian Archaeology." *Palestine Exploration Quarterly* (January–June 1979): 2–10.

—. *Excavation in Palestine.* Grand Rapids, MI: William B. Eerdmans Publishing Company, 1981.

—. *A Century of Biblical Archaeology.* Louisville, KY: Westminster/John Knox Press, 1991.

—. "British Women in Near Eastern Archaeology: Kathleen Kenyon and the Pioneers." *Palestine Exploration Quarterly* (July–December 1992): 91–100.

Moorey, P. R. S., and Peter Parr, eds. *Archaeology in the Levant: Essays for Kathleen Kenyon.* Warminster, England: Aris & Phillips Ltd., 1978.

Morgan, F. C. "Reports of Sectional Editors for 1949. Archaeology." *Transactions of the Woolhope Naturalists' Field Club* XXXIII Part I (1949).

Morris, R. "Breathing the Future: The Antiquaries and Conservation of the Landscape, 1950–1950." In *Visions of Antiquity: The Society of Antiquaries of London 1707–2007,* edited by Susan Pearce, pp. 328–351. Society of Antiquaries of London.

Myres, J. N. L. "Verulamium." *Antiquity* 12 (1938): 16–25.

"Notes and Notices." *The Museums Journal* 43, September (1943): 89–90.

Oates, Joan. "Review of *Excavations at Jericho,* Vol. 3." *Antiquity* LVII, No. 221 (November 1983): 222–223.

—. "Review of *Excavations at Jericho,* Vol. 4 and Vol. 5." *Antiquity* 61, No. 232 (July 1987): 341–343.

Palestine Exploration Fund. *The Survey of Western Palestine,* 7 vols. London: PEF, 1881–1888.

—. *Quarterly Statement of the Palestine Exploration Fund* (1930).

Parr, Peter. "Proto-Urban Jericho: The Need for Reappraisal." In *The Archaeology of Jordan and Beyond: Essays in Honor of James A. Sauer,* edited by Lawrence E. Stager, Joseph A. Greene, and Michael D. Coogan, Winona Lake, IN: Eisenbrauns, 2000.

Perdue, Leo G., Lawrence Toombs, and Gary L. Johnson, eds. *Archaeology and Biblical Interpretation. Essays in Memory of D. Glenn Rose.* Atlanta: John Knox Press, 1987.

Pitt Rivers, Augustus Henry Lane-Fox. *Excavations in Cranborne Chase.* 3 vols. London: [Harrison and Sons, Printers] printed privately, 1887–1905.

Prag, Kay. "Kathleen Kenyon and Archaeology in the Holy Land." *Palestine Exploration Quarterly* (July–December 1992): 107–123.

—. "Moving Onward. Australians Uncovering Ancient Jordan." In *Australians Uncovering Ancient Jordan,* edited by Alan Walmsley. Sydney: The Research Institute for Humanities and Social Sciences, The University of Sydney, 2001.

Randall-MacIver, David. *Mediaeval Rhodesia.* London, New York: Macmillan and Co., 1906.

Reich, Ronny, and Eli Shukron. "Light at the End of the Tunnel." *Biblical Archaeology Review* 25 (1999): 23–33, 72.

—. "The Jerusalem City Dump in the Late Temple Period." *Zeitschrift des Deutschen Palästina-Vereins* 119 (2003): 12–18.

"Revealing Biblical Jerusalem." In *Biblical Archaeology Today*. Proceedings of the International Congress on Biblical Archaeology, Jerusalem, April 1984. Jerusalem: Israel Exploration Society, 1985.

Rose, Kenneth. *King George V*. London: Weidenfeld and Nicolson, 1983.

Ruby, Robert. *Jericho: Dreams, Ruins, Phantoms*. New York: Henry Holt and Company, 1995.

Sandars, Nancy. "Gordon Childe at St. John's Lodge: Some Early Recollections." *Archaeology International* (1999/2000): 11–12.

Shanks, Hershel. *The City of David: A Guide to Biblical Jerusalem*. Washington, DC: The Biblical Archaeology Society, 1973.

—. "Kathleen Kenyon's Anti-Zionist Politics—Does It Affect Her Work?" *Biblical Archaeology Review* 1, No. 3 (1975): 3–13, 21.

—. "The City of David After 5 Years of Digging." *Biblical Archaeology Review* 11, No. 6 (1985): 22–38.

—. "The Jerusalem Wall that Shouldn't be There." *Biblical Archaeology Review* 8, No. 3, (1987): 47–57.

—. "An Archaeological Romance: An Interview with Moshe and Trude Dothan." *Biblical Archaeology Review* 19, No. 4 (1993): 22–31.

—. "The Mistress of Stratigraphy Had Clay Feet." *Biblical Archaeology Review* 29, No. 3 (2003): 53–58, 70.

Sharp, Maisie. *British Red Cross Hammersmith. 1939–1994*. London: British Red Cross, London Branch, Hammersmith & Fulham Centre, 1995.

Shiloh, Yigael. *Excavations at the City of David*. Qedem 19 (1984).

Silberman, Neil Ashur. *A Prophet from Amongst You: The Life of Yigael Yadin: Soldier, Scholar, and Mythmaker of Modern Israel*. Reading, MA: Addison-Wesley Publishing Co., 1993.

Steele, Ann. "The College Head Who Doesn't Mind Digging for Facts." *The Daily Telegraph*, 18 January (1968): 15.

Steiner, M. L. *Excavations by Kathleen M. Kenyon in Jerusalem 1961–1967*, Vol. III. *The Settlement in the Bronze and Iron Ages*. Continuum International Publishing Group.

Stern, Ephraim, ed. *The New Encyclopedia of Archaeological Excavations in the Holy Land*. 4 vols. Jerusalem: Israel Exploration Society, 1993.

Stutchbury, Howard E. "Excavations in the Kidron Valley." *Palestine Exploration Quarterly* 93 (1961): 101–113.

Talbot, Geraldine. "Crystal Bennett: An Appreciation." *Levant* XIX (1987): 2.

—. "Memories: The Institute, 1946–1947." *Bulletin of the Institute of Archaeology* 24 (1987): 27–28.

Tappy, Ron E. *The Archaeology of Israelite Samaria I: Early Iron Age through the Ninth Century BCE*. Harvard Semitic Studies. Atlanta: Scholars Press, 1992.

—. *The Archaeology of Israelite Samaria* II. Harvard Semitic Museum, 2001.

—. "Samaria." In *The Oxford Encyclopedia of Archaeology in the Near East*, edited by Eric M. Meyers. American Schools of Oriental Research. Oxford and New York: Oxford University Press, 1997

Taylor, M. V., and Richard Goodchild. "Review of *Excavations at the Jewry Wall Site, Leicester.*" *Journal of Roman Studies* XXXIX. (1949):142–145.

Trickett, Rachel. "Dame Kathleen Kenyon." Address delivered at the Memorial Service for Dame Kathleen Kenyon on 10 November 1978 in the University Church of St. Mary the Virgin, Oxford. *St. Hugh's Chronicle* (1978/1979): 35–40.

Tubb, Jonathan. "The MB IIA Period in Palestine: Its Relationship with Syria and Its Origin." *Levant* XV (1983): 49–62.

Tushingham, A.D. "Excavations at Old Testament Jericho." *Biblical Archaeologist* XVI, no. 3 (1953): 46–67.

—. *ASOR Jerusalem and Baghdad Newsletter* #8, 2 April 1953.

—. "Kathleen Mary Kenyon." *Proceedings of the British Academy* 71 (1985): 555–582.

Tushingham, A. D., and Maggie. "Dame Kathleen Kenyon: A Personal Appreciation." In *Archaeology in the Levant: Essays for Kathleen Kenyon,* edited by P. R. S. Moorey and Peter Parr. Warminster, England: Aris & Phillips Ltd., 1978.

"Under the Ground." *The Times* (London). 11 July 1960.

Ucko, Peter. "The Biography of a Collection: The Sir Flinders Petrie Palestinian Collection and the Role of University Museums." *Museum Management and Curatorship* 17, No. 4 (1998): 351–399.

Warnock, Mary. *Mary Warnock: A Memoir.* London: Duckworth, 2001.

Watkins, Trevor. "Review of *Excavations at Jericho,* Vol. 3." *Institute of Archaeology Bulletin* 18 (1982): 205–206.

—. "Review of Kenyon and Holland, *Excavations at Jericho.* Vol. 4. *The Pottery Type Series and Other Finds,* and *Excavations at Jericho.* Vol. 5. *The Pottery Phases of the Tell and Other Finds.*" *Institute of Archaeology Bulletin* 23 (1986), review supplement, 40.

Webster, Graham. *Archaeologist At Large.* London: B. T. Batsford, Ltd., 1991.

West, Priscilla. "Reminiscences of Seven Decades." In *St. Hugh's: One Hundred Years of Women's Education at Oxford,* edited by Penny Griffin. London: Macmillan, 1986.

Western, A. C. "Dame Kathleen Kenyon, D.B.E." *Levant* 11 (1979): iii–iv.

Wheeler, Margaret. "The Lighter Side of Dig Life" *Palestine Exploration Quarterly* (1955): 184–185.

—. *Walls of Jericho.* London: Readers Union and Chatto & Windus, 1958.

Wheeler, Mortimer. *Archaeology from the Earth.* Harmondsworth: Pelican Penguin, 1956.

—. *Still Digging.* New York: E. P. Dutton & Co., Inc., 1956.

Wheeler, R. E. M. "Anniversary Address." *Antiquaries Journal* 36 (1956): 166.

—. *The British Academy 1949–1968.* London and Oxford: Oxford University Press for the British Academy, 1970.

Wheeler, R. E. M., and T. V. Wheeler. *Verulamium: A Belgic and Two Roman Cities.* Reports of the Research Committee of the Society of Antiquaries of London, No. XI. Oxford: The Society of Antiquaries, 1936.

"When the Two Dames Met." *Wrexham Leader.* 8 September (1978).

White, Roger, and Philip Barker. *Wroxeter: Life and Death of a Roman City.* Stroud, Gloucestershire: Tempus Publishing Ltd, 1998.

Wilkes, John. "Kathleen Kenyon in Roman Britain." *Palestine Exploration Quarterly* (July–December 1992): 101–108.

266

Wilkins, Penelope, compiler. *Kenyon Family Histories*. Published by Penelope Wilkins, PO Box 10, Campbell ACT 2612, Australia, 2000.

Withers, Audrey. *Lifespan: An Autobiography*. London: Peter Owens Ltd., 1994.

Wood, Bryant. "Did the Israelites Conquer Jericho?" *Biblical Archaeology Review* 16, no. 2 (March–April 1990): 45–59.

"Wrekin's Old British City." *Wellington Journal & Shrewsbury News*, 19 August 1939.

Wright, G. E. "Archaeological Method in Palestine – An American Interpretation." *Eretz-Israel* 9 (1969): 120–133.

—. "Israelite Samaria and Iron Age Chronology." *Bulletin of the American Schools of Oriental Research* 155 (October, 1959): 13–29.

Yadin, Yigael, ed. *Jerusalem Revealed: Archaeology in the Holy City 1968–1974*. New Haven and London: Yale University Press and the Israel Exploration Society, 1976.

Zeuner, F. E. "Notes on the Bronze Age Tombs of Jericho – I." *Palestine Exploration Quarterly* 87 (May–October 1955): 118–128.

INDEX

Bennett, Crystal: 169, 184, 189, 219, 221
Benoit, Père Pierre: 194
Bent, Theodore: 28
Bentwich, Muriel: 57
Bible: 14, 20, 54, 56, 101, 104, 117, 135, 136, 161, 224. *See also* Kings, Book of; Old Testament
The Bible and Recent Archaeology: 224
Biblical Archaeology Review: 201
Biddle, Martin: 211
Biran, Avraham: 196, 199
Blake, Robert: 57
Bliss, Frederick: 55, 158–160, 179
Boudica: 49, 55
Bowman, Kathleen: 108
Braidwood, Robert: 149
Breedon-on-the-Hill: 95, 100
British Academy:
    Amman Institute, 221
    British government, 91,
    Dead Sea Scrolls, 165, 166
    Frederic Kenyon, 14, 72
    Joint Expedition to Samaria, 56, 65
    KK made representative on PAM board, 162
    R. E. M. Wheeler, 103,136, 204
British Association for the Advancement of Science: 29, 30, 33, 38, 39, 40
British Embassy: 192
British Foreign Office: 162, 192, 203
British Mandate: 55, 97, 160, 161, 162. *See also* Mandate Palestine
British Museum:
    bronze buckets sent to, 191–192
    Christopher Hawkes at, 90
    Frank Francis, director of, 165, 166
    Frederic Kenyon as director of, 14–15, 18, 72
    Institute of Archaeology moves closer to, 181
    KK as Trustee, 222
    KK borrows slides belonging to, 26
    KK does research in, 43
    KK grew up in, 21, 224
    KK meets GCT at, 30
    "Land of the Bible" exhibit at, 135
    Neolithic portrait skulls sold to, 140
    scrolls exhibit at, 166
    specialist to help with Dead Sea Scrolls, 203
    Zimbabwe china identified by, 38
British Red Cross: 85–88, 89, 94, 135, 183
British School of Archaeology in Jerusalem (BSAJ):
    Basil Hennessey, director of, 195–196

building in Jerusalem, 146
consequences of Israeli takeover for, 220–221, 256 n. 21
Crystal Bennett, assistant director of, 219
established, 55
excavation at Damascus Gate, 189
excavations of, 155
Frederic Kenyon on executive committee, 72
Jericho excavations, 103–104
Jerusalem excavations, 156, 157, 169, 191
John Allegro, 164, 165
John Crowfoot as director of, 56
KK and, 102, 103–104, 128, 135, 136, report on first season at Jericho to, 127; KK retires as Chairman, 225
Peter Parr, Secretary/Librarian, 171
Pontiac, 212
publication of Jerusalem excavations, 209
Samaria excavation, 56
Six Day War, 195–196, 200, 203–205
students of at Samaria, 56, 57
British School at Athens: 90
British School at Rome: 97, 100
British Treasury: 164, 166, 167
Brogan, Dennis: 98
Brogan, Olwyn: 98
Bronze Age: 93, 104, 114, 186, 210
    Early Bronze Age: pottery, 63; walls at Jericho, 101, 102, 114–117; tombs, 121, 124; Jericho during, 148, 151
    Middle Bronze Age: walls at Jericho, 101, 102, 150; Canaanites of, 117, 148, 151; tombs, 120–122; wall at Jerusalem, 174, 186
    Late Bronze Age: period of Joshua, 101, 117–118, 145–146, 148; town, 138; pottery at Jericho, 102; Jerusalem terraces, 177, 210
Broshi, Magen: 202, 253–254 n. 25, 254 n. 40
Buchanan, Archie: 57
Buildings of Samaria, Samaria-Sebaste Vol. I. *See under* Samaria-Sebaste I
Bull, General Odd: 191, 196
Buried Treasure: 143
Butcher, Sarnia: 124
Byzantine period: 181, 186, 188, 205

Caesar: 48–49, 53
Callaway, Joe: 134, 219, 224
Calvary: 179
Canaan: 101

ABOUT THE AUTHOR

M iriam C. Davis first worked on an archaeological dig at the age of seventeen. She first visited the Middle East at the age of sixteen. After graduating Magna Cum Laude from Emory University with a degree in history, she spent a year in Scotland at the University of St. Andrews on a Bobby Jones Scholarship, studying history and archaeology. After receiving an M.A. in history from the University of California at Santa Barbara, she spent a year at the University of York (England) as a Fulbright fellow, taking an M.A. in medieval archaeology. She then received a Ph.D. in medieval history from UCSB in 1995. Her scholarly work has concentrated on waste disposal and city cleaning in late medieval English towns, but she has also written for the popular press on archaeology and travel. Since 1995 she has taught at Delta State University in Cleveland, Mississippi. Dr. Davis has participated in archaeological excavations in Alabama, Mississippi, England, and Scotland.